W9-AQQ-104

The Romance of the Fungus World

An Account of Fungus Life in its numerous guises, both real and legendary

BY

R. T. ROLFE

F.I.C., ETC.
Member of the British Mycological Society

AND

F. W. ROLFE

Member of the British Mycological Society

WITH FOREWORD BY

J. RAMSBOTTOM

O.B.E., M.A., F.L.S.

*Past President of the British Mycological Society, and
Mycologist to the British Museum (Natural History)
South Kensington*

Dover Publications, Inc.
New York

GREENWOOD LIBRARY
LONGWOOD UNIVERSITY
REDFORD & RACE STREET
FARMVILLE, VA 23909

To the Memory of
GEORGE EDWARD MASSEE,
V.M.H., A.L.S.

to whom the Authors are indebted for their first glimpses of the Fungus World, and in whose company, in field and by fireside, they spent many delightful hours.

This Dover edition first published in 1974, is an unabridged republication of the work first published in 1925 by Chapman & Hall.

International Standard Book Number: 0-486-23105-4
Library of Congress Catalog Card Number: 74-81401

Manufactured in the United States of America
Dover Publications, Inc.
180 Varick Street
New York, N. Y. 10014

GREENWOOD LIBRARY
LONGWOOD UNIVERSITY
REDFORD & RACE STREET
FARMVILLE, VA 23909

Foreword

THE authors of the present work have done me the honour of requesting a foreword to their volume. Though doubting whether such a preamble ever has any significance other than showing a kindly feeling towards authors, I accede to the request because it gives me an opportunity of supporting their plea as to the interest and importance of those bizarre members of the plant kingdom, the toadstools and their like. Quite apart from the great scientific interest of these organisms—particularly attractive in that more problems are encountered and are being investigated among them than in any other group of plants—there are in addition matters of enormous economic importance touching organic existence in all its forms. Further, it is a field into which the amateur as such can enter and find a hobby; a hobby moreover, which, with a minimum of expense, gives opportunity of adding materially to our knowledge of fungi. Many of the most important discoveries of the past have been made by amateurs, and some of the outstanding mycologists of the day are amateurs in every sense of the word. It is to be hoped that the following pages will add to the number of those who find pleasure and friendships in matters mycological.

J. RAMSBOTTOM,
Department of Botany, British
Museum (Natural History).

December, 1924.

iii

LONGWOOD LIBRARY

1000443434

Preface

IN launching a new book upon the sea of public criticism, it is customary to give some reasons for its appearance. At times an apology has even been offered. In the hope that the reader will consider the latter superfluous, we may give some explanation as to the former.

Though by most people little known or regarded, the toadstools and their allies concern mankind, in many of his daily doings, not only intimately but also enormously. Indeed, they are linked up with his destinies by bonds which, although hidden, are nevertheless infinitely strong. In spite of this, and of the fact that a vast quantity of information concerning them has long been accessible, general interest in them has remained small. It has never gained strength because the literature dealing with them is too frequently unpalatable. The ordinary reader is appalled when he turns over the leaves of many of the very excellent text-books of fungi which have been published. Yet, we can assure him, the subject is not necessarily so precise, inhuman, not to say *desiccated*, as some well-intentioned laboratory mycologists would make it appear.

On the contrary, it is a *human* subject. Many are the quaint fantasies which have been interwoven by man into its lore, and thus, *its* history is almost *his* history. It starts with Adam and Eve, and it will continue after the ultimate man has looked his last on a dying world. It embraces not only our first ancestors, but such diverse characters as Judas Iscariot and the Devil, Pliny and

Erasmus Darwin, the fairies and the witches, and Baron Munchausen and Sir John Mandeville. With such associations, real and imaginary, it is a subject which should provide interesting, indeed fascinating reading ; not only for the botanist, not only for the Nature-lover, but for everyone. It is in the hope of demonstrating this fact that this book was undertaken.

So much for the conception. In endeavouring to materialize it, a difficulty at once presented itself, for to do the subject justice, it was obvious that the utmost limits of several volumes would be required. The choice thus lay between a compressed and, therefore, indigestible résumé, and a selection of the more salient features. The latter course was chosen. The work is thus not a text-book, nor even an " Introduction to the Fungi," at least in the sense in which such a title would be generally understood. Nor does it pretend to supply an answer to the question " What fungus is this ? " It is merely an attempt to portray these plants in some of their numerous guises ; to show them, not only as they *seem* and as they really are, but also as they have appeared to other folk in other times.

The mode of treatment of the theme must be left to the judgment of the reader. If he considers it, as some may, strictly from the botanical standpoint, it must be obvious that a good deal of explanatory matter has, of necessity, had to be omitted. For, as we are well aware, to any general statement there are often a number of qualifications. The book may thus appear a little superficial in places—an appearance inevitable in any popular treatment of the theme. An enormous amount of material has, however, been sifted, and although, for reasons of space, a quantity of interesting information

has been rejected, there are doubtless some matters
which have been overlooked, and we should be glad to
have information of these.

On the other hand, the reader who previously has
considered these plants as unworthy of the slightest
regard, will find plenty to enforce an interest. If, in
any case, the book affords a fresh view-point from which
these peculiar plants may be surveyed, and thus creates
a more universal interest in them, it will have
accomplished all that was hoped of it.

In any book of this character, the questions of
technical terms and of *names* are burning ones, and,
therefore, deserve some comment. The former are always
a bugbear to the layman and for this reason their use has
been reduced to a minimum. At the same time, a certain
number are almost inevitable, since by their use one is
often able to convey, in a single word, the essence of a
sentence, or more, of descriptive matter, the continued
repetition of which would become tiresome to the reader.
Such terms, when used, have always been carefully
explained.

The names of fungi also present a certain amount of
difficulty. Owing to the unpopularity of these plants,
few of them have English names, and recourse has,
therefore, to be had to the scientific ones. Where a
fungus *has* an English name by which it is usually known,
we have referred to it as such. A number of " popular "
names which have been used from time to time are,
however, purely the invention of a particular author,
and are *not* in general use. These " coined " designations
have, as far as possible, been avoided.

With regard to the many references to fungi in
classical literature, mycologists are indebted for much of

this knowledge to the researches of the Rev. W. Houghton, recorded in an article entitled "Notices of Fungi in Greek and Latin Authors" (*Annals and Magazine of Natural History*, Series 5, Vol. 15, pp. 22-49). This we have freely consulted.

We also wish to record our indebtedness to the many other writers on mycological and other matters, whose works have been made use of, and who are too numerous to specify here; and to the almost equally numerous friends and correspondents who have rendered assistance in various ways. Particularly must we mention:

The authorities of the Royal Botanic Gardens, Kew, and of the British Museum (Natural History), South Kensington, who have granted facilities in many directions. To the Trustees of the latter institution we are indebted for permission to reproduce the text figures, the whole of which are from W. G. Smith's "Synopsis of the British Basidiomycetes."

Mr. Ernest Bramah, Sir Arthur Conan Doyle, and Messrs. Rudyard Kipling, E. Phillips Oppenheim, Eden Phillpotts, and H. G. Wells, who have given us permission to reproduce extracts from their works.

H.M. Office of Works, The Proprietors of the *Bristol Times and Mirror*, and of *The Fruit Grower*, and Messrs. Buckhurst, Langley, Lévy and Neurdein, Millard, and A. E. Peck, who have supplied photographs. Of these, it should be noted that Mr. A. E. Peck, of Scarborough, Honorary Secretary to the Mycological Committee of the Yorkshire Naturalists Union, has provided a large number, and we are especially indebted to him for the unselfish way in which he has placed at our disposal the fruits of many years of labour.

Last, but by no means least, we desire to express our

gratitude to Mr. John Ramsbottom, O.B.E., M.A., F.L.S., mycologist to the British Museum (N.H.), who has not only read the proofs, and offered many valuable criticisms and suggestions, but who has throughout the whole course of the work acted as guide, philosopher and friend, to such a degree, indeed, that he must view the culmination of our efforts with as much relief as we ourselves feel.

Contents

CHAPTER   PAGE

I.   INTRODUCTION   I

II.   THE FUNGI IN MYTHOLOGY AND FOLK-LORE   7

III.   THE FUNGI IN FICTION   18

IV.   THE FUNGI IN REALITY : THEIR STRUCTURE
        AND CHARACTERISTICS   39

V.   THE FUNGI IN REALITY : THEIR MODES
        OF EXISTENCE   76

VI.   THE DAMAGE CAUSED BY FUNGI AND ITS EFFECT
        ON MANKIND   93

VII.   THE USES OF FUNGI : IN MEDICINE .   .   127

VIII.   THE USES OF FUNGI : IN INDUSTRY .   .   148

IX.   THE USES OF FUNGI : AS FOODS   .   .   166

X.   THE CULTIVATED FUNGI AND OTHER FUNGUS
        FOODS OF COMMERCE   197

XI.   THE POISONOUS FUNGI   225

XII.   THE CURIOUS PHENOMENA EXHIBITED BY
        FUNGI   246

XIII.   THE STUDY OF THE FUNGI AS A HOBBY .   260

XIV.   SOME FURTHER HISTORICAL ASPECTS OF THE
        FUNGI   273

XV.   THE DERIVATION OF FUNGUS NAMES .   .   292

List of Illustrations

FIG.   PAGE

1. Forest tree attacked by Dryad's Saddle (*Polyporus squamosus*) . . . . . Frontispiece
2. *Mycena galericulata,* on an old stump . . . 4
3. Earth-stars (*Geaster fimbriatus*) 4
4. *Marasmius ramealis,* on dead twigs . . . 5
5. Miniature birds' nests (*Crucibulum vulgare*) . . 5
6. A lesser puffball (*Lycoperdon gemmatum*) . . . 14
7. " And little fleas have lesser fleas," (*Cordyceps capitata* on *Elaphomyces granulatus*) 14
8. The Jew's Ear (*Hirneola Auricula-Judae*) . . 15
9. A small puffball (*Lycoperdon pyriforme*) . . . 15
10. A Fairy Ring of *Collybia maculata* . . . 22
11. Some Elf-cups (*Peziza vesiculosa*) 22
12. *Calocera viscosa,* on an old pine stump . . . 23
13. The Sulphur Tuft (*Hypholoma fasciculare*) . . 23
14. The Common Stinkhorn (*Phallus impudicus*) . . 34
15. The Fly Agaric (*Amanita muscaria*) . . . 34
16. *Cordyceps Taylori,* on a caterpillar 35
17. The Coral Spot (*Nectria cinnabarina*) . . . 35
18. *Polystictus versicolor* 35
19. Development of the Common Mushroom (*Psalliota campestris*) 44
20. Spores of *Psathyrella prona* 47
21. Section through Puffball 50
22. Section through Mushroom 50
23. Section through spore-bearing surface of Mushroom 51

xii LIST OF ILLUSTRATIONS

FIG.   PAGE

24. Ascus of Common Morel (*Morchella esculenta*) . 51

25. Agaricaceae. *Amanita phalloides* 58

26. Agaricaceae. *Coprinus comatus* and *spp.* . . 59

27. Agaricaceae. *Lenzites betulina* 61

28. Polyporaceae. *Boletus spp.* 62

29. Polyporaceae. *Fistulina hepatica* 62

30. Polyporaceae. *Merulius lacrymans* . . . 63

31. Hydnaceae. *Hydnum spp.* 64

32. Hydnaceae. *Phlebia merismoides* 65

33. Thelephoraceae. *Craterellus cornucopioides* . 65

34. Thelephoraceae. *Stereum spp.* 66

35. Clavariaceae. *Clavaria spp.* 67

36. Tremellinaceae. *Tremella lutescens* . . . 68

37. Phalloidaceae. *Phallus impudicus* 69

38. Lycoperdaceae. *Lycoperdon spp.* 70

39. Sclerodermaceae. *Scleroderma vulgare* . . 71

40. Nidulariaceae. *Crucibulum vulgare* . . . 72

41. Hymenogastraceae. *Rhizopogon rubescens* . . 73

42. Fungus gall caused by *Frankiella alni* . . . 108

43. Corky Scab of Potatoes (*Spongospora subterranea*) . 108

44. Brown Rot of Fruit (*Monilia fructigena*) . . 109

45. Spraying fruit trees 109

46. Damage to woodwork of a building caused by " Dry rot " (*Merulius lacrymans*) 118

47. Wood destroyed by " Dry rot " 118

48. *Fomes fomentarius*, employed as counter-irritant and styptic, and in the manufacture of tinder . . 119

49. *Polyporus betulinus*, occasionally used by apiarists as anaesthetic 119

50. A larger duffball (*Lycoperdon caelatum*) formerly used as a styptic 136

FIG.   PAGE

51. " Cramp Balls " (*Daldinia concentrica*)   .   .   .   136

52. *Hirneola polytricha*, as exported from New Zealand
    and the South Sea Islands.   137

53. Ergot. of rye (*Claviceps purpurea*)   137

54. " German Tinder " as prepared from *Fomes fomen-
    tarius*   158

55. *Daedalea quercina*, a natural curry-comb .   .   .   158

56. The Champignon (*Marasmius oreades*)   .   .   .   159

57. The Horse Mushroom (*Psalliota arvensis*)   .   .   159

58. *Helvella crispa*   180

59. *Gyromitra esculenta*   180

60. The " Shaggy Cap " (*Coprinus comatus*)   .   .   181

61. The " Blewitt " (*Tricholoma personatum*)   .   .   181

62. *Sparassis crispa*   190

63. *Clavaria abietina*   190

64. A dish of Morels (*Morchella esculenta*)   .   .   .   191

65. " Black-fellow's Bread " (*Polyporus Mylittae*)   .   .   191

66. Corsham Mushroom Industry : View of entrance to
    quarries   204

67. Corsham Mushroom Industry : Pickers at work   .   204

68. Corsham Mushroom Industry : Part of the day's crop   205

69. Truffle hunting in Périgord   205

70. Poisonous fungi and serpents : an old woodcut   .   230

71. *Entoloma lividum*, a poisonous species   .   .   .   230

72. *Amanita phalloides*, the most poisonous fungus known   231

73. *Stropharia aeruginosa*, a suspicious species   .   .   231

74. *Lepiota procera*, in young state   250

75. The same, twenty-four hours later   .   .   .   250

76. A " Shaggy Cap " (*Coprinus comatus*) in old state   .   251

77. The Dog Stinkhorn (*Mutinus caninus*)   .   .   .   251

78. A Giant Puffball (*Lycoperdon Bovista*)   .   .   .   258

FIG.   PAGE

79. The Candle-Snuff Fungus (*Xylaria hypoxylon*) . 258

80. The Oyster Fungus (*Pleurotus ostreatus*), at home . 259

81. The Common Parasol (*Lepiota procera*), at home . 259

82. *Boletus edulis* 286

83. *Boletus scaber* 286

84. *Lactarius deliciosus* 287

85. The Common Morel (*Morchella esculenta*) . . 287

CHAPTER I

Introduction

" Where I was wont to seeke the honey Bee,
Working her formall rowmes in wexen frame,
The grieslie Tode-stoole growne there mought I se
And loathed Paddocks lording on the same."
—1579, SPENSER, *The Shepheard's Calendar.*

" December," 12., 67–70.

" When Flora's lovelier tribes give place,
The Mushroom's scorn'd but curious race
Bestud the moist autumnal earth ;
A quick but perishable birth,
Inlaid with many a brilliant die
Of Nature's high-wrought tapestry."
—BISHOP MANT.

IN the autumn, when woods are bare, and " when, o'er the half-world, Nature seems dead," the toadstools and the like appear ; at first a scattered few, and later, if the weather be kind to them, in their hosts. True, at all seasons some representatives of this peculiar tribe are to be found, but it is in the decline of the year, when all Nature is damp and dripping, that these queer fellows spring up in such profusion as to force themselves upon the attention of even the least observant. Nurtured in death and decay, often bizarre of form and lurid of colour, some bloated and leering, others dainty and graceful, all appearing and often disappearing in such uncanny fashion, these pariahs of the plant world have been for ages at once a source of wonder and of loathing to the uninitiated. In a day

1

gone by, their appearance in unwonted numbers was of ill-augury to mankind, not that they wrought the evil, but the mischance which brought the one may well have increased the ravages of the other. Thus in the year 1348, when the Black Death devastated the country, it is recorded in the olden chronicles that, after the lowering of a mighty storm-cloud until it filled the heavens, rain fell almost unceasingly for over two months, so that the crops rotted in the fields, and ruin and desolation brooded over all. " The rain had ceased at last, and a sickly autumn sun shone upon a land which was soaked and sodden with water. Wet and rotten leaves reeked and festered under the foul haze which rose from the woods. The fields were spotted with monstrous fungi of a size and colour never matched before—scarlet and mauve and liver and black. It was as though the sick earth had burst into foul pustules ; mildew and lichen mottled the walls, and with that filthy crop, Death sprang also from the water-soaked earth." [1]

That these foul fungi spring up from the ruin of all that is fair and beautiful is, perhaps, a not unnatural belief; but whether or no, it is one which has gradually erected against them a barrier of prejudice, through which only a few useful members have been allowed to creep. In 1857, Berkeley, the father of British mycology, referred to the popular antipathy to fungi, " which, from the poisonous qualities, the evanescent nature, and the loathsome mass of putrescence presented in decay by many species, have become a byword among the vulgar," [2] and thirty years later Hay expressed excellently the same

---

[1] 1906, Conan Doyle, *Sir Nigel*, ch. i.
[2] 1857, Berkeley, *Introduction to Cryptogamic Botany*, p. 241.

popular view-point : " Among this vast family of plants, belonging to one class, yet diverse from one another, comprising more than a thousand distinct species indigenous to these islands, there is but one kind that Englishmen condescend to regard with favour. All the rest are lumped together in one sweeping condemnation. They are looked upon as vegetable vermin, only made to be destroyed. No eye can see their beauties ; their office is unknown ; their varieties are not regarded ; they are hardly allowed a place among Nature's lawful children, but are considered something abnormal, worthless, and inexplicable. By precept and example children are taught from earliest infancy to despise, loathe, and avoid all kinds of ' toadstools.' The individual who desires to engage in the study of them must boldly face a good deal of scorn. He is laughed at for his strange taste among the better classes, and is actually regarded as a sort of idiot among the lower orders. No fad or hobby is esteemed so contemptible as that of the ' fungus-hunter ' or ' toadstool-eater.'

" This popular sentiment, which we may coin the word ' Fungophobia ' to express, is very curious. If it were human—that is, universal—one would be inclined to set it down as an instinct, and to reverence it accordingly. But it is not human—it is merely British. It is so deep and intense a prejudice that it amounts to a national superstition. Fungophobia is merely a form of ignorance, of course ; but its power over the British mind is so immense, that the mycologist, anxious to impart the knowledge he has gleaned to others, often meets with scarcely credence or respect." [1]

---

[1] 1887, W. D. Hay, *British Fungi*, p. 6.

Although education has more recently swept away many misconceptions, this distaste still lingers on, and finds outlet even nowadays in the insensate wrath with which these outcasts are often shattered by a militant walking-stick, or ground to pulp 'neath a hostile heel.

Yet these denizens of the woodland and meadow are something more than mere blots upon an autumnal landscape, for, on closer observation, many of them are seen to be of curious form and singular beauty. Thus they may appear as cups and goblets, as globes, as a bird's nest filled with eggs, as corals and sponges, as a delicate network resembling a diminutive cage, and indeed of an infinite variety of form and shade.

> " Whose tapering stems, robust or light,
> Like columns catch the searching sight ;
> Like fair umbrellas, furl'd or spread
> Display their many-coloured head,
> Grey, purple, yellow, white or brown,
> A Grecian shield, or prelate's crown,
> Like Freedom's cap or friar's cowl,
> Or China's bright inverted bowl."

The most common form with stalk and cap may display the most brilliant tints of crimson or golden, often diversified with spots or patches of a different colour, or may exhibit that delicacy of form which only Nature can give. And thus for their beauty alone they have appeared to some in very different guise than that of abhorrence, as being no less worthy than the trees and the flowers of the attention of the Nature-lover.

> " He that high grouth on cedars did bestowe,
> Gave also lowly mushrumpes leave to growe." [1]

It was the beauty of the scarlet and orange elf-cups

---

[1] 1595, Robert Southwell, *Spirituall Poems*, Grosart, 69.

Photo by A. E. Peck, Scarborough

Fig. 2.—" Like Freedom's cap or friar's cowl." *Mycena galericulata*, on an old stump.

Photo by A. E. Peck, Scarborough

Fig. 3.—Earth-stars (*Geaster fimbriatus*), an autumn inhabitant of pine and beech woods.

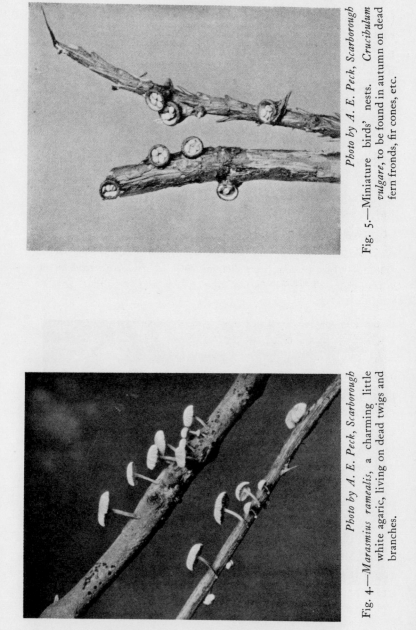

Photo by A. E. Peck, Scarborough

Fig. 5.—Miniature birds' nests. *Crucibulum vulgare*, to be found in autumn on dead fern fronds, fir cones, etc.

Photo by A. E. Peck, Scarborough

Fig. 4.—*Marasmius ramealis*, a charming little white agaric, living on dead twigs and branches.

(*Pezizae*) (Fig. 11), which first directed the attention of two distinguished mycologists, Persoon and Battarra, to the study of the fungi, Persoon being one of the first to systematize the classification of these plants.

Nor are they merely ornamental, or, as some would have it, the reverse, and the curious observer may speculate as to the place they fill in the great scheme of Nature. And since every heap of decaying vegetable matter will be found sustaining a multitude of these growths, many small or even of microscopic dimensions, it is evident that they are the agents of dissolution, not only breaking down the dead matter which would otherwise cumber the soil with an ever-increasing mass of débris, but converting it to a form which can again be absorbed to make fresh growth. To appreciate something of their work, one need but imagine for a moment the woods free of toadstools and their allies, and, therefore, free from decay ; the ground choked with the leaves and branches of countless ages which refuse to moulder, the trees themselves stark and lifeless, smothered from above by their own substance and starved below by the lack of necessary liquid food for their roots. Such a scene would be even more desolate than that which normally presents itself in the fall of the year. These plants thus act as vegetable vultures, and as such, help to preserve Nature's balance, by removing the remains of those which have fallen in the great ever-raging battle for existence.

The relatively harmless and even beneficent toadstools and puff-balls, so numerous in themselves, are, however, but a small section of that large and ubiquitous tribe, the fungi, and of these as a whole the vast majority, unfortunately for man, have linked forces against him, and these, although generally so small as to be quite unnoticed and unknown, are legion in number, great in power and devastating in effect. Of them the rusts, smuts and mildews decimate his crops, the moulds spoil his foods, while others more daring attack even himself. His progress through life is dogged by these diminutive marauders, who only await conditions suitable for attack, and who are responsible for incalculable losses to him.

True, it is to some of these minute fungi that man owes his ale, wine, and all such " hot and rebellious liquors," his vinegar and the lightness of his bread ; but the number so ministering to his needs is few, and their virtues are apt to pale into insignificance beside the vices of the many.

Small wonder is it, then, in the absence of that knowledge which brings tolerance, and which it will be our aim to supply, that the fungi in general have been regarded with the antipathy to which reference has already been made, an antipathy so strong that it has been woven into our folk-tales, and finds expression in the pages of our writers, both of prose and of poem.

CHAPTER II

The Fungi in Mythology and Folk-lore

" Now shift the scene to moonlight glade,
Where dapper elves beneath the shade
Of oak or elm, their revels keep,
What time we plodding mortals sleep."
—*Spirit of the Woods.*

" They in their courses make that round,
In meadows and in marshes found,
By them socalled the Fairy ground."
—1627, DRAYTON, *Nymphidia,* 71.

THE first observers of the fungi had obviously little exact knowledge of the workings of the natural world. It is thus not surprising that they had recourse to the supernatural to account for the extraordinary characters of these plants. Certainly such was the case, and their association with those mythical beings, the fairies, witches and so forth, was the result. This probably originated in times of which no records now remain, but in mediaeval times, when superstition was rife, and even until quite recently, the belief in the supposed connection of toadstools, and the like, with fairies, was a very common one, and many are the references founded upon this basis.

The Fairy Rings.—An ancient tradition has it that after the wee people had joined hands and danced together in a ring on a midsummer evening, their tracks

were to be seen as fairy-rings on the meadows, and the
toadstools growing in them did but serve as seats for
tired elves :

> " And nightly, meadow-fairies, look you sing
> Like to the Garter's compass, in a ring
> Th' expressure that it bears, green let it be
> More fertile fresh than all the field to see." [1]

The beauty and regularity of outline of these rings,
which, of course, are caused by the growth of the
toadstools, have often excited the wonder of the casual
observer, and it is not surprising that various strange
conjectures have been made concerning them. In those
days of early superstition in Europe it was generally
held that they were caused by the dancing of the fairies,
and to this belief, picturesque expression has often been
given in poem and fable, indeed, until long after our
faith in fairies had deserted us, and the more prosaic
explanation of the rings had become well known. Thus
Browne describes :

> " A pleasant mead,
> Where fairies often did their measures tread,
> Which in the meadows made such circles green,
> As if with garlands it had crownèd been.
> Within one of these rounds was to be seen
> A hillock rise, where oft the fairy-queen
> At twilight sat." [2]

Pope, in that inimitable example of ludicrous poetry,
" The Rape of the Lock," speaks :

> " Of airy elves, by moonlight shadows seen,
> The silver token and the circled green." [3]

---

[1] 1602, Shakespeare, *The Merry Wives of Windsor*, Act V., Scene v.
[2] 1613—16, Browne, *Britannia's Pastorals*.
[3] 1711, Pope, *The Rape of the Lock*, i., 31.

Collins relates that "twilight fairies tread the circled green," [1] which might almost owe its inspiration to the last quotation, and Tennyson also refers to "the fairy footings on the grass." [2] Shakespeare more than once suggests that the making of rings was one of the fairy duties, and not merely a daytime memory of their moonlight revels, and in "A Midsummer Night's Dream," a fairy says to Puck :

> "And I serve the fairy queen
> To dew her orbs upon the green." [3]

Superstitions concerning the Rings. In the sixteenth century, however, the belief in fairies was falling on evil days, and until its recent curious revival, it had generally almost disappeared as a popular superstition in this country, although occasionally still surviving here and there, while certain curious beliefs relating to the rings were current in quite recent times.

Most people have heard of the old West-country superstition, which holds that if a maiden desires to improve her complexion, it is only necessary to go out early on a May morning, and rub the dew from the grass on her face. It is doubtless still practised. It is, however, not so generally known that, for this purpose, one must avoid the grass growing within the circles, or the fairies may revenge themselves on the rash intruder into their sanctuaries by spoiling her complexion. A similar idea is expressed by the old Scots' proverb :

> "He wha tills the fairy green,
> Nae luck again sall hae." [4]

---

[1] 1743, Collins, *Epistle to Sir T. Hanmer*, 98.
[2] 1864, Alfred Tennyson, *Aylmer's Field*, 90.
[3] 1594, Shakespeare, *A Midsummer Night's Dream*, Act II., Scene i.
[4] 1819, *Edin. Mag.*, July 19.

It was a further popular belief that even by stepping inside the rings, one would put oneself within the fairies' power, perhaps with unfortunate results. Whether sheep *do* avoid the grass of the rings, the coarser growth found encircling the bare ring being presumably that in question, we have not been able to observe. Shakespeare certainly says so in the following passage :

> " You demy-puppets, that
> By moonshine do the green sour ringlets make,
> Whereof the ewe not bites ; and you, whose pastime
> Is to make midnight mushrooms." [1]

Even as recently as the year 1869, a contributor to " Notes and Queries " appears fully to believe in the fairy origin of the rings, and says :

> " My informant stated that he had often seen the rings left on the grass where they had been dancing, but he had never seen any of the little folks himself." [2]

A variant of the usual legend, which was believed in some parts of Devonshire not many years ago, was that the rings were caused by the fairies catching the colts found in the fields and riding them round and round.

Other superstitions connected with the rings are mentioned by Ramsbottom as current in different countries :

> " That in England was that the circular growths marked the paths of dancing fairies . . . and that they brought good luck to the houses built in fields in which they occurred. French peasants could not be induced to enter the rings because enormous toads with bulging eyes abounded there . . . In Germany the

---

[1] 1611, Shakespeare, *The Tempest*, Act V., Scene i.
[2] 1869, *Notes and Queries*, 4th Ser., IV., Aug. 14.

bare portion of the ring marked the place where a glowing dragon had rested after his nocturnal wanderings. A very prevalent belief was that such rings marked the presence of treasures which could not be obtained without the aid of the fairies or witches. The earliest scientific explanations were almost as fantastic— thunder, lightning, whirlwinds, ants, moles, haystacks, animal urine and such being considered the causal agents." [1]

There has lately been a recrudescence of faith in the existence of fairies, and the rings also figure in the story. The great protagonist of the case for the fairies, Sir Arthur Conan Doyle, although agreeing that the belief that these circles are caused by the beat of the fairy feet is certainly untenable, somewhat ingeniously, but not altogether convincingly, advances the following idea :

> " It might be asserted and could not be denied that the rings once formed, whatever their cause, would offer a very charming course for a circular ring-a-ring dance. Certainly from all time these circles have been associated with the gambols of the little people." [2]

Nor is it only in this country that popular belief has connected toadstools with fairies, and as far away as India the same relationship is found, one of the vernacular names for the Common Mushroom (*Psalliota campestris*) being recorded by Watt [3] as " Kullalic-div," " the Fairies' Cap."

Puff-balls and Fairies. Elves and toadstools are in truth indissolubly linked together, not only in the matter of meadow rings, for other tricksy sprites were said to sow the puff-balls. Here, if any introduction be needed,

---

[1] 1923, Ramsbottom, *A Handbook of the Larger British Fungi*, p. 6.
[2] 1923, Conan Doyle, *The Coming of the Fairies*, p. 101.
[3] 1889, Watt, *Dictionary of Economic Products of India*, Vol. I., p. 130.

let us present Puck—a fairy, and merry wanderer of the night, " rough, knurly-limbed, faun-faced, and shock-pated, a very Shetlander among the gossamer-winged " fairies around him.   He deserves adequate recognition because, according to some, it was Puck who gave his name to the puff-ball.[1]

Fairy Butter, etc. Several different fungi have at various times been associated with the fairies, as is shown by the local names under which they are stated to be known.   Thus Brand tells us that

> " there is a substance found . . . in crevices of limestone rocks . . . near Holywell . . . which is called Menyn Tylna Teg or Fairies' Butter.   So also in Northumberland the common people call a certain fungous excrescence, sometimes found about the roots of old trees, Fairy Butter." [2]

It is probable, however, that the first-named is not of fungus origin, but is limestone in a loose or semi-indurated form, resembling a fungus.   Fairy Butter is also mentioned by Friend, possibly describing the same fungus just alluded to as found in Northumberland, for he says that

> " in the northern counties of England there is a plant called Fairy Butter, . . . receives its name from the supposition that it is made in the night, and scattered about by the fairies." [3]

The plant in question may be *Tremella albida*, although Friend mentions *Exidia glandulosa* as bearing the same popular name,

> " and a broad species of fungus, probably the same as that called Fairy Butter in some parts, is in others known as Pixy-puff." [4]

---

[1] See ch. xv. : The Derivation of Fungus Names.
[2] 1777, Brand, *Popular Antiquities* (1813) II., 339.
[3] 1883, Friend, *Flowers and Flower Lore* (1886), p. 19.
[4] *Loc. cit.*, p. 20.

The same author states :

> " In Lincolnshire we find that a kind of fungus like a cup or old-fashioned purse with small objects inside is called a ' Fairy Purse.' " [1]

This would be either a *Nidularia, Cyathus* or *Crucibulum*. On the next page of the same work, there is a picturesque reference to the Elf-cup or Fairies' Bath (*Peziza coccinea*). We put these statements on record on the strength of the evidence in question, but with reservation, having some doubts as to whether the particular fungi *were* known so extensively under these names as the writers would lead one to suppose.

Fungi and Witches. Leaving the fairies, we may next consider the witches, particularly as *Exidia glandulosa*, already mentioned as " Fairy Butter," is said in some countries to be associated instead with the latter, and termed " Witches' Butter." Dr. Prior asserts that the name was given it from its buttery appearance

> " and unaccountably rapid growth in the night, which has given rise to a superstitious belief, still prevalent in Sweden (where it is called " troll smör " or Troll's Butter), that witches (and trolls) milk the cows and scatter about the butter." [2]

Referring to the same country, Brand tells us that the devil gives them (the witches)

> " a beast about the bigness and shape of a young cat, which they call a carrier. What this carrier brings they must receive for the devil. These carriers fill themselves so full sometimes, that they are forced to spew by the way, which spewing is found in several gardens where Colworts grow, and not far from the houses of these witches. It is of a yellow colour like gold and is called ' Butter of Witches.' " [3]

---

[1] *Loc. cit.,* p. 33.

[2] 1863, Prior, *Popular Names of the British Plants* (1870), p. 252.

[3] 1777, Brand, *Popular Antiquities,* Bohn ed. ; Sir H. Ellis, Relation of the Swedish Witches, Vol. III. (1882), p. 7.

The description might refer equally well to several species of *Tremella*, and these may presumably be also known under the same popular name.

Witches' Brooms. There is another indirect relation between fungi and witches, for the malformed growths, generally known as "witches' brooms," frequently found on many different species of trees, are due to the growth of fungi, mainly various species of *Exoascus*, and it was once believed that trees becoming so affected were those over which witches had flown on their nocturnal excursions. This would incidentally afford a plentiful supply of brooms for future flights.

In reality these malformed growths in their origin bear some relation to the plant galls, and are the result of an irritation set up by the fungus, which stimulates the affected regions to a much more intensive growth, a thick bunch or tangle, usually consisting of a large number of small slender twigs, being formed ; sometimes, but not always, round a hard central core, and generally on the upper side of a branch.   The twigs are sometimes few in number, but may

> " be so numerous and continually divided as to produce between three and four hundred branchlets each not less than 15 inches long.   When the twigs arise from a solid core . . . the weight [may be] very great and [may cause] the branch to bend." [1]

These twigs when young are soft and pliable, but later become hard and brittle, and the brooms may continue growing for many years, sometimes living as long as the tree itself. They occur on the alder, beech, birch, cherry, bullus, elm, laburnum, fir, larch, pine, and spruce.

---

[1] 1909, Connold, *Plant Galls*, p. 76.

Photo by A. E. Peck, Scarborough

Fig. 7.—" And little fleas have lesser fleas." One fungus, *Cordyceps capitata*, growing upon another subterranean fungus, *Elaphomyces granulatus*.

Photo by Authors

Fig. 6.—*Lycoperdon gemmatum*, one of the lesser puffballs.

Photo by A. E. Peck, Scarborough

Fig. 8.—The Jew's Ear (*Hirneola Auricula-Judæ*) the origin of an old superstition.

Photo by A. E. Peck, Scarborough

Fig. 9.—*Lycoperdon pyriforme*, a small puffball commonly found clustered on decaying stumps, in late summer and autumn.

Other Legendary Associations. It is only natural that part of the ill-fame, often attaching to the fungi in popular estimation, should be an association with the Devil. Thus the evil-smelling stinkhorn (*Phallus impudicus*), shown in Fig. 14, is said to be known in Yorkshire as " The Devil's Stinkpot," and in Norfolk as " The Devil's Horn " ; while a puff-ball in some parts of the country is termed " The Devil's Snuff-Box," as it is also by the coloured people in the vicinity of Washington, U.S.A. In Scotland, puff-balls are known as " Blind Men's Een," and Friend records that

> " if by any means the dust from one should enter the eyes it is believed to cause certain blindness " [1]

and no doubt it *is* very irritating.

The Jew's Ear. Another ancient myth connects one of the fungi with Judas Iscariot, who was supposed to have hanged himself upon an elder[2] after betraying Our Lord, in consequence of which this tree frequently bears an appendage strongly resembling a human ear, known as " Judas's Ear," corrupted to " Jew's Ear." This is *Hirneola Auricula-Judae* (Fig. 8), the botanical name of which is merely a translation of the popular one. Mandeville tells us that

> " under mount Syon toward the vale of Josaphat is a well that men call Natatorium Sylo [= The Pool of Siloah], there was our Lord washed after he was baptised. And thereby is the tree on which Judas hanged himselfe for dispaire when he had soulde Christ " ; [3]

---

[1] 1883, Friend, *Flowers and Flower Lore* (1886), p. 327.

[2] This ignominy is divided with the Judas Tree, *Cercis siliquastrum*.

[3] *circa* 1355–1371, *The Voiage and Travayle of Sir John Maundeville, Knight*, 1887 ed., p. 69.

while Friend gives us the following slightly different version of the same passage, apparently from another edition :

> " Mandevile says that between Jerusalem and the valley of Jehoshaphat is Zit the tree of Eldre, that Judas henge himself upon." [1]

At the risk of digressing to the medicinal aspects of the fungi, which are dealt with later, we may refer to Bacon's description of the Jew's Ear as

> " an herb that groweth upon the roots and lower parts of the bodies of trees ; especially of Elders and Ashes.   It hath a strange propertie : for in warm weather it swelleth and openeth extremely. It is not green, but of a duskie brown colour.   And it is used for squinancies and inflamations in the throat : whereby it seemeth to have a mollifying and lenifying vertue." [2]

Thus by a kind of poetic justice, the elder, by means of which Judas died from a throat trouble, later provided a means of remedying indispositions of the same in others.   It is incidentally not quite clear why Judas's Ear, and not his tongue, should commemorate his evil deed, for the latter would have seemed more appropriate.

The Beef-Steak Fungus.   A fungus growth on trees, generally found on an oak, which in the young stage *does* often resemble a tongue, has doubtless played its part in mythology in the past.   This is *Fistulina hepatica*, the Beef-Steak, which varies in colour from flesh-pink to blood-red, is soft, clammy and sticky to the touch, sometimes only two inches or so across, when the

---

[1] 1883, Friend, *Flowers and Flower Lore* (1886), p. 225.
[2] 1627, *Bacon, Sylva Sylvarum, or a Naturall Historie in Ten Centuries*, § 554.

resemblance may be most striking, but often much larger. Of this fungus, Badham says that

> " in the days of enchanted trees you would not have cut it off to pickle or eat on any account, lest the knight to whom it belonged should afterwards come to claim it of you." [1]

In these decadent latter days, when fairies no longer haunt the groves as of yore, and when no more do witches career merrily on broomsticks overhead, it has been pleasant to consider them for a moment, and with them the queer beliefs associating them with the toadstools, for, since a knowledge of the early history of a subject is necessary before one can do full justice to its present state, one should be neither scornful nor unmindful of such fantasies as we have endeavoured to chronicle, and which may otherwise become lost in the vast quantity of material dealing with these plants which has now accumulated.

---

[1] 1847, Badham, *Esculent Funguses of England*, p. 10.

CHAPTER III

The Fungi in Fiction

" And plants, at whose names the verse feels loath,
Filled the place with a monstrous undergrowth,
Prickly and pulpous, and blistering, and blue
Livid, and starred with a lurid dew.

And agarics and fungi, with mildew and mould
Started like mist from the wet ground cold ;
Pale, fleshy, as if the decaying dead
With a spirit of growth had been animated !

Their moss rotted off them, flake by flake
Till the thick stalk stuck like a murderer's stake
Where rags of loose flesh yet tremble on high,
Infecting the winds that wander by."

—1820, SHELLEY, *The Sensitive Plant*, III., 62.

THE mythology and folk-lore of a country is reflected, to a great or lesser degree, in its fiction, and, if we pursue the fungi into this realm, we find both the plants themselves, and the imaginary and fantastic properties with which they have popularly been credited, finding frequent application. They figure in various guises, sometimes appearing as quaint and grotesque curiosities of the countryside, sometimes dreaded as things of evil with deadly attributes, now having magic power in themselves or being created by supernatural forces ; again, as the material for a gourmet's feast ; at times even affording a means of indulgence in intoxication, but generally a little strange and unusual.

Strangeness.   In the first aspect we may recall that Florence Dombey, on her first visit to the Toodles' home in Staggs's Gardens, was

> " conducted forth by the young Toodles to inspect some toadstools and other curiosities of the Gardens." [1]

Great use is made of the fungi in a similar manner in Wells' fantasy " The First Men in the Moon," for they are in their proper environment in such an eerie setting as is there depicted, where their growth, speedy enough under terrestrial conditions, is represented as stimulated to a truly fearsome degree. The quickly-changing appearance of the landscape under this rapid growth is described by Bedford as follows :

> " And all this time the lunar plants were growing around us, higher and denser and more entangled, every moment thicker and taller, spiked plants, green cactus masses, fungi, fleshy and lichenous things, strangest radiate and sinuous shapes." [2]

Later on, when they heard the bellowings of the moon-calves and did not know what frightful monsters might be uttering them, they got down on their hands and knees, and began to crawl through the jungle, still searching for their lost home.   Bedford goes on :

> " We crawled through stony ravines . . . amidst fungi that ripped like thin bladders at our thrust, emitting a watery humour, over a perfect pavement of things like puff-balls, and beneath interminable thickets of scrub. And ever more hopelessly our eyes sought for our abandoned sphere." [3]

Another writer of what we may advisedly describe

---

[1] 1848, Charles Dickens, *Dombey and Son*, ch. vi.
[2] 1900, H. G. Wells, *The First Men in the Moon*, ch. ix.
[3] *Loc. cit.*, ch. xi.

as " fiction," also refers to the mushrooms on the moon, and Baron Munchausen relates of its inhabitants, that,

> " in making war, their principal weapons are radishes, which are used as darts. Those who are wounded by them die immediately.
> " Their shields are made of mushrooms, and their darts (when radishes are out of season) of the tops of asparagus.
> " Some of the natives of the dog-star are to be seen here ; commerce tempts them to ramble . . ." [1]

and the artist has depicted one of them, armed with the lunar weapons in question.

Rapidity of Growth. One aspect of the fungi, the rapidity with which they may grow, has received some attention in fiction, and this rapidity, often marvellous enough in reality, is represented in Wells' book, " The Food of the Gods," as enormously increased by the absorption of the growth-accelerating food prepared by Professor Bensington. And so, with the giant wasps and stupendous rats that were thus let loose upon a peaceful country-side, it is not surprising to find that while common weeds developed to an enormous degree, so puff-balls were found of such portentous dimensions as to astound their first discoverer, the Vicar of the village of Cheasing Eyebright :

> " They were scattered at intervals up and down the path between the near down and the village end—a path he frequented daily in his constitutional round. Altogether, of these abnormal fungi there were, from first to last, quite thirty. The Vicar seems to have stared at each severally, and to have prodded most of them with his stick once or twice. One he attempted to measure with his arms, but it burst at his Ixion embrace.
> " He spoke to several people about them, and said they were

---

[1] 1786, (Rudolph E. Raspe), *Baron Munchausen's Narrative of his Marvellous Travels and Campaigns in Russia, etc.*, reprinted by John Dicks, complete from the original edition, ch. xviii., p. 31.

' marvellous !' and he related to at least seven different persons
the well-known story of the flagstone that was lifted from the
cellar floor by the growth of fungi underneath. He looked up
his Sowerby to see if it was *Lycoperdon coelatum* or *giganteum*—
like all his kind since Gilbert White became famous, he Gilbert-
Whited. He cherished a theory that *giganteum* is unfairly named
. . . The growth of the puff-balls following on the expansion of
the Caddles' baby really ought to have opened the Vicar's eyes."

But he realised some days later, when he found

" another puff-ball, one of the second crop, rising like a roc's egg
out of the abnormally coarsened turf. The thing came upon
him in a flash." [1]

An abnormal growth of fungi is also depicted by
Jules Verne in " A Journey to the Centre of the Earth,"
as occurring on the shores of the vast Central Sea.
Harry relates :

" After we had gone about five hundred yards, we suddenly
turned a steep promontory, and found ourselves close to a lofty
forest ! It consisted of straight trunks with tufted tops, in shape
like parasols. The air seemed to have no effect upon these trees—
which in spite of a tolerable breeze remained as still and motionless
as if they had been petrified.

" I hastened forward. I could find no name for these singular
formations. Did they not belong to the two thousand and
more known trees—or were we to make the discovery of a new
growth ? By no means. When we at last reached the forest,
and stood beneath the trees, my surprise gave way to admiration.

" In truth, I was simply in the presence of a very ordinary
product of the earth, of singular and gigantic proportions. My
uncle unhesitatingly called them by their real names.

" ' It is only,' he said, in his coolest manner, ' a forest of
mushrooms.'

" On close examination I found that he was not mistaken.
Judge of the development attained by this product of damp hot
soils. I had heard that the *lycoperdon giganteum* reaches nine
feet in circumference, but here were white mushrooms, nearly

---

[1] 1904, H. G. Wells, *The Food of the Gods.* Book II., ch. i. : The
Food in the Village.

forty feet high, and with tops of equal dimensions. They grew
in countless thousands—the light could not make its way through
their massive substance, and beneath them reigned a gloomy and
mystic darkness." [1]

Here, undoubtedly, these arborescent fungi appear in
noble guise, and to borrow from another writer :

" Jules Verne at any rate was alive to the possibilities of fungi,
and his outlook is to be preferred to that which holds the group
to be devoid of initiation and crippled by degeneracy." [2]

Some huge fungi are also found in " Peter Pan," where
the infamous Captain Hook, while concocting a plan of
revenge against the Lost Boys,

" sat down on one of the enormous forest mushrooms (in the
Never-Never-Never Land mushrooms grow to a gigantic size)." [3]

Desolation and Ruin.   The fungi have always been
considered as queer fellows, but probably the greatest
play has been made with them as objects of loathing,
to strike a note of tragedy, and especially to intensify
an air of desolation and ruin.   Thus when Florence
Dombey, after the death of her brother, lived in her
father's great dreary house, while it fell gradually into
decay, its desolate condition is indicated by the fact
that—

" mildew and mould began to lurk in closets.   Fungus trees grew
in corners of the cellars," [4]

and it was no doubt most dismal, and eminently suitable
for the flourishing of the fungi.

---

[1] 1864, Jules Verne, *A Journey to the Centre of the Earth* (1921),
ch. xxvii., p. 160.

[2] 1923, F. T. Brooks, Pres. Address to Brit. Myc. Soc., *Trans. Brit.
Myc. Soc.*, Vol. IX., p. 26.

[3] 1907, J. M. Barrie, *loc. cit.*, Part II.

[4] 1848, Charles Dickens, *Dombey and Son*, ch. xxiii.

Photo by Authors

Fig. 10.—A Fairy Ring, formed by *Collybia maculata*.

Photo by Authors

Fig. 11.—Some Elf-cups (*Peziza vesiculosa*).

Photo by Authors

Fig. 12.—" On the wreck of the year they flourished, sucked strange
life from rotten stick and hollow tree." *Calocera viscosa*, on
an old pine stump.

Photo by Authors

Fig. 13.—" Clustered like the uprising roof-trees of a fairy village in
dingle and in dene." The Sulphur Tuft (*Hypholoma
fasciculare*).

In Poe's tale, " The Fall of the House of Usher,"
every stone in the doomed building seemed to show a
sense of its impending fate :

> " The discolouration of ages had been great. Minute fungi
> overspread the whole exterior, hanging in a fine tangled web-work
> from the eaves. Yet all this was apart from any extraordinary
> dilapidation. No portion of the masonry had fallen, and there
> appeared to be a wild inconsistency between its still perfect
> adaptation of parts and the crumbling condition of the individual
> stones. In this there was much that reminded me of the specious
> totality of old woodwork which has rotted for long years in some
> neglected vault with no disturbance from the breath of the
> external air."

Toadstools and such are indeed fit denizens of ruins,
and Eden Phillpotts thus describes the present appearance
of that tragic dwelling-place, Dagger Farm :

> " Now the ruin fades back into nature like a cloud and peers
> ill-favouredly from lush green things. Great umbel-bearing
> plants, blackthorns, and briars strive to bury each lower wall ;
> hart's-tongue ferns loll from the empty joist-holes ; fungus lifts
> its livid cowls beneath." [1]

As attendants on death and decay, the fungi are
portrayed in another of Phillpotts' books in the following
passage :

> " Beneath trees and hedgerows the ripe mosses gleamed, and
> coral and amber fungi, with amanita and other hooded folk. In
> companies and clusters they sprang, or arose misshapen, sinister,
> and alone. Some were orange and orange-tawny ; others white
> and purple ; not a few peered forth livid, blotched, and speckled,
> as with venom spattered from some reptile's jaws. On the wreck
> of the year they flourished, sucked strange life from rotten stick
> and hollow tree, opened gills on lofty branch and bough, shone
> in the green grass rings of the meadows, thrust cap and cowl
> from the concourse of the dead leaves in ditches, clustered like
> the uprising rooftrees of a fairy village in dingle and in dene." [2]

[1] Eden Phillpotts, *The Farm of the Dagger*, ch. i.
[2] 1896, Eden Phillpotts, *Children of the Mist*, Book IV., ch. vii.

A tone of tragedy is again intensified by fungi in "The Song of Hiawatha," where the hero :

> "Wounded, weary and desponding,
> With his mighty war-club broken,
> With his mittens torn and tattered,
> And three useless arrows only,
> Paused to rest beneath a pine-tree,
> From whose branches trailed the mosses,
> And whose trunk was coated over
> With the Dead-man's Mocassin-leather,
> With the fungus white and yellow." [1]

In Stevenson's fable, " The House of Eld," Jack was searching for the sorcerer's house in the Wood of Eld,

> " so he came to that wood and entered in, and he was aware of a house in a low place, where funguses grew, and the trees met, and the steaming of the marsh arose about it like a smoke," [2]

and the "funguses" certainly add to the weirdness of the scene. In " The Vanished Messenger," E. Phillips Oppenheim employs a fungus to enhance the bizarre character of the underground chamber at the tower near Salthouse in which the vanished messenger has been temporarily imprisoned :

> " There was a thick carpet upon the floor, a sofa piled with cushions in one corner, and several other articles of furniture. The walls, however, were uncovered and were stained with damp. A great pink fungus stood out within a few inches of the bed, a grim mixture of exquisite colouring and loathsome imperfections. The atmosphere was fetid." [3]

The supposition that these loathsome fellows arise from the decay of more beautiful things is supported by

---

[1] 1855, H. W. Longfellow, *The Song of Hiawatha*, ix., 195.
[2] 1896, R. L. Stevenson, *The House of Eld* (1906), p. 181.
[3] 1916, E. Phillips Oppenheim, *The Vanished Messenger*.

Shelley, and in his poem " The Sensitive Plant," he describes a lovely garden, guarded with every tender care by a lady, who died, leaving it to fall into neglect and decay. The progress of the disorder is indicated in the verses at the head of this chapter.

Evil Smell. In the last verse [1] is an indirect reference to another evil attribute of the fungi, the intolerable smell possessed by some of them, the odium of which is partly shared by nearly all. Of this theme, Oppenheim makes considerable use in " The Great Impersonation," in order to create an atmosphere of horror and repugnance. In this book, Middleton, the gamekeeper, is describing to Sir Everard Dominey the Black Wood, in which Roger Unthank was supposed to have met his death, and which his ghost was said to haunt, as follows :

> " ' There's nowt like this wood in the world, sir,' the old man asserted doggedly. ' The bottom's rotten from end to end and the top's all poisonous. The birds die there on the trees. It's chockful of reptiles and unclean things, with green and purple fungi, two feet high, with poison in the very sniff of them. The man who enters that wood goes to his grave.' " [2]

Later on, when Sir Everard is questioning the foreman regarding the same wood, which his men are clearing at the former's instructions, the latter says :

> " And there's fungus there which, when you touch it, sends out a smell enough to make a strong man faint." [3]

---

[1] This verse refers to the method of ' decay ' of the Shaggy-cap, *Coprinus comatus* (Fig. 76). It is curious that the verse in question, although appearing in the first edition in 1820, is not found in several later editions, and it is suggested that it seemed over-horrible when Shelley first saw it in print. This may well be the case.

[2] 1920, E. Phillips Oppenheim, *The Great Impersonation*, p. 208.

[3] *Loc. cit.*, p. 296.

Tennyson does not despise a similar use of fungi, and it was probably the odour emitted by the stinkhorn (*Phallus impudicus*) which inspired him when he wrote the passage describing the contempt expressed by Lynette for Gareth, for she behaved :

> " As one
> That smells a foul-flesh'd agaric in the holt,
> And deems it carrion of some woodland thing,
> Or shrew, or weasel, nipt her slender nose
> With petulant thumb and finger, shrilling, ' Hence ! ' " [1]

It was undoubtedly the same evil-smelling toadstool that is referred to by Fragrantia, in discussing, with Baron Munchausen, Dr. Johnson's visit to the Hebrides, when the former says :

> "Oh, 'twas base ! to be treated everywhere with politeness and hospitality, and to return invidiously to smellfungus them all over." [2]

More Pleasing Aspects. But very few toadstools have a really bad odour and it was probably the pleasant earthy smell possessed by many which Andrew Black had in mind when he spoke of

> " a moist odour of toadstools and fern " [3]

and which made Thomas Hardy write of

> " an afternoon which had a fungous smell out of doors." [4]

Nor do the toadstools always grow amid unhappy surroundings, linked with decay and desolation, and in

---

[1] 1859, Alfred Tennyson, *Gareth and Lynette*, 728.
[2] *Loc. cit.*, Part II., ch. x., p. 67.
[3] 1872, Andrew Black, *Strange Adventures of a Phaeton*, ch. xxii.
[4] 1876, Thomas Hardy, *The Hand of Ethelberta* (1890), p. 84.

a rather more cheerful strain may we refer to Kipling's
story of " The Cat that Walked by Himself," in the
illustration of which he is most excellently pictured in
the act of so doing, together with some toadstools,
which

"had to grow there because the woods were so wet." [1]

Legendary Associations. We may next consider
the toadstools in fiction as thought to be created by
supernatural forces, and the classical example of this is
the tradition of the fairy rings. These were known in
folk lore long before they were in fiction, and the former
aspect has been dealt with in the previous chapter. In
fiction, however, it is best illustrated in Kipling's story,
" Puck of Pook's Hill." [2] You may remember that the
two children, Dan and Una, were acting as much as
they could remember of " A Midsummer Night's
Dream," to an audience of three cows :

"The Theatre lay in a meadow called the Long Slip. A little
millstream, carrying water to a mill two or three fields away,
bent round one corner of it, and in the middle of the bend lay a
large old fairy Ring of darkened grass, which was the stage . . .

"Their play went beautifully . . . They were both so pleased
that they acted it three times over from beginning to end before
they sat down in the unthistly centre of the Ring to eat eggs and
Bath Olivers. This was when they heard a whistle among the
alders on the bank, and they jumped.

"The bushes parted. In the very spot where Dan had stood
as Puck they saw a small, brown, broad-shouldered, pointy-eared
person with a snub nose, slanting blue eyes, and a grin that ran
right across his freckled face. He shaded his forehead as though
he were watching Quince, Snout, Bottom and the others rehearsing
Pyramus and Thisbe, and, in a voice as deep as Three Cows asking
to be milked, he began :

---

[1] 1902, Rudyard Kipling, *The Just So Stories*, pp. 206–207.

[2] 1906, Rudyard Kipling, *Puck of Pook's Hill*, ch. i : Weland's
Sword.

" ' What hempen homespuns have we swaggering here,
        So near the cradle of our fairy Queen ? '

" He stopped, hollowed one hand round his ear, and, with a
wicked twinkle in his eye, went on :

" ' What, a play toward ? I'll be auditor,
        An actor too, perhaps, if I see cause.'

" The children looked and gasped. The small thing—he was
no taller than Dan's shoulder—stepped quietly into the Ring.

" ' I'm rather out of practice,' said he ; ' but that's the way
my part ought to be played.'

" Still the children stared at him—from his dark blue cap,
like a big columbine flower, to his bare, hairy feet. At last he
laughed.

" ' Please don't look like that. It isn't my fault. What else
could you expect ? ' he said.

" ' We didn't expect anyone ' Dan answered slowly. ' This is
our field.'

" ' Is it ? ' said their visitor, sitting down, ' Then what on
Human Earth made you act *Midsummer Night's Dream* three
times over, *on* Midsummer Eve, *in* the middle of a Ring and
under—right *under* one of my oldest hills in Old England ?
Pook's Hill—Puck's Hill—Puck's Hill—Pook's Hill ! It's as plain
as the nose on my face.' " [1]

And after further converse, said Dan :

" ' Then there's the verse about the Rings. When I was
little it always made me feel unhappy in my inside.'

" ' Witness those rings and roundelays, do you mean,' boomed
Puck, with a voice like a great church organ.

" ' Of theirs which yet remain,
        Were footed in Queen Mary's days
        On many a grassy plain.
        But since of late Elizabeth,
        And later James came in,
        Are never seen on any heath,
        As when the time hath been.' " [2]

The fairy ring is also found in fiction in an old book

---

[1] *Loc. cit.*
[2] *Loc. cit.*

which purports to relate the curious adventures of a
certain Tom Whigg, who was apparently a more ancient
prototype of Gabriel Grub, but who fell into the hands
of kindlier spirits, in whose revels he joined, for we are
told that :

> " Tom . . . trod out Fairy Circles at the Head of each Tribe." [1]

and if there were not mushrooms growing in these rings
thereafter, there should have been.

The traditional side of the associations of fairies
with toadstools is told elsewhere, but they have not
always been considered as made by the magic of fairies,
and Harrison Ainsworth, in " The Lancashire Witches,"
relates how, by the machinations of the witches :

> " all the sallets are turned to Jewes-Ears, Mushrooms and
> Puckfists."

It is but a step from the mushroom produced by
supernatural arts to that having magical properties, and
readers of Lewis Carroll will need no introduction to
the mushroom on which Alice found the caterpillar.
You will remember that, after the usual desultory
conversation, the caterpillar informed her :

> " ' One side will make you grow taller, and the other side
> will make you grow shorter.'
> " ' One side of *what* ? The other side of *what* ? thought
> Alice to herself.'
> " ' Of the mushroom,' said the Caterpillar, just as if she had
> asked it aloud ; and in another moment it was out of sight." [2]

And on experiment, Alice found that it was so.

---

[1] 1711, *Acc. Distemper Tom Whigg*, II., 44.
[2] 1865, Lewis Carroll, *Alice's Adventures in Wonderland*, ch. v :
Advice from a Caterpillar.

Foods. Not the least important aspect in which
the fungi are presented in fiction is the gastronomic one.
They are generally introduced as luxurious adjuncts to
the feast, and pride of place may be given to those
toothsome delicacies, the morels and truffles. Gay tells
us that :

> " Spongy morells in strong ragousts are found,
>   And in the soup the slimy snail is drown'd." [1]

This sounds as if it might be nourishing, but a little
glutinous. As a contrast, we may cite Countess
Winchelsea to the effect that :

> " in the plain unstudied sauce, Nor Treufle, Nor Morillia was," [2]

evidently an adjunct to more spartan fare. At a slightly
later period, Pope apostrophizes :

> " Thy Truffles, Périgord ! thy Hams, Bayonne ! " [3]

Readers of Thackeray will remember that, at Mrs.
Perkins's ball, Mr. M. A. Titmarsh says :

> " I gave Miss Bunion, with my own hands, four bumpers of
> champagne : and such a quantity of goose-liver and truffles that
> I don't wonder she took a glass of cherry-brandy afterwards." [4]

But it is in the justly-named " Memorials of
Gormandising " that the truffles really come into their
kingdom, and Mr. Titmarsh thus describes his
appreciation of the truffled partridge that, in company
with a friend, he consumed at the Café Foy in Paris :

> " We were kept waiting between the steak and the partridge
> some ten minutes or so . . . Presently, we were aware of an
> odour gradually coming towards us, something musky, fiery,

---

[1] 1716, Gay, *Trivia*, III., 203.
[2] 1713, Countess Winchelsea, *Misc. Poems*, 35.
[3] 1742, Pope, *Dunciad*, IV., 558.
[4] 1847, Thackeray, *Mrs. Perkins's Ball*, p. 17.

savoury, mysterious,—a hot drowsy smell, that lulls the senses,
and yet inflames them, the *truffles* were coming ! Yonder they
lie, caverned under the full bosom of the red-legged bird. My
hand trembled as, after a little pause, I cut the animal in two.
G—— said I did not give him his share of the truffles ; I don't
believe I did. I spilled some salt into my plate, and a little
cayenne pepper—very little ; we began, as far as I can remember,
the following conversation :—

"*Gustavus.* Chop, chop, chop.

"*Michael Angelo.* Globlobloblob.

"*G.* Gobble.

"*M.A.* Obble.

"*G.* Here's a big one.

"*M.A.* Hobgob. What wine shall we have ? I should
like some champagne.

"*G.* It's bad here. Have some Sauterne.

"*M.A.* Very well. Hobgobglobglob, &c.

"*Auguste* (opening the Sauterne). Cloo-oo-oo-oop   The
cork is out ; he pours it into the glass, glock, glock, glock.

"Nothing more took place in the way of talk. The poor
little partridge was soon a heap of bones—a very little heap. A
trufflesque odour was left in the room, but only an odour." [1]

But there are certainly good and bad truffles, and
on another occasion, Titmarsh records that :

"the poulet á la Marengo is bad—too oily by far ; the truffles
are not of this year, as they should be, for there are cartloads in
town : they are poor in flavour, and have only been cast into the
dish a minute before it was brought to table, and what is the
consequence ? They do not flavour the meat in the least ; some
faint trufflesque savour you may get as you are crunching each
individual root, but that is all, and that all not worth the having ;
for as nothing is finer than a good truffle, in like manner nothing
is meaner than a bad one. It is merely pompous, windy, and
pretentious, like those scraps of philosophy with which a certain
eminent novelist decks out his meat.

"A mushroom, thought I, is better a thousand times than
these tough flavourless roots. I finished every one of them,
however, and the fine fat capon's thigh which they surrounded." [2]

---

[1] 1841, Thackeray, *Memorials of Gormandising, Works* (1885), Vol.
XXV., p. 387.

[2] *Loc. cit.*, p. 393.

To verify whether mushrooms were really superior to those tasteless truffles, Titmarsh ordered a dish to try, and apparently found that they were, for he ate such an immense quantity of them, that he began to be afraid of the consequences.

Thackeray was not the only author who was fond of truffles, and they are placed on a gastronomic pinnacle by Elinor Glyn, when she refers to :

" truffled partridge in aspic." [1]

Other writers have been content with less aristocratic members of the fungus tribe, and when the Pickwickians had arrived at the Bull Inn at Rochester, Mr. Pickwick addressed their fellow-traveller, the versatile Jingle, as follows :

" 'You rendered us a very important service this morning, sir,' said he, 'will you allow us to offer a slight mark of our gratitude by begging the favour of your company at dinner ? '
" ' Great pleasure—not presume to dictate, but broiled fowl and mushrooms—capital thing ! what time ? ' " [2]

However, it is not only as luxuries that we may find fungi as foods in fiction, but also as necessities. In " The First Men in the Moon," when Cavor and Bedford were hiding from the Selenites, they had become ravenous with hunger, and had recourse to a fungus to relieve their pangs. Bedford says :

" Ever and again I was seized with fits of hungry yawning. We came to flat places overgrown with fleshy red things, monstrous coralline growths ; as we pushed against them they snapped and broke. I noted the quality of the broken surfaces. The confounded stuff certainly looked of a biteable texture. Then it seemed to me that it smelt rather well . . . ' I'll chance it,' I

---

[1] 1902, Elinor Glyn, *The Reflections of Ambrosine*, II., viii.
[2] 1836, Dickens, *Posthumous Papers of the Pickwick Club*, ch. ii.

said. . . . For a time we did nothing but eat. The stuff was not unlike a terrestrial mushroom, only it was much laxer in texture, and, as one swallowed it, it warmed the throat. At first we experienced a mere mechanical satisfaction in eating ; then our blood began to run warmer, and we tingled at the lips and fingers, and then new and slightly irrelevant ideas came bubbling up in our minds. . . . I felt that my head swam, but I put this down to the stimulating effect of food after a long fast. ' Ess'lent discov'ry yours, Cavor,' said I. ' Se'nd on'y to the " tato." '

" ' Whajer mean ? ' asked Cavor. ' Scovery of the moon— se'nd on'y to the " tato." '

" I looked at him, shocked at his suddenly hoarse voice, and by the badness of his articulation. It occurred to me in a flash that he was intoxicated, possibly by the fungus. . . .

" From that point my memory of the action of that abominable fungus becomes confused. I remember vaguely that we declared our intention of standing no nonsense from any confounded insects, that we decided it ill became men to hide shamefully upon a mere satellite, that we equipped ourselves with huge armfuls of the fungus—whether for missile purposes or not I do not know— and, heedless of the stabs of the bayonet scrub, we started forth into the sunshine." [1]

Intoxicants. From the mythical mushroom of the moon, we may turn to a terrestrial one capable of producing a similar result when eaten. Here we are on surer ground, for the physiological effects of the toadstool which Wells describes in " The Purple Pileus " are practically identical with those produced by a small quantity of the flesh of the Fly Agaric (*Amanita muscaria*).[2] Under the temporary effects of fungus poisoning, one of Wells' characters plays strange pranks, and in a truly diverting vein does he relate, in the story in question, the tribulations of Mr. Coombes, a little harassed and hen-pecked draper, and how from adversity he rode to triumph by the aid of toadstools. Our hero

---

[1] *l.c.*, ch. xi.
[2] See page 233.

led an unhappy life, being handicapped in his struggling business by a lack of support from his pleasure-loving spouse; while he also suffered greatly, both in pocket and reputation, from his wife's visitors. One Sunday afternoon, he had vainly protested against the playing of banjo tunes, and

> " the end was, that Mr. Coombes ordered his visitors out of the house and they wouldn't go, and so he said he would go himself,"

which he did, to the accompaniment of the same insulting strains.

Now he found himself going along a muddy path under some firs :

> " it was late October, and the ditches and heaps of fir needles were gorgeous with clumps of fungi."

Mr. Coombes was sick of life, and as he communed with himself and thought wildly of drowning, or of other means by which he might escape so intolerable an existence, the purple pileus caught his eye.

> " They were wonderful fellows, these fungi, thought Mr. Coombes, and all of them the deadliest poisons, as his father had often told him."

But having in his desperation consumed some, with the fell intent of making away with himself,

> " he was no longer dull—he felt bright, cheerful. And his throat was afire. He laughed in the sudden gaiety of his heart. Had he been dull ? He did not know ; but at any rate he would be dull no longer. He got up and stood unsteadily, regarding the universe with an agreeable smile. He began to remember. He could not remember very well, because of a steam roundabout that was beginning in his head. And he knew he had been disagreeable at home, just because they wanted to be happy. They were quite right ; life should be as gay as possible. He would go home, and make it up, and reassure them. And why not take some of this delightful toadstool with him, for them to eat. A hatful, no less. Some of those red ones with white spots

Photo by Authors

Fig. 14.—" A foul-flesh'd agaric in the holt." The Common
   Stinkhorn (*Phallus impudicus*).

Photo by Authors

Fig. 15.—" The purple pileus caught his eye." The Fly Agaric
   (*Amanita muscaria*).

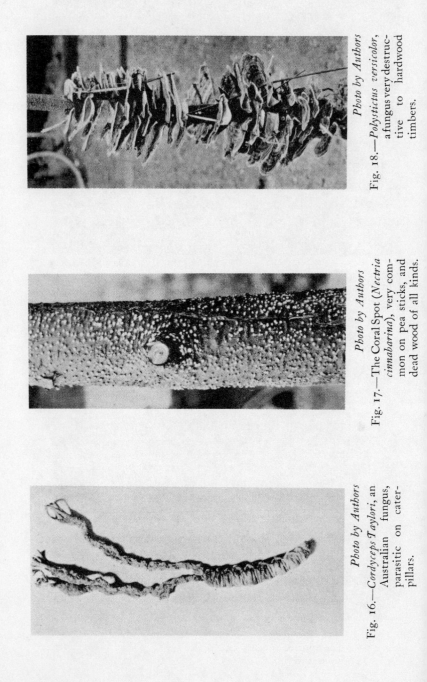

Photo by Authors

Fig. 18.—*Polystictus versicolor*, a fungus very destructive to hardwood timbers.

Photo by Authors

Fig. 17.—The Coral Spot (*Nectria cinnabarina*), very common on pea sticks, and dead wood of all kinds.

Photo by Authors

Fig. 16.—*Cordyceps Taylori*, an Australian fungus, parasitic on caterpillars.

as well, and a few yellow. He had been a dull dog, an enemy to merriment ; he would make up for it. It would be gay to turn his coat-sleeves inside out, and stick some yellow gorse into his waistcoat pockets. Then home—singing—for a jolly evening."

But when he arrived, his visitors, very startled by his new appearance—his face

" was livid white, his eyes were unnaturally large and bright, and his pale blue lips were drawn back in a cheerless grin"—

showing no inclination to partake of the offering of friendship he had brought them, he became mad with fury, shouting

" in such a huge voice as Mrs. Coombes had never heard before . . . ' My house. I'm master 'ere. Eat what I give yer ! ' "

Whereupon the two women fled to safety, the luckless Clarence, now showing himself a coward, remaining in the hands of Mr. Coombes after a similar but futile attempt to escape.

" Mr. Clarence is singularly reticent of the details of what occurred. It seems that Mr. Coombes' transitory irritation had vanished again and he was once more a genial playfellow. And as there were knives and meat choppers about, Clarence very generously resolved to humour him and to avoid anything tragic. It is beyond dispute that Mr. Coombes played with Mr. Clarence to his heart's content . . . He insisted gaily on Clarence trying the fungi, and, after a friendly tussle, was smitten with remorse at the mess he was making of his guest's face. It also appears that Clarence was dragged under the sink and his face scrubbed with the blacking brush—he being still resolved to humour the lunatic at any cost—and that finally, in a somewhat dishevelled, chipped, and discoloured condition, he was assisted to his coat and shown out by the back door."

The subsequent proceedings of Mr. Coombes, sufficiently enlivening though they were, are too lengthy to chronicle here, but his evening ended in the coal cellar, in a deep and healing sleep.

And having thus valiantly asserted himself (" Now you know what I'm like when I'm roused," as he told Mrs. Coombes next morning) his wife was changed from a hindrance to a helpmate, and success smiled on him thereafter. Some years later he was walking along under the same firs, and recounting to his brother Tom, home from Australia, the tale of his early struggles and how he was finally successful, but with no mention of the toadstools.

> " ' What a lot of these funguses there are about here ! ' remarked Brother Tom presently. ' I can't see what use they are in the world.'
> " Mr. Coombes looked. ' I dessay they're sent for some wise purpose,' said Mr. Coombes.
> " And that was as much thanks as the purple pileus ever got for maddening this absurd little man to the pitch of decisive action, and so altering the whole course of his life." [1]

Poisons. We have referred already to the manner in which various authors, in making use of the fungi, have embroidered their theme ; even when keeping fairly accurately to the subject, they have often not been able to refrain from painting in a few high lights. This is particularly well illustrated in a description of another case of toadstool poisoning, also ascribed to an *Amanita*, which on this occasion has fatal effects.

Thus Ernest Bramah [2] in " The Mystery of the Poisoned Dish of Mushrooms " records the evidence of a doctor in the following manner :

> " Dr. Slark was the next witness. . . . He understood that the case was one of convulsions and went provided for that contingency, but on his arrival he found the patient already dead. From his own examination and from what he was told he had no

---

[1] H. G. Wells, *The Purple Pileus.*
[2] 1923, Ernest Bramah, *The Eyes of Max Carrados*, p. 126.

hesitation in diagnosing the case as one of agaric poisoning. He
saw no reason to suspect any of the food except the mushrooms,
and all the symptoms pointed to bhurine, the deadly principle
of *Amanita Bhuroides*, or the Black Cap, as it was popularly called,
from its fancied resemblance to the head-dress assumed by a judge
in passing death sentence, coupled with its sinister and well-
merited reputation.   It was always fatal."

This account is evidently intended to depict *Amanita
phalloides* (Fig. 72), sometimes known as the Death Cap,
which in all conscience is deadly enough in itself.   The
author has, however, endeavoured to increase the
gruesomeness of his subject by changing the white cap
of this species to a sombre blackness, presumably to
intensify the warning which its appearance should
convey.

Figurative Uses.   Before leaving the fungi in
fiction, we should refer to their figurative uses.   The
employment of the term " mushroom " (and " puff-ball,"
etc.) to describe anything which has suddenly risen to
prominence, and which, like the mushroom, may be
expected to vanish as suddenly into the obscurity from
which it sprang, is of course an obvious one.   There is,
however, another usage which came into being by
reason of the almost universal contempt with which in
older days the fungus family was regarded, and which
led to the word " mushroom " being often personally
applied, in fiction as well as in fact, as a term of
disparagement.   This use is now quite obsolete, but
we cannot forbear to quote some quaint examples of
it :

" Summon a parley sirs, that we may know
Whether these Mushroms here will yeeld or no." [1]

---

[1] 1594, Greene *Selimus* Wks. (Grosart) xiv., 282.

" Come Ladies, I'le be your Gaurdian ;
　　Let these Musrumes stand if they dare." [1]

Curiously enough, an exactly parallel usage, which is discussed later,[2] existed among the Romans in the third century B.C.

There are naturally many other allusions in fiction to fungi, under their various aspects, but we have sufficiently shown that they have often played their own distinctive part " to adorn a tale," in which we may find, either tragedy or comedy, according to the author's bent.

[1] 1676, D'Urfey, *Mad. Fickle*, II., i.
[2] See ch. xiv : Some further Historical Aspects of the Fungi.

CHAPTER IV

The Fungi in Reality:

THEIR STRUCTURE AND CHARACTERISTICS.

O NE is loath to shatter these charming fantasies, but truth must prevail, for despite the queer properties with which they have been invested, and the romantic tales woven around them in the past, fungi are, after all, only commonplace natural objects, holding a definite position in the plant world. Since, however, they differ so materially from the popular conception of a plant, it is interesting to consider, by comparison with their associates, what these differences really are.

Mode of Reproduction of the Flowering Plants. Of the vast multitude of apparently dissimilar plant forms, which comprise the vegetable kingdom, few fail to exhibit certain characteristics by means of which their affinities may be traced. Thus, considered from one standpoint—that of the way in which the individual reproduces its kind—all plants fall into one or the other of two definite classes. The more familiar plants produce flowers, which eventually ripen into fruits bearing seeds. *Each seed contains an embryo plant,* capable, under suitable conditions, of developing into a new individual. The group of plants having this common characteristic is known as the *flowering plants* or *phanerogams*. Its members exhibit a high degree of development, and a corresponding complexity of structure, one aspect of which is the differentiation of the plant body into root, stem, and leaves. The flowering plants cover a wide range of forms, extending from the most majestic forest tree to the humblest wayside weed.

Mode of Reproduction of the Flowerless Plants. The second group, the *flowerless plants* or *cryptogams*, comprises plants of a lower order. These bear no flowers of any kind, and reproduce themselves normally by means of microscopic bodies, known as *spores, which contain no embryos*, but which, like seeds, are capable of germinating and producing new individuals. This group contains plants of such diverse organizations as those of the ferns, horse-tails and club-mosses ; the true mosses and liverworts ; the algae, including seaweeds ; the bacteria ; the fungi ; and the slime-moulds. With the exception of the first three classes, these plants are of simple cellular structure, showing no development of vessels or true tissue, and possessing no roots, stems, or leaves, as these terms are generally understood.

Mode of Nutrition of the Flowering Plants. Considering the plant world from another standpoint—that of the mode of nutrition of its members—we find that most plants obtain the starchy and other organic foods on which they live, by building them up from the gaseous constituents of the atmosphere and the mineral salts of the soil. This they are enabled to do by the presence in their tissues of a green colouring matter, chlorophyll, contained in granules. The primary

function of these granules is, under suitable conditions
of warmth, moisture and light, to convert carbon dioxide
and water into the carbohydrates which form the chief
food of these plants. To emphasize the importance of
chlorophyll, it may be said that, without it, the members
of this group could not exist, and with their passing, all
human and animal life, as it is to-day, would cease,
since organic food is necessary for it. It is also of
interest to note that it is this chlorophyll or " leaf-
green " which supplies these plants with the green
pigment which strikes the universal colour-note of
vegetation.

Mode of Nutrition of some Flowerless Plants.
A smaller group of plants, of which the fungi are the
chief representatives, are, however, destitute of
chlorophyll, and are thus incapable of manufacturing
their food in the manner described.   They are, therefore,
compelled to absorb it in the form of the complex
organic compounds already elaborated by other plants,
either *directly*, from these plants, or *indirectly*, from
animals which have fed on them. This somewhat
immoral habit, of living on the energies of their neigh-
bours, renders it unnecessary for them to perform many
of the duties of the flowering plants, and this has caused
their evolution to develop on simpler lines. These facts
explain why the fungi are so primitive in growth, when
compared with the higher and infinitely more
complex development exhibited, for example, by an oak
tree.

**Essential Differences between a Flowering Plant
and a Fungus.** If then, in the light of these facts, we
compare a typical flowering-plant with a typical fungus,
we find that the two are, in a sense, diametrically

opposed to one another, the material differences being as follows :

Typical Flowering Plant.	Typical Fungus.
Plant body of root, stem, leaves and flowers.	Plant body variously shaped.
Reproduction by seeds.	Reproduction by spores.
Chlorophyll present.	Chlorophyll absent.
Food manufactured from simple inorganic materials.	Food absorbed in complex organic state.
Light essential for development.	Light not essential.

Evolution of the Fungi. These being thus so diverse from the flowering plants, one may well enquire how they originated ; and on this point there is a conflict of opinion. The oldest and most widely-accepted theory is that they have degenerated from the algae, or " seaweeds," and, by the gradual adoption of their present mode of life, have lost the need for chlorophyll, and, therefore, the chlorophyll itself. The more modern line of thought, and one that is probably nearer the truth, is that the fungi have evolved directly from the *protists*, that indefinite and indefinable group of primitive forms of life, which exist on the borderline of the animal and vegetable kingdoms. In the latter case, they naturally never possessed chlorophyll. Whichever view is taken, there is little doubt that the early ancestors of the fungi emerged from the primeval slime, and, gradually adapting themselves, by various biological changes, to their new surroundings, have developed in course of time into the multitude of diverse types existing to-day.

Extent of the Fungi. It is this multiplicity of forms, many of whose life-cycles are extremely complicated, and of which some have never been elucidated, together with the vast number of individuals concerned, that renders the intensive study of the fungi as a whole the work of a lifetime. It is thus obvious that, in the limited space here available, it is only possible to discuss the botanical aspects of this huge subject very broadly, and even then our remarks must be considered as referring more particularly to that sufficiently numerous class commonly designated—the larger British fungi. Of these, the most familiar is of course the Common Mushroom (*Psalliota campestris*) and since this species is typical of the vast majority of the kinds under immediate consideration, it will simplify matters if first we trace out its life history and structure before attempting any comprehensive description of the fungi in bulk.

Life History of the Common Mushroom. If, then, a brick of mushroom spawn, which acts as the basis for the cultivation of this esculent, is obtained from a nurseryman, and is carefully examined, it will be found to consist of a compressed mass of compost, permeated in all directions by a vast network of minute interwoven branching whitish threads, in appearance not unlike a loose weft of wadding. This system, which is known as the *mycelium*, constitutes the vegetative portion of the mushroom plant, and is the part concerned with growth and nutrition. The function of this organ is to absorb, from the organic materials of the mushroom bed, the food requisite for its own development, and for the eventual production of the fruiting bodies. It is in this respect analogous in a sense to the root, stem, and leaves of a flowering plant.

Production of Fruiting Bodies. When, as described elsewhere (p. 207), the spawn is placed in a mushroom bed, this dormant mycelium springs into life and " runs " or spreads in all directions, gradually permeating the compost, as it did the " brick." Having reached a suitable stage of development, the threads of

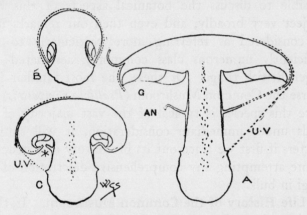

Fig. 19.—THE DEVELOPMENT OF THE FRUITING BODY IN THE COMMON MUSHROOM (*Psalliota campestris*).   Half natural size.

A, full grown specimen, AN = annulus, or ring; UV = universal veil : B, young specimen ("button"): C, half-grown specimen, showing rupture of veil at *.

the mycelium near the surface of the bed bunch themselves together, here and there, into small knots, which enlarge, take shape, and eventually burst through the surface of the bed in the form of " button " mushrooms. The " buttons " continue to expand, resulting in the mature specimens with which everyone is familiar.

These mushrooms constitute the reproductive portion of the fungus, and may be termed the fruiting-bodies. Their function is to produce and liberate the spores, the microscopic mushroom "seeds." If we examine one of these fruiting-bodies more closely, the mechanism for accomplishing this task becomes obvious. A mushroom consists of an umbrella-like *cap*, supported on a stout *stem*, and bearing on its lower surface, radiating outward like the spokes of a wheel, a number of vertical knife-like plates, known as the *gills*, which are covered with the spore-bearing surface or *hymenium*. During the "button" stage, these delicate gills are protected from injury, partly by the convexity of the cap, and partly by a veil-like membrane, which joins the edge of the cap to the stem. In expanding, in order to liberate the spores, the cap tears this membrane, some remnants of which remain attached to the edge of the cap, while the major portion is left on the stem in the form of a *ring*. The gills are thus completely exposed and the spores have access to the air. The latter bodies are liberated from the gills in vast numbers,[1] and are so impalpable that they are carried away on the lightest puff of air, and scattered far and wide. On reaching a suitable substratum—a thing which obviously seldom occurs—the spore germinates, and produces a new mycelium, the life-cycle being thus complete. This, then, is briefly the story of the mushroom, and what is true of it is equally true, with but varying details, of almost all of the larger species of fungi. It is seen that, fundamentally, a fungus plant consists of two distinct parts; the vegetative system or mycelium,

---

[1] Buller has computed the number of spores resulting from a single mushroom as 1,800,000 000.

and the reproductive system or fruiting body. The mycelium may, and frequently does, live for years, without producing any fruiting-bodies; while, on the other hand, the latter can only arise from a mycelium.[1]

These basic facts having been clearly grasped, we may pass on to the consideration of these two systems, vegetative and reproductive respectively, as they appear in the larger fungi as a whole.

THE SPAWN OR MYCELIUM.

The spawn or mycelium of a fungus, as has already been seen in the case of the Common Mushroom, is necessary to its nutrition and is, therefore, a constant feature in the life history of the plant. True, in some of the microscopic forms it may be so rudimentary as to be almost indistinguishable, and even in the larger fungi, it is, owing to its subterranean mode of growth, a not very obvious feature. Nevertheless, it is always present. In most places where undisturbed organic matter abounds, a careful search will usually reveal the mycelium of one fungus or another; while in its more usual haunts—the woods and forests—every fragment of leaf-mould, every hedge-bottom, every decaying stump or log, will be found to be literally teeming with it.

Mode of Development of Mycelium. The mycelium usually arises from a spore in the following

---

[1] It is necessary that this matter should be quite clear, since a very common but quite erroneous belief is that the fruiting bodies (the mushrooms, puff-balls, etc.) are complete plants, any mycelium which remains attached after pulling them up being considered as " roots." We are aware that the term " fungus " *is* frequently applied to these fruiting bodies alone, and, in the absence of a more suitable word, this is quite permissible, if the actual facts are not overlooked.

manner. On germination the spore throws out one or more minute germ-tubes, which elongate by apical growth and branch into a number of filaments or *hyphae*, these continuing to ramify until a typical mycelium is formed. With those fungi which inhabit decaying wood and the like, the mycelium is naturally confined by the limits of the host. In terrestrial species, however, especially where no obstacles impede growth, the general tendency is for the mycelium to spread in all directions, so that it gradually assumes the form of a large subterranean rosette, of ever-increasing size. In course of time, the area around where the spore originally

Fig. 20.—SPORES OF *Psathyrella prona* GERMINATING. ×350.

alighted becomes exhausted of available nutriment and the mycelium in this area dies. The rosette thus becomes a ring of mycelium, whose outer filaments are continually pushing forward into areas of fresh nutriment, and whose inner filaments are equally continuously dying of starvation. Since the mycelium requires oxygen for its growth, it remains near the surface of the soil, and the chemical and physical changes which it produces, react on the local vegetation and cause the appearance on the surface of a bare ring corresponding to the ring of growing mycelium. This bare ring is the "fairy ring" of mythology. Ritzema Bos has very aptly compared the formation of a fairy ring, to the circular flame which results from dropping a lighted match in dry grass, where, on a still day, the flame spreads regularly outward. A fairy ring is usually bordered by vegetation of a more vigorous growth, while that within the area of the ring is often quite rank. Shantz and Piemeisel account for these three zones in the following manner : 1. (Outer)—Acceleration of growth of vegetation, owing to the chemical action of the mycelium on the organic contents of the soil. 2. (The actual ring)—Death of vegetation, owing to the drought brought about by the physical action of the mycelium. 3. (Inner)—Stimulation of the vegetation, owing to the decay of fungus mycelium and fruiting-bodies, and the subsequent chemical changes.

The advance of the mycelium in fairy rings is, of course, extremely slow, and naturally varies with the season. In the case of the Champignon (*Marasmius oreades*) Bayliss found the rate to vary from three to thirteen and a half inches a year. Thus, comparing the size of rings with the average annual increase, it seems probable that their age often exceeds a century. In Colorado, Shantz and Piemeisel calculated that certain rings were 250 and 420 years old respectively, whilst certain fragmentary rings would appear to be about 600 years old. The mycelia of some hundred species of the larger fungi are known to grow in this annular formation, and to this number might probably be added many more, did not their natural habitats possess obstructions of various kinds which interfere with this tendency.

In the case of those fungi which do not appear to grow in rings, it is probable that the mycelium ramifies either in a mass insufficiently dense to cause surface reaction, or in a more erratic fashion. It should be also noted that many rings grow in woods where there is no grass, and where the reactive effect is therefore missing.

The Function of Mycelium—Storage Bodies. As we have already indicated, the primary work of the mycelium is to absorb food, of which it requires little for its normal growth, but naturally much more at the fruiting period. Some fungi have learned to provide for this heavy demand by storing large supplies of nutriment, which can be rapidly drawn on for the production of fruiting-bodies, and which will also tide them over adverse periods, when growing conditions are unfavourable. The storage organs used for this purpose consist of densely-compacted mycelium, and take various forms in the different species in which they occur. Some, known as *sclerotia*, appear usually as dark-coloured, rounded or elongated tubercles, varying in size from that of a pin's head in some species to that of a man's fist, or even his head, in others. Examples of these may be found in the " ergot of rye " (*Claviceps purpurea*), or the " black fellows' bread " (*Mylitta australis* = *Polyporus Mylittae*). Other kinds, called from their root-like appearance, *rhizomorphs*, consist of thick and tough cord-like strands, as in the " dry rot fungus " (*Merulius lacrymans*), the honey-tuft (*Armillaria mellea*), etc. In the latter cases, besides acting as storage organs, they facilitate the wide distribution of the fruiting-bodies, by reason of the distances over which they frequently extend.

Except, however, when such special adjuncts as those mentioned are present, the mycelia of the vast bulk of the larger fungi are similar, both in character and in general appearance, to that of the Common Mushroom ; indeed, so great is this similarity that in spite of variations of colour and habitat, it is usually impossible to establish the identity of a fungus from this organ alone ; and hence the characters necessary for this purpose must be sought in the fruiting-bodies.

THE FRUITING BODIES OR SPOROPHORES.

The fruiting-bodies—the "mushrooms," "toad-stools," "puffballs," etc.—comprise the reproductive system of the fungus. They are the structures by whose means the subterranean mycelium is enabled to produce

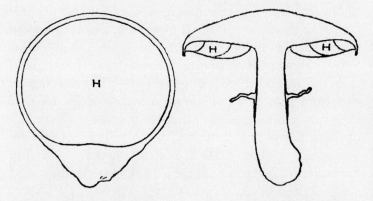

Fig. 21.—Section through Puffball, showing spore-bearing surface (H) enclosed in the body of the plant. One-quarter natural size.

Fig. 22.—Section through Mushroom, showing exposed spore-bearing surface (H). One-half natural size.

and liberate its reproductive bodies—the spores—above the surface of the leaf-mould, decaying wood, or other material in which the plant is living, so giving them access to the air. Essentially, these structures consist of complex, compact masses of mycelium, bearing in, or upon some portion of them, the spore-producing layer or *hymenium*, on which the spores are generated, in one of the two following manners. In the Common Mushroom, the spores are budded off and set free from the tips of minute horns, which are borne, in fours, on the extremities of club-shaped cells, called *basidia ;* while in the Morel, the spores are produced, usually

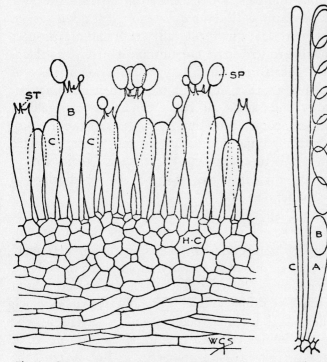

Fig. 23.—Section through Spore-bearing Surface of the Common Mushroom (*Psalliota campestris*). × 1000.
B = basidia ; SP = spores ; C = cystidia or barren basidia ; ST = sterigmata ; H.C = hymenial cells.

Fig. 24.
An Ascus of the Common Morel (*Morchella esculenta*), showing enclosed spores. × 500.
A = ascus ; B = spore ; C = paraphysis.

eight together, within cylindrical sac-like cells, known as *asci,* and are liberated at maturity by the rupture of these sacs. These characters, which are naturally microscopic ones, provide the division between the two great primary groups of the larger fungi, viz. : the *Basidiomycetes* and the *Ascomycetes*. Whichever mode of production is adopted, the spores are liberated in prodigious numbers, a fact which can be accounted for by the peculiar conditions requisite for their germination. Fungus spores are microscopically small and are in most cases unable to withstand circumstances adverse to them. Unless, therefore, they encounter conditions of substratum, weather, etc., suitable for their germination, they die, and, since all these conditions are seldom contemporaneously propitious, it follows that for every spore which produces a mature fungus plant, myriads do not. It is to counteract this state of affairs that a beneficent providence has arranged this prodigality of spore production.[1]

Spore Dispersal. These two factors, their minute size, and the numbers in which they are liberated, render the distribution of fungus spores an extremely simple, and in most cases a very haphazard proceeding ; yet it is undoubtedly *to* these factors that the cosmopolitan character of the fungi is due. The distances over which such light and invisible bodies can be carried by the wind, and by insects, birds, animals and so on, is of course a matter of pure conjecture. But it must be very great, and is certainly far in excess of the distances covered by the larger and less portable seeds of the flowering plants. This is supported by the fact that there are hundreds of species of fungi which are ubiquitous throughout the world, at any rate where

---

[1] Other computations made by Buller are that a single Shaggy Cap (*Coprinus comatus*) produced 5,000,000,000 spores ; a Dryad's Saddle (*Polyporus squamosus*) 11,000,000,000 spores ; and a large example of the Giant Puffball (*Lycoperdon Bovista*) 7,000,000,000,000 spores.

climatic conditions are suitable, whereas very much more limited habitats are found in the case of many flowering plants which climatically are equally favoured.

As would be natural to suppose, the vast majority of fungi have their spores disseminated by the wind. In most of these species we find the same tremendous degree of spore production, a fact which presupposes a large spore-bearing surface. This is obtained with, at the same time, an economy of structure, by having this surface spread over corrugations, projections or convolutions of various kinds, such as the gills of the Agarics, the tubes of the Polypores, the teeth of the Hydnums, etc. These projections are usually on the lower surface of the fruiting body, so that the spores as they reach maturity may drop free and be carried away. In some species, notably the puffballs, the spore-bearing surface occupies the greater part of the interior of the " plant," and, at maturity and under suitable atmospheric conditions, the spores emerge from an apical vent in puffs, often visible as small clouds resembling smoke.

The members of another group of fungi have specialized in the employment of insects for the distribution of their spores, by producing the latter in sugary secretions on which these insects feed. A notable example of these is the Stinkhorn (Figs. 14 and 37), the spores of which are embedded in a green viscid mucus of powerful carrion-like odour, having a great attraction for flies. So greedily do they devour it that they become almost comatose. Eventually the spores, which are quite unharmed in the bodies of the insects, are deposited, often at a great distance from the parent fungus, and, moreover, in a medium suitable for their germination.

In the case of spore dispersal by animals, it must be admitted that the results undoubtedly obtained are largely fortuitous. Even so, they must take a prominent position, for slugs are proverbial mycophagists, and after feeding they carry away great numbers of spores with them in much the same way as do insects ; while squirrels, rabbits, and other rodents, which feed at times on fungi, also play their part in this work. Man, however, is a much more powerful agent of distribution. His various commercial transactions ; the transhipment of grain and other commodities ; the introduction of plants, bulbs, seeds, etc., from other countries, all lead to the distribution of millions of fungus spores over distances which no natural means could so readily traverse. The most serious aspect of this unwilling transportation is the introduction of fungus diseases from an infested country to another which was formerly immune.

There is, lastly, a class which is by no means the least interesting, those fungi which, by various expulsive methods, actually hurl their spores to a distance, greater or less, according to the efficiency of the apparatus employed, and the degree of assistance rendered by the wind. Most of these fungi are minute and thus hardly come within our purview. The ingenuity displayed, however, renders them worthy of at least passing reference, and we may consider two examples here : In the case of *Empusa Muscae*, the fungus parasitic on flies, which causes the death of such multitudes of these insects, the spores, at maturity, are shot off from the tips of their hyphae like the bullet from a rifle. These spores can often be seen in the form of a whitish halo, round a fly which has died on a window pane. With *Sphaerobolus*, a minute puffball, the inner spore case is thrown, as from a catapult, a yard or more into the air by the bursting and sudden inversion of the outer coats of the fruiting body.

The varying methods of production, liberation and dispersal of spores are naturally expressed in a varying structure of the fruiting body, and thus this organ provides a series of characters, the permutations and combinations of which serve as the basis for the classification of the fungi. This scheme of classification, when viewed in tabular form, gives a graphic summary of the main groups of the larger fungi, and the relationship they bear to each other. It must, however, be borne in mind that essential characters are not necessarily the most obvious ones, and, therefore, the following tabulation should be read in conjunction with the fuller descriptions given at the pages indicated.

It should further be remarked that the *English* names we have given must not be considered as strictly correct, or even as " popular " names, although some undoubtedly *are* so, but merely as a rough indication of some prominent characteristic. They are frequently an approximate rendering of the botanical ones. To the strict botanist, such names are objectionable, in certain aspects rightly so.

CLASSIFICATION OF THE LARGER BRITISH FUNGI.

CLASS I. **Basidiomycetes.**—Spores borne on the exterior of more or less club-shaped *basidia*, usually in fours.

Order I. **Hymenomycetes.**—Spore-bearing surface (*hymenium*) superficial, exposed either from the first, or at a very early stage of development.

Family 1.—*Agaricaceae* (The Agarics or Gill Fungi) : Spore-bearing surface covering radiating plates or gills (p. 57).

Family 2.—*Polyporaceae* (The Polypores or Pore Fungi) : Spore-bearing surface lining the interiors of tubes or tube-like recticulations, the mouths of which appear as pores (p. 61).

Family 3.—*Hydnaceae* (The Toothed Fungi) : Spore-bearing surface spread over spines, teeth or papillae (p. 63).

Family 4.—*Thelephoraceae* (The Leathery Fungi) : Spore-bearing surface covering a firm, smooth or corrugate surface (p. 64).

Family 5.—*Clavariaceae* (The Fairy Clubs) : Spore-bearing surface smooth, covering erect club-shaped or variously-branched fruiting bodies (p. 66).

Family 6.—*Tremellinaceae* (The Jew's Ears, etc.) : Spore-bearing surface spread over smooth or irregularly-folded gelatinous surface (p. 67).

Order II. **Gasteromycetes.**—Spore-bearing surface produced in " tissue " (the *gleba*) within the more or less globular body of the plant (the *peridium*).

Family 1.—*Phalloidaceae* (The Carrion Fungi) : Peridium globular, with a middle gelatinous layer. At maturity the foetid mucilaginous gleba, containing the spores, is raised above the ruptured peridium by the elongation of a stalked or latticed receptacle (p. 68).

Family 2.—*Lycoperdaceae* (The Puffballs) : Peridium usually globular, of two or more layers ; dehiscing at maturity by an apical vent or by the rupture of the walls. Spores when ripe a powdery mass intermixed with a web of threads (*capillitium*) (p. 70).

Family 3.—*Sclerodermaceae* (The Earth Balls) : Peridium usually globular, thick, of a single layer, dehiscing irregularly ; capillitium absent or rudimentary (p. 71).

Family 4.—*Nidulariaceae* (The Bird's Nest Fungi) : Peridium bell- or cup-shaped, containing usually several egg-like spore chambers (*peridiola*), each sometimes attached by a thread (*funiculus*), but free at maturity (p. 72).

Family 5.—*Hymenogastraceae* (The False Truffles) : Sub-terranean ; peridium globular or nodular, indehiscent. Spores released by the decay of the plant (p. 72).

CLASS II. **Ascomycetes.**—Spores produced *within* cylindrical, spherical or club-shaped *asci*, usually in eights.

Order I. **Discomycetes.**—Spore-bearing surface exposed on a flat, cup-shaped or convex receptacle. (The Cup Fungi, Morels, etc. : see pp. 73 and 74).

Order II. **Pyrenomycetes.**—Spore-bearing surface lining minute flask-shaped bodies (*perithecia*); of which, in the larger species, many hundreds are borne embedded in a fleshy, corky, or carbonaceous receptacle (the *stroma*).

Order III.—**Tuberaceae.** (The True Truffles) Subterranean. Spore-bearing surface lining chambers in a globular or nodular peridium, the decay of which releases the spores (p. 74).

A short account of each of these families is given below :—

THE BASIDIOMYCETES.

The Agarics or Gill Fungi (*Agaricaceae*), comprising the mushrooms and toadstools proper, form the most numerous class of the larger fungi, and are represented in Britain by over fifteen hundred species, contained in fifty-eight genera. Their common distinguishing feature is the presence, on the fruiting body, of vertical knife-like plates, the gills, which carry the spore-bearing layers. The fruiting body takes most frequently the parasol-like form of a convex cap, supported on a stem, and is well exemplified by the Common Mushroom (*Psalliota campestris*) ; or, less frequently, appears as a shelf-like or bracket-shaped organ, as in the Oyster fungus (*Pleurotus ostreatus*) (Fig. 80) ; the gills being carried on the lower surface, radiating outward from the stem, or in the stemless species, from the point of support.

In *Amanitopsis*, the entire fruiting body when young is enclosed in a veil-like covering, called the " volva," which ruptures during development and remains as a sheath surrounding the base of the stem ; particles of it being sometimes carried upward on the cap, on which they remain as loose patches.   In others, such as the

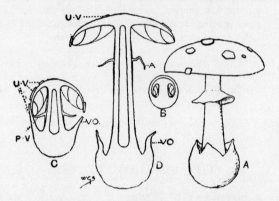

Fig. 25.—AGARICACEAE.   *Amanita phalloides.*   One-third natural size.

A, perfect plant : B, section of young plant showing universal veil : C, section of half-grown specimen showing rupture of universal veil : D, section of mature specimen.

U.V. = universal veil ; P.V = partial veil, becoming annulus, or ring ; A = annulus ; VO = volva, or sheath.

Common Mushroom, only the gills are enclosed, and in these the ruptured veil is left on the stem, as a collar or " ring," while fragments are often found hanging to the edge of the cap.   In *Amanita*, both of these characters are present ; in other genera, neither.

In the classification of the Agarics, the primary character selected is that of the colour of the spore mass. If the cap of a mature specimen is placed, gills downwards on a sheet of paper, and left undisturbed for a few hours, the spores are deposited in such vast numbers that they form on the paper a complete plan of the gills.[1] This plan will be in one of five colours, viz. : (1) White ; (2) Pink ; (3) Ochre, cinnamon or rust ; (4) Purple ; or

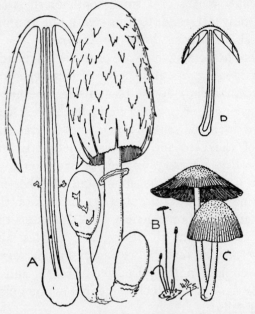

Fig. 26.—AGARICACEAE. A, *Coprinus comatus*, entire and in section : B, *C. radiatus :* C, *C. domesticus ;* D, ditto in section. One-third natural size.

(5) Black. This somewhat laborious process is not, however, always essential, since the colour of the spores is usually the same as that of the gills, although some species with dark coloured gills produce white spores. Lest this colour character be considered to constitute an extremely artificial means of classification, it may be pointed out that not only is it very stable, but it possibly indicates the degree of evolution of the individual.

The mode of attachment of the gills is another

[1] See page 267.

character of importance ; whether they are completely free from the stem (*free*) ; partially attached to the stem (*adnexed*) ; attached for their whole width (*adnate*) ; attached by means of a small tooth or sinus (*sinuate*) ; or, not only attached to the stem, but running for a considerable distance down it (*decurrent*).

Other characters which are of service in distinguishing the individual genera and species of this huge group are : (1) The consistency of the plant itself, whether soft and soon decaying ; or, membranous, leathery or corky, and therefore more persistent. (2) The general shape and colour of the cap, and further, whether its surface is viscid or dry, smooth, warted, or scaly, etc. (3) The general character of the stem, and whether furnished with a ring and/or volva ; and (4) the size of the plant, its habitat, etc.   Some genera have characteristics which separate them from all others, and in this connection reference may be made to the species of *Lactarius* which exude a copious milky juice when broken, and to those of *Schizophyllum*, in which the edges of the gills are split longitudinally.

However, it is not the purpose of this book to supply a catalogue of diagnoses, and the examples given will demonstrate sufficiently how the identity of the members of this great family is arrived at.

The habitats selected by the Agarics are numerous and varied.   The majority, it is true, prefer the moist, shady, and relatively warm situations afforded by woods ; a number inhabiting the trees themselves.   But even so, a sufficiently large number are found in other localities, and pastures, heaths, farmyards, gardens, dunghills, old gate-posts and fences, old thatch, dead leaves and fir-cones, are but a few of the sites which demand their share of attention. In short, it is hardly an exaggeration to say that some species of the Agarics will be found in any situation which is capable of supporting fungus life. The preferences of individual species become, therefore, a special factor in their detailed study.

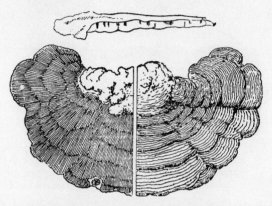

Fig. 27.—AGARICACEAE. *Lenzites betulina,* entire and in section. Lower surface on left, upper on right. One-third natural size.

The Polypores (*Polyporaceae*). This group comprises some two hundred and fifty British species, contained in eleven genera. In superficial appearance many of them are not unlike some of the Agarics, but the gills of the latter are here replaced by a mass of compacted tubes, of which the lower surface appears punctured by a multitude of pores, round or angular, occasionally sinuate or torn. In some genera, as *Boletus,* the plant is terrestrial, and has an umbrella-shaped cap, supported on a stout central stem. In others, such as *Merulius* and *Poria,* the fruiting body is flat and crust-like ; the mouths of the pores, which in some species are mere shallow depressions, appearing on the free surface. In the vast majority, however, are those forms, like

Polyporus, Polystictus, Fomes and *Fistulina,* which appear as bracket-shaped, or hoof-like masses, adhering to trees,

Fig. 28.—POLYPORACEAE. A, section of *Boletus luteus,* showing gelatinous membranous veil. B, section of *B. edulis,* showing at * tubes separating from cap. C, section of *B. cyanescens;* young specimen showing universal veil. One-third natural size.

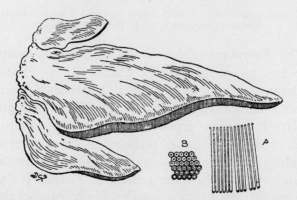

Fig. 29.—POLYPORACEAE. *Fistulina hepatica,* in section. One-third natural size.
A, tubes × 3. B, mouths of ditto × 6.

both living and dead. In the Polypores, the fruiting body shows every variation of consistency, from the soft and juicy, through the leathery varieties, to those really woody. The latter are perennial, and their annual layers of growth may be easily traced. On account of their arboreal habits, many of these species are very destructive in woods and forests. *Merulius lacrymans* is the agent of " dry rot " in houses, and is discussed more fully elsewhere.

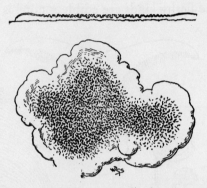

Fig. 30.—POLYPORACEAE. *Merulius lacrymans,* entire and in section above. One-third natural size.

The Toothed Fungi (*Hydnaceae*). In this group, the spore-bearing surface is spread over spines, teeth, tubercles, papillae, or wart-like folds, which take the place of the gills in the Agarics and the tubes in the Polypores. The Hydnaceae are represented in Britain by nine genera, containing in all about one hundred species. Of these, a few have a central stem, and conform more or less to the orthodox parasol-like shape ; but most of them resemble hedgehog-like masses, or else fleshy or leathery crusts of various shapes, bearing the spine-like process on the lower, or the free, surface. In the largest and best known genus, *Hydnum*, of which there are some fifty species, the spines are large and almost awl-like. From this, they vary in shape and prominence, in the different genera, down to *Phlebia*, which has radiate veins or wrinkles. The consistency of the fruiting body shows also every variation and may be gelatinous, fleshy, membranous, wax-like or leathery. Many of them are terrestrial and are found in woods or on heaths ; others inhabit decaying logs, while some are known to attack living trees. Most of the fleshy kinds are edible ; none is considered poisonous.

Fig. 31.—HYDNACEAE. A, *Hydnum repandum*, section, one-half natural size. B, *H. auriscalpium*, entire, one-half natural size. C, ditto, section through cap, natural size. D, *H. erinaceus*, section, one-half natural size. E, *H. ochraceum*, entire, one-half natural size. F, ditto, section, one-half natural size. G, *H. squalinum*, section, one-half natural size.

The Leathery Fungi (*Thelephoraceae*) comprise a heterogeneous collection of fungi, numbering about one hundred and fifty species, contained in eleven genera, whose identity, in the absence of a micro-

scope, is often difficult to determine. In general they
have a smooth, flat or slightly undulating hymenium,

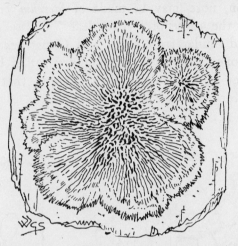

Fig. 32.—HYDNACEAE. *Phlebia merismoides*, two-thirds natural size.

spread over the *exterior* of an irregular cup-like
body, the free surface of a prostrate crust, or the
lower surface of a
bracket-shaped body.
In most cases their
consistency is mem-
branous or leathery,
though occasionally
waxy or even gelatin-
ous. The members of
the order have no
particular points of
interest except that
all the species of
Craterellus are edible,
C. cornucopioides being

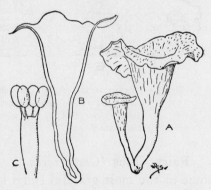

Fig. 33.—THELEPHORACEAE. A, B, *Craterellus
cornucopioides*, entire and in section,
one-third natural size. C, basidium
and spores.   × 500.

formerly sold in Covent Garden market, while of the
other genera, many species are destructive pests.   In this
connection, note may be made of *Stereum purpureum*,
which is the cause of "silver leaf" disease of plum,
apple, and similar fruit trees, and *Coniophora cerebella*,
which is one of the fungi causing dry rot in buildings.
The latter is particularly dangerous in that it paves
the way for *Merulius lacrymans*.

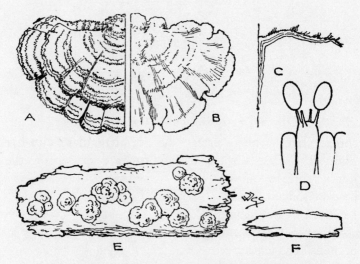

Fig. 34.—THELEPHORACEAE.   A, B, C, *Stereum hirsutum*, upper and lower
surfaces and section, two-thirds natural size.   D, basidium and
spores, × 660.   E, F, *S. Pini*, upper surface and section, two-
thirds natural size.

Fairy Clubs (*Clavariaceae*). This group contains
some of the most graceful fungi known. Most of them
are small in stature, delicate in appearance and often
bright in colour. Of the sixty or so British species,
comprised in six genera, forty alone are contained in the

genus *Clavaria*, in which the fruiting bodies occur as
small erect tufts of simple or much branched clubs;
many of the latter having
an elaborate antlered or
coral-like appearance. In
Sparassis, the fruiting body
is so much divided that it
resembles a cauliflower.
(See Fig. 62). In *Calocera*,
which has a superficial resemblance to Clavaria, the
clubs are gelatinous, be-
coming horny when dry
(Fig. 12).

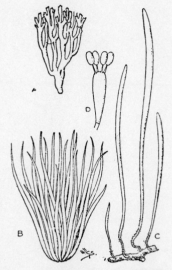

Most of the Club fungi
are found among grass in
meadows or woods, or
upon lawns. A few inhabit
decaying stumps, dead
leaves, etc. All of the
larger kinds are edible:
none is known to be
poisonous.

Fig. 35.—CLAVARIACEAE. A, *Clavaria
coralloides*; B, *C. vermicularis*;
C, *C. fistulosa*, one-third natural
size. D, *C. pistillaris*, basidium
and spores, × 330.

The Jew's Ears, etc. (*Tremellinaceae*). In these
fungi, of which there are some three dozen British
species, contained in eleven genera, the fruiting bodies
are of gelatinous consistency, becoming rigid and
horny in dry weather, and regaining their original
condition when moistened. In shape they are very variable and extremely irregular. In *Tremella*, the largest
genus, the fruiting bodies are often brightly coloured and
appear as irregular, lobed or brain-like masses. In
Exidia, *Hirneola* and *Auricularia* they are irregularly

cup-shaped, or convoluted like a human ear. Others appear as small variously-shaped lumps of jelly. Most of these fungi inhabit decaying logs, the stumps of trees, old fence posts, etc.

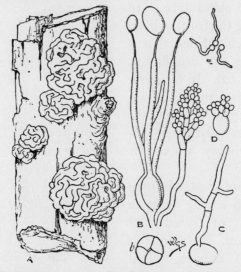

Fig. 36.—TREMELLINACEAE. A, *Tremella lutescens*. One-half natural size. B, basidium, with surface view, b, spores and conidia. C, spore germinating and producing hyphae. D, ditto, producing sporidiola. E, sporidiola germinating. × 500.

The Carrion Fungi (*Phalloidaceae*) constitute a family whose affinity with the puffballs would not be suspected by the casual observer. When young, the complete fungus is enclosed in a gelatinous " egg," which eventually bursts open and permits the erection of a stem-like or latticed receptacle, which bears the spores, embedded in an evil-smelling mucus, the last being responsible for making the presence of these fungi *known* long before they are seen. There occur in Britain five genera, containing seven species, of which three are introductions from abroad.

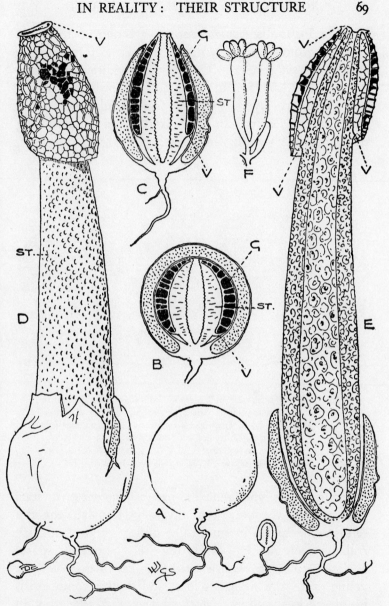

Fig. 37.—Phalloidaceae. *Phallus impudicus.* Two-thirds natural size. A, young plant. B, section of ditto, showing veil at V. C, ditto, showing cap emerging from volva, veil at V. D, mature plant, remains of veil at V. E, section of ditto. F, basidium and spores, × 1000. G, gleba; ST, stem or receptacle.

The Puffballs (*Lycoperdaceae*) are one of the most familiar groups of fungi, numbering some forty British species, of six genera. The fruiting bodies are usually more or less spherical in shape and are provided with a cuticle of two layers. In *Lycoperdon* and *Bovista*, the outer coat flakes away in spine-like tufts or warts during development; while in *Geaster*, it is permanent,

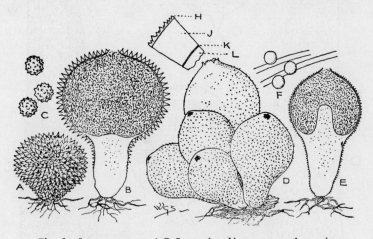

Fig. 38.—LYCOPERDACEAE. A, B, *Lycoperdon echinatum*, young plant entire and mature plant in section. One-half natural size. C, spores. × 750. D, E, *L. pyriforme*, entire and in section. One-half natural size. F, spores and threads of capillitium. × 750. G, section through cortex of *L. gemmatum* × 5; H, outer scurfy coat; J, inner coat; K, membrane over gleba; L, gleba.

becoming split and reflexed like a conventional star. At maturity, the inner coat opens by a apical vent and releases the spores in smoke-like puffs ; or the top may collapse completely, exhibiting the powdery spores enclosed in a brownish wadding-like mass. In the young state the flesh is white, and in this condition is in most cases edible. Most of the puffballs grow in pastures, though a number occur on the ground in woods, and one species on decaying stumps.

The Earth Balls (*Sclerodermaceae*) are close allies of the puffballs, from which they differ chiefly in their thick, hard, leathery rind, and by the absence of a capillitium. The flesh when young is generally more or less white, becoming darker with age; while the

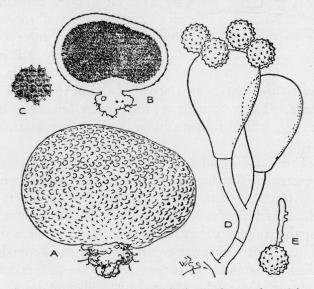

Fig. 39.—SCLERODERMACEAE. A, B, *Scleroderma vulgare*, entire and in
section. One-half natural size.
C, cells of gleba. × 5. D, basidia and spores; E, spore
germinating. × 750.

peridium opens at maturity by splitting irregularly, releasing a mass of dark violet spores. There are two British genera, *Scleroderma* and *Polysaccum*, containing respectively five and one species, the last being extremely rare. All are terrestrial and appear to favour a sandy soil.

The Birds' Nest Fungi (*Nidulariaceae*). This group contains a number of charming little fungi, which, despite their affinity, would hardly be recognised as akin to the puffballs. At maturity, most of them appear as miniature, fanciful birds' nests, containing minute eggs, well shown in Fig. 5. The three chief genera occurring in Britain are *Cyathus*, *Nidularia* and *Crucibulum*, containing respectively two, three and one species. The remaining genus, *Sphaerobolus*, has only one egg, which at maturity is hurled away as from a catapult.

Fig. 40.—NIDULARIACEAE.   *Crucibulum vulgare*, section showing young and mature specimens.   × 3.

The False Truffles (*Hymenogastraceae*). This family is remarkable for the underground habit of its members. The fruiting bodies, which are usually just below the surface, and are found near trees, appear as globose or irregular tubers, somewhat resembling a small warted potato. There are some twelve British species contained in half that number of genera. They are seldom found except by those who are making deliberate search for them.

THE ASCOMYCETES.

This class contains a tremendous number of fungi, whose characteristics are too varied to consider in detail. Most of them are minute and, therefore, require the aid of a microscope for their determination and study. So distinctive in appearance are most of them, and so unlike the ordinary conception of a toadstool, that a popular description will almost certainly fail to conjure up the plant we have in mind.

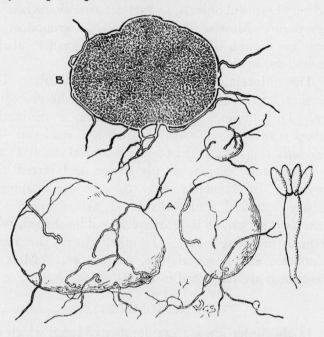

Fig. 41.—Hymenogastraceae. A, B, *Rhizopogon rubescens*, entire and in section. Four-thirds natural size. C, basidium and spores. × 660.

THE DISCOMYCETES.

The Cup Fungi (*Pezizae*). As their name suggests, these fungi have fruiting bodies more or less cup-shaped in form, though often shallow and distorted, or even disc-like; the hymenium being carried on the inner or the upper surface. They are mostly soft and fleshy in consistency and brilliant in colour. In the largest and best-known genus, *Peziza*, which contains some dozen British species, the cups vary from bright scarlet, through various shades of orange to lemon yellow, and from scarlet to brown. They are thus very striking and very beautiful objects, and attract attention wherever they occur. Most of them grow on the ground or on decaying stumps, though some of the smaller inhabit dead sticks, herbaceous stems, etc.

The Morels and Helvells (*Helvelleae*). The members of this group are close allies of the preceding one. They differ, however, in having a distinctly-stalked fruiting body, with a variously-shaped cap. In *Morchella* (Fig. 85), it is irregularly conical and is a mass of ridges and hollows, deeply folded and pitted like a sponge. In *Gyromitra* (Fig. 59), the cap is approximately spherical and convoluted like a brain. In *Helvella* (Fig. 58), it is grotesquely saddle-shaped, with irregular drooping lobes. In other genera, this organ is smooth, and is spatula-like, conical, etc. Most of these fungi are terrestrial in woods.

THE PYRENOMYCETES.

In this order are a great number of fungi which are of little interest to folk other than those engaged in their actual study. Most of them are small, and even the larger ones are far from attractive. The best known is probably the Candle Snuff fungus, *Xylaria hypoxylon*, (Fig. 79) a small, branched, fungus common on old stumps.

THE TRUE TRUFFLES (*Tuberaceae*).

In superficial appearance, these fungi have almost all of the attributes of the *Hymenogastraceae* ; from which they differ, however, in the spores being produced in *asci*. Like them, these plants are subterranean and grow near, and often associated with, the roots of trees. The principal genus is *Tuber*, which comprises the edible truffles, a subject dealt with elsewhere (p. 215).

In this brief survey of the classes of the larger fungi we have not attempted to go very deeply into the matter, for to do so would be belying the sentiment which we expressed in our preface. It is, however, desirable that the reader should understand something of the numerous and varied kinds of fungi which exist, even if only to bring realisation that these larger kinds comprise considerably more than the class which he has perhaps formerly lumped together, under the comprehensive term, " toadstool."

CHAPTER V

The Fungi in Reality :

THEIR MODES OF EXISTENCE.

THE common characteristic of all living organisms is that they possess metabolic power, i.e., they continually use up and renew the materials of which their bodies are composed; and thus, to sustain life, they need constant and unfailing supplies of food as fuel for their vital energies. These foods, which are essentially the same in both plants and animals, and which consist of carbohydrates, proteins, fats, etc., with mineral salts and water as vital adjuncts, can only be constructed, as we have already shown, by " green " or chlorophyll-bearing plants. Thus all other forms of life, including such widely divergent organisms as fungi and animals, are directly or indirectly dependent on green plants for *their* supplies of these necessary foods. In the case of the fungi, this complete dependence has done much to shape their destinies. Because of it, they themselves can never be pioneers, but must remain— to continue the simile—the camp followers of the plant world ; for until other organic life has first occupied a location, no fungus can there find subsistence. Further, this very dependence has served to evolve a variety not only of form, but also of habit, probably greater than that of any other form of life—a variety so great that concise description would fail in the task of depicting it.

We have, in this matter, likened the fungi to animals, and if we turn for a moment to the latter, we find that, in feeding, certain creatures are herbivorous or "vegetarians"; while others are carnivorous or "meat-eaters." Of the latter, again, some are predatory, others are "carrion-feeders." The members of each class select that type of food to which, in course of time, they have become accustomed or adapted, and normally feed only upon it. In so doing, they are not exercising individual choice so much as following natural instinct.

Fungi, of course, do not ingest their food, but absorb it through the cell walls of the mycelium, after it has been converted, by means of the ferments or enzymes which they secrete, into a suitable soluble form: the starch into sugar or glucose; the albumen into other nitrogenous compounds, and so forth. But, in this matter of "choice" of foods, we find among them a state of affairs somewhat similar to that existing among animals.

A fungus spore, under suitable weather conditions, will germinate almost anywhere, but unless the resultant germ tube almost immediately encounters a hospitable medium, i.e., one capable of furnishing the accustomed type of food, it soon perishes, for, unlike the animals, it naturally cannot roam in search of its food. This factor of natural selection plays an important part in the lives of fungi, since it tends to correlate a fungus with its host substance, and, through the latter, to fix its habits and habitat. Moreover, this factor proves a safeguard in preventing these plants from completely overrunning the earth.

Pursuing our theme, we find, excluding for the moment certain rather exceptional cases, that the fungi have evolved into two fairly distinct types, viz. : (1) *parasitic fungi*, which obtain their food by attacking and preying on the living organism, either animal or vegetable ; and (2) *saprophytic fungi*, which live on its dead and decaying remains, or on the various waste and reserve materials produced during its life. These respective habits are not, however, wholly common to definite systematic groups of fungi ; neither do the compositions of the foods utilised by each group vary greatly. Yet in other ways so distinct are the methods adopted by the members of the respective groups for the acquisition of these foods, and so marked are the effects of the various methods on the individual fungi, that for purposes of comparison a very useful line may be drawn between the two.

SAPROPHYTIC FUNGI.

True saprophytes (Gr. *sapros*=rotten), as their name suggests, live on rotting or decaying matter. They are incapable of attacking living tissues and are, therefore, forced to draw their supplies of food from one or other of that wide range of organic but inanimate substances which result from animal or vegetable life : in the case of the former, dead carcasses, dung, wool, horn, feathers, cheese, etc. ; and in that of the latter, leaf-mould and general plant débris, rotting timber, ripe fruit, jams, and so forth. Each of these substances appears to offer attractions to certain fungi, and therefore each provides sustenance for its quota of species.

Terrestrial Saprophytes. The vast majority of the larger fungi—the class with which we are immediately concerned—grow on the ground, and, after the manner of the Common Mushroom, absorb their nourishment from the humus ever present in the soil, and arising from dead grass and decaying plant débris generally. The composition of this humus naturally varies with its original source, and as, within limits, the food requirements of individual species of fungi also vary, it is found that meadow fungi, like the Common Mushroom, never occur in woods ; while woodland species seldom invade pastures. Again, in the woods, as the tree formation changes, so do the kinds of fungi encountered. The fungus flora of a beech wood differs materially from that of an oak wood, while a plantation of conifers supplies yet another range of species. Another factor which has a marked effect on the prevalence of individual species, is the composition of the soil, whether chalk, sand or clay. It will be readily seen that the combination of these characters tends to segregate these fungi into a number of communities, more or less well defined ; and thus the chaotic profusion in which they appear to occur is more orderly than might at first be supposed.

Wood-destroying Saprophytes. A further large class of fungi confine their attention to wood—old fence rails and posts, fallen logs, tree stumps, and the like. The mycelia of such fungi secrete ferments which break down the woody tissues of these materials, and in this way not only liberate quantities of nutrient substance for their own use, but in course of time reduce the timber to a powdery mass which mingles with the soil, and thus becomes available for the sustenance of other plants. This process, however laudable when applied to useless tree stumps, is naturally not appreciated when exercised on useful timbers (the woodwork of a house, railway ties, etc.), and among this class of fungi are to be found the agents of many of the wood rots referred to elsewhere (p. 116).

Dung Saprophytes. The dung of certain animals affords an excellent medium for the growth of many fungi, both large and minute. Many of these result from spores deposited from the air, but, in other cases, the spores pass through the animal with its food. In the latter case, not only are the spores unharmed, but their germinative powers are frequently increased by the action of the digestive juices of the animal.

Other Saprophytes. Although the former classes cover most of the larger fungi, some consideration should be given to a large number of microscopic fungi, which live saprophytically on foods, clothes, feathers and various other materials, when conditions are suitable. Among those quite familiar to the housewife are the blue and green moulds (certain of the *Aspergillaceae*) often found growing on the surface of jams, preserved fruits, potted meats and other foods, and arising from the development of spores deposited thereon from the air. The germination of these air-borne spores results in a film of mycelium, carrying enormous numbers of bluish spores, to which the colour of the mass is due. Of the same type are the black moulds (certain of the *Mucorineae*) of bread, cake, cheese, etc.

This list might be extended almost indefinitely, for, as we have said, there is no form of organic material which does not, under suitable conditions, provide the necessary food materials for the existence of some fungi. Sufficient examples have, however, already been given, to illustrate the versatility of saprophytic fungi as a whole, and the variety of the substances on which they can take up their abode.

PARASITIC FUNGI.

Parasitism (Gr. *parasites* : one who sups at another's table) may be defined as that property which causes an organism to attach itself to another, and to nourish itself at its host's expense. When, as is usually the case, this dual strain is brought to bear on resources which were only designed to cater for one, the results can hardly fail to be detrimental to the host. Indeed, so serious may be the check to its vital processes that a state of disease is provoked. It is this power of causing disease, both in animals and plants, which forms the heaviest item in the indictment which can be made against the parasitic fungi.

At the same time, this parasitic habit, though admittedly degenerate, is one which often entails considerable adaptation to the vicissitudes of the host, and it is this necessity for adaptation which has caused the parasitic fungi to exhibit in most cases a degree of specialisation, and a variability of life methods, greater than that shown by the saprophytic kinds.

While not necessarily characteristic of them, parasitism is found chiefly among the more minute groups of fungi, and since these provide a complete and an intricate study in themselves, we do not propose to deal with other than general principles.

The power of attacking, which obviously precedes their existence on living organisms, is manifested by parasitic fungi in varying degrees; but in all cases it appears to be due primarily to a definite, if unwilling, attraction exercised by the host, rather than to any innate pugnacity on the part of the fungus. This attraction is furnished by certain chemical substances, present in the tissues of the host, which react on the germ tube of a fungus spore, and supply this organ with the necessary impulse to attack. Conversely, when these substances are inimical to the fungus, no stimulus is received, and the germinating spore soon dies from lack of nourishment. Thus it is the composition of the host which is the potential deciding factor in regulating the number and the kinds of parasitic fungi which can subsist upon it. The only hosts available are members of either the animal or the vegetable kingdoms, and these form convenient headings for their further consideration.

Fungi parasitic on Animals. Of the thousands of known fungus parasites, those which are capable of subsisting on the tissues of living animals—the term is used in its widest sense—are in the vast minority. The explanation of this relative immunity is found in the operation of several factors, of which the chief are :

(i) The alkaline reaction of animal tissues—fungi generally prefer acid or neutral media.

(ii) Their comparative freedom from air cavities in which the fungus mycelium can develop readily.

(iii) The body temperature, which, in the higher animals, is greater than that at which most fungi develop.

(iv) The natural combative powers of the white corpuscles of the blood.

In view of these facts, it is correct to assume that of the fungus parasites of animals, the larger proportion is supported by the lower members of the animal world, insects being especially vulnerable. Even so, there is hardly a class of animal, from the smallest unicellular organisms of our ponds, right up to man himself, which does not contain potential hosts for these fungi. Lest, however, the reader should imagine himself in the light of a peripatetic mushroom bed, let us hasten to add that in almost every case these fungi are microscopic growths. He will obtain an impression of their activities by consulting the following chapter.

Fungi parasitic on Plants. The vast proportion of parasitic fungi have linked their destinies with those of other plants, and it is here that we find the most remarkable examples of adaptation to a parasitic existence. The versatility exhibited by many individuals is really extraordinary, for not only do they change their complete forms two or three times during the course of their life, but in the same time even utilise two distinct host plants. Some idea of the completeness of this apparent change of identity may be gathered from the fact that the three stages of the Wheat Rust (*Puccinia graminis*) were considered by early investigators to be three distinct species of fungi.

Even the mycelium, which is usually the most stable organ, participates in this versatility. In the simplest forms (the ectoparasites), it remains external, merely ramifying on the surface of the plant, usually the leaves, in the form of a loose web, and taking up nourishment, either by means of small suckers (*haustoria*), which are thrust beneath the surface of the plant, or by direct osmotic absorption through the epidermis, which in this case naturally remains unbroken.

In the more advanced section of parasites (the endoparasites), the mycelium itself lives wholly within the tissues of the plant, where it has not only greater facilities for feeding, but also greater opportunities for harm. Even so, it is not in the interest of the fungus to kill its host plant—although this too frequently is the result—and many species, apparently in an attempt to obviate this dilemma, have in the past confined their attention chiefly to one organ of the host plant, and on this organ alone have they now the power to live.

Leaf Parasites. Of the various parts of a plant, the leaves are the organs most open to attack. Their tender tissues ; the breathing pores (stomata) which communicate with the outer air, and which, therefore, give convenient ingress to marauding fungi ; the numerous moist air cavities ; and the proximity of the starch-making apparatus (the chlorophyll) : all assist in rendering the leaves ideal breeding places for parasitic fungi. Thus it is they who have to support the most extensive, and, for the same reason, the most destructive group of parasites. In this group are the various rusts, mildews, leaf-curls, leaf-spots, etc., and although their actual presence usually passes unnoticed, the damage which they cause is only too evident. The various coloured spots, scabs, etc., on the surfaces of leaves, as well as the wilting and yellowing of these organs, are due mostly to the action of these fungi.

Stem Parasites. The conditions existing in the leaves are in part reproduced in the younger shoots, which have, therefore, to accommodate the same or a similar band of parasites. As the stem gets older, the tissues firmer, and a tough outer rind or cuticle is formed, the difficulties of entrance on the part of the fungus are increased, and, therefore, the liability to attack is lessened. Finally, when the stem becomes truly woody, it can only provide a satisfactory medium for those fungi which develop wood-destroying ferments.

Root Parasites. The roots of a plant do not provide conditions so suitable to fungus attack, yet many parasites which prefer the moister conditions provided by the soil make their homes in these organs, where they often cause such damage as to prevent their proper functioning.

Flower and Fruit Parasites. A sufficiently large number of fungi infest the flowers and especially the fruits of plants. The latter are particularly susceptible, for not only are they, in their later stages, often gorged with foods intended as an attractive present to those animals and birds on which they rely for the distribution of their seeds—foods which prove equally acceptable to many fungi—but there is the additional advantage that resting spores or dormant mycelium may be carried with the seeds, the fungi being thus enabled to repeat their life cycles on the new plants.

The Effects of Parasitic Fungi on their Hosts. Many parasitic fungi have little or no effect on their host plants, but others, as has been shown, have tremendous disease-causing propensities. With regard to the latter, speculation may arise as to how this damage is brought about. The mycelium of the invading fungus may nourish itself by drawing on the foods which the plant is producing for its own future use, in which case the ill-effects on the host are not pronounced ; or, it may destroy and absorb the complete structures of the host in its immediate vicinity. In the latter event, the amount of injury caused depends upon the activities of the fungus. In some cases the area occupied by the fungus may be small, the result being merely the production of unsightly, decayed patches, which reduce by this amount the utility of the organs on which they occur.   In other cases the damage is very considerable, extending frequently to areas widely separated from the immediate seat of the fungus.   This extended field is due to toxic substances liberated in the vessels of the plants and carried along them to more distant parts ; or, to interference with the normal flow of foods to these parts.   The irritation set up by the fungus frequently causes reaction on the part of the host, which reaction usually takes the form of a greatly-increased production of tissue, resulting in the appearance of fungus galls (Fig. 42), " witches' brooms," etc.   In short, parasitic fungi have, in most cases, a distinctly injurious effect upon their hosts, and this injury is evidenced by certain external symptoms, the chief of which are given below.[1]

Rot, due to the breaking down of tissue, is probably the most common symptom of disease to be noted in any plant part.   It has numerous forms, and may be of a wet, dry, soft, or hard character, and may be accompanied by an offensive odour, or be odourless.

Blight is a symptom often exhibited by leaves, roots, stems, flowers or fruits.   It indicates complete death of the part affected, may be local or general, and may or may not be followed by rot.

Wilt of stems or leaves is caused usually, either by a plugging, or other interruption, of the sap-carrying vessels, or by some injury to the absorbing root system.

Spots on leaves, bark or fruits, may be caused by

---

[1] We are indebted to Stevens & Hall, *Diseases of Domestic Plants*, 1910, pp. 14–16, for the substance of this tabulation.

local blight, rot of tissue, imperfect coloration, or by local over-development or under-development of colour.

Scab in fruit, leaves, or bark, is due to the growth of the causal parasite upon or near the surface, or to thickening of the outer layer or layers of tissue caused by the irritation of the parasite.

Mildew upon any plant surface consists of a whitish powdery fungus growth.

Burn is a general term applied to all cases where the leaves turn red or brown, especially if the edge first shows the symptom.

Smut consists of a mass of spores, usually black and powdery. It is most common in the ovaries and other floral parts of various grasses.

Rust should properly be applied to the diseases caused by the rust fungi (the *Uredineae*). These are accompanied by rust-coloured streaks due to the appearance of the spore clusters. Yellowing of leaves, due to diminution in green colouring matter, is a common symptom of disease.

Chlorosis is also a lack of proper green, the normal green tissues becoming bleached.

Canker is a roughening and splitting of the bark.

The Effects of the Host upon the Fungus. When such powerful influences are at work, it might well be assumed that any effect which the host plant has upon the fungus would be negligible; yet such an assumption would be far from the truth. Certainly, when once infection has taken place, the fungus is usually able to proceed without much interference from its victim. But, for all that, plants have had a very considerable effect in controlling the life methods of the parasitic fungi which prey upon them. We have already seen that the attractive power of the host tends to restrict the fungi which can exist upon it, but in addition to this, a factor controlled by the seasons is introduced. The dependence of these fungi on plants which themselves have a restricted season of growth forces the fungi to experience, and, therefore, to make provision for, the periods during which the host plant is unavailable. These "close" seasons they have learned to meet in a number of ways, by means of sclerotia, resting spores, dormant mycelium, etc., all of which entail a degree of hibernation. A more active manner of bridging the gap is found among certain of the rusts (*Uredineae*), where the fungus abruptly changes its character just before the hiatus, and passes on to another host plant which *is* available in the interim, or at least in part of it. This mode of existence is known as heteroecism (Gr. *heteros* = different and *oikos* = a house) and is well exemplified in the Black Rust of Wheat (*Puccinia graminis*). Here the spring form of the fungus occurs on the barberry ; the summer and autumn stages on wheat or similar grasses ; while the winter or resting stage, when neither host is available, is passed on the dead wheat straw, etc., or upon the surface of the soil. This alternation of host, however, is not absolutely necessary to the existence of the fungus, for, in the absence of the alternative host, this stage of the life cycle can be omitted. For example, the black rust of wheat has been prevalent in Australia for almost a century, yet no barberry bushes occur there. The exact advantage of heteroecism to the fungus is in this case not obvious, while in certain other instances it is almost as obscure.

Intermediate Forms. Since parasitism is an acquired character, it would be natural to suppose that, between the two extremes of true saprophytism and true parasitism, would occur a number of intermediate forms in various transition stages of development. Of such forms two main types may be distinguished : the *hemi-saprophytes*, which are capable of completing their life cycles as saprophytes, but which, under certain conditions, have the faculty of attacking living tissues ; and, the *hemi-parasites*, which usually feed on living organisms, but which can, if necessary, pass part of their lives as saprophytes.

Hemi-saprophytes. Of this class of fungi, the most important section comprises species known as " wound-parasites," of which, again, the majority are ravagers of trees. These fungi are unable to attack uninjured, healthy trees, but if access can be gained by means of a wound—a broken branch, an abrasion caused by browsing animals, or an insect puncture—the mycelium lives first on the dead and rotting tissue at the seat of the injury, and, having gained a firm footing at this point, is then able to pass on to the healthy tissue, and may, in this way, soon involve the whole tree. Among the larger wound parasites of note are various polypores, such as *Fomes igniarius*, *F. fomentarius*, *F. applanatus*, *Polyporus betulinus*, *P. squamosus*, etc., various species of *Hydnum*, *Stereum*, and many others.

Hemi-parasites. These fungi, while normally acting as parasites, are able at need to exist saprophytically, although when reduced to the latter existence, they are seldom able to complete their full development. Of this type are the smuts, which, in the absence of a living host, are able to live for a considerable time upon the

soil.   Many of the ripe fruit rots, which exist
saprophytically on ripe fruits, commenced their life as
parasites upon the living tissues of the unripe fruits.
In both of these groups the parasitism displayed is
frequently of an exceedingly weak order, in that the
plant parts selected for attack are seldom in their full
vigour.

SYMBIOTIC UNIONS.

The living together in intimate association of two
organisms does not lead always to a benefit for one at
the expense of the other.   In some cases a partnership
is formed, in which each participant undertakes certain
work for their mutual benefit.   Such unions are termed
symbiosis (Gr. *syn* = together : *bios* = life) and that
they probably arose as abortive attempts at parasitism,
does not alter the fact that the ultimate result has, in
almost every case, been so advantageous that the dual
organism is stronger, and better able to battle for
existence, than would be either organism independently.
Symbiotic unions are found in all sections of life.   Among
the fungi the best-known examples of this phenomenon
are (1) the lichens, which are unions between fungi and
algae ; and (2) *mycorrhiza*, unions between fungi and
the higher plants.

Lichens.   In the lichens, those foliaceous incrusta-
tions commonly seen on rocks and on the bark of trees,
the component organisms are usually one of the green
algae such as are found on flower pots, or as scums on
ponds, and a member of the Ascomycetes ; the dual
entity being quite unlike either of the participant
organisms.   In the economy of these dual plants, to the
alga, since it contains chlorophyll, is assigned the task of

starch-making for itself and its partner; while the filaments of the latter not only supply a protective coat, but also absorb the water and mineral salts necessary for both. It is interesting to note that, while this partnership is of joint benefit, the fungus is apparently the predominant organism, in that, in most cases, it alone is capable of producing reproductive bodies.

Mycorrhiza. During the past eighty years, numerous cases of symbiosis between fungi of various kinds and the higher plants have come to light. The fungi are usually found associated with the roots of the plant, and, therefore, are termed mycorrhiza ("fungus-roots"). Of these, probably the most universal examples occur in the case of forest trees growing in soil rich in humus. In these, parts of the mycelium of the fungus appear as compact sheaths around the root tips, the remainder acting as the absorbent medium. In this way, nutrient materials obtained from the humus by the fungus can be utilised by the tree, and the reliance which the latter places on this mode of nutrition is illustrated by the loss of its root hairs which would normally perform this function. In a somewhat similar manner, many bog-loving plants employ mycorrhiza for obtaining part of their food. In other instances, notably with the orchids and the heaths, the mycelium dwells actually within the root-cells, which supply the necessary organic food, and in return are enabled to absorb waste material resulting from the death of parts of the fungus.

It is of interest to note that mycorrhiza are most abundant in plants which inhabit localities rich in humus, and may be entirely absent from other plants of the same species growing in places relatively devoid of this material. That in all cases the plants so infected not only suffer no inconvenience, but rather gain by the presence of the fungus, is shown by the fact that infected plants are, on the whole, more vigorous and more fertile than uninfected ones. This is especially the case with orchids, where the presence of the appropriate fungus is absolutely necessary for the successful raising of seedlings. It should be noted, however, that the fungus can be artificially replaced by the presence of certain carbohydrates in solution.

Conclusion. This brief sketch of the life methods of the fungi is, of necessity, extremely curtailed, and for this reason much of interest has had to be omitted. It is hoped, however, that, short as it is, it will serve to illustrate some of the vagaries of these peculiar plants, and the manner in which they live and have their being.

CHAPTER VI

The Damage Caused by Fungi and its Effect upon Mankind

"When rust is falling on the hearbes, then
Beritius in his husbandry instructions, willeth . .
to make a great smoake forthwith round about
the garden."—1563, HYLL, *Art Garden*, (1593) 28.

"This oure bred . . . was new . . . but now lo, it
is harde and moulde."—1535, COVERDALE, *Josh.* ix.,12.

WHEN a survey is made of the extensive feeding-grounds utilised by the fungi, encompassing as they do every corner of the earth, and every form of organic material upon it, one is immediately struck by the general similarity between *their* wants and our own. Man himself and his animals are of course organic, while the enormous use made by him of other organic materials hardly needs elaboration : his plants and trees, his food, his clothing, and his furniture, are but a few of the appurtenances which fall within this category. When, therefore, the fungi use any of these articles as a means of sustenance, they naturally encroach on what man regards as rightly his—an encroachment which he, equally naturally, resents and combats. In the warfare which ensues, the casualties are not wholly with the attackers. On the contrary, the losses sustained by ourselves, not only of material and money, but even of human life, are sufficiently grave to afford ground for furious thought.

The operations of the fungus forces, which are in this way arrayed against us, are dominated by their method of attack—in other words, by the manner in which they feed. Thus, from our point of view, they may be divided into three armies, comprising respectively :

(1) Those fungi which attack and cause disease in man and animals.

(2) The fungi which carry out these same processes on plants.

(3) The fungi which confine their attentions to the inanimate organic substances which man employs, viz., timber, foods, clothing, etc.

THE FUNGUS DISEASES OF MAN, AND OF OTHER ANIMALS.

Of these three classes, the most insidious foes—and therefore, in one sense, the most important—are the fungi which, by direct infection or by the contamination of staple foods, jeopardize the health, or even the life, of man himself ; or the health and well-being of the domestic animals with which he has surrounded himself. Fortunately, this class is not large, and their evil effects have been greatly reduced by modern prophylaxis. Yet their activities, even now, are by no means negligible ; while the harm which they have wrought in the past has often had very serious consequences. So far as man himself is concerned, the disease which has been most epidemic is undoubtedly ergotism, a malady brought about by the continued use of cereal foods, notably rye flour, which have become contaminated by the sclerotia of Ergot (*Claviceps purpurea*) (Fig. 53). This disease is a form of chronic poisoning, which is frequently accompanied by mortification of the fingers and toes. In earlier times, when people were wholly dependent on the produce of local harvests, which were frequently scanty and of poor quality, and when the milling of flour was not carried out with the care which is now exercised, this disease was extremely common. During the Middle Ages, many of the malignant plagues, which ravaged Europe after seasons of rain and scarcity, may be attributed to the presence of ergots in the cereals consumed by the inhabitants. Those recorded by chroniclers of the 6th and 8th centuries were possibly due, in several instances, to this cause ; while less doubt exists concerning the epidemics which prevailed in the 10th century in France and the 12th in Spain. In 1596, Hesse and the adjoining regions experienced a terrible pestilence, which was attributed by the Medical Faculty of Marburg to ergotism. The same disease appeared in France in 1630; in Voigtlandia (Saxony) in the years 1648, 1649, and 1675 ; and again in various parts of France, as Aquitaine and Sologne, in 1650, 1670, and 1674. Freiburg and its surroundings were visited by the disease in 1702, other parts of Switzerland in 1715–16, Saxony and Lusatia in 1716 ; and many districts of Germany in 1717, 1722, 1736, and 1741–42. The last epidemic in Europe occasioned by ergot is apparently that which, after the rainy season of 1816, descended on Lorraine and Burgundy, where it proved fatal to many of the poorer classes. To-day, although cases from time to time occur, ergotism in man is comparatively rare— thanks to the more careful milling of grain, and to the transport facilities which tend to make famine, and the use of damaged grain to which it leads, a thing of the past.

Less preventible, but also less dangerous, are those skin diseases of man, the *dermycoses*, which arise from infection by fungi. The "ringworm" of children— that human fairy-ring—and the "barber's itch" of adults, are both due to minute fungi, *Trichophyton tonsurans* and other species. That form of eczema known as *Favus* is brought about by another, *Achorion Schonleinii;* while thrush, the white pellicle which develops in the mouths of infants, is merely the crust-like mycelium of *Oidium albicans*. All these diseases are almost universal, and are spread by the use of insanitary appliances, e.g., dirty towels, feeding bottles, etc. The leprosy mentioned in Leviticus,[1] as causing baldness of the head and beard, may ·possibly have been brought about by a parasitic fungus.

The fungus diseases of the tropics are much more severe than those common to temperate regions, for the causal organism is frequently more acute and more deeply seated. Of this type is the dreaded "Madura foot," a disease especially common in Southern India, but occurring also in other tropical regions, and due to various different species of *Madurella*, *Indiella*, etc. This organism attacks the feet, in which it causes deformity and fungus tumours. The details are singularly revolting to the non-medical mind and may well be passed over. It is, however, of interest to note that the disease known as "Trench feet," suffered by our troops during the late war, was of fungus origin and therefore allied, in a measure, to "Madura foot." These are but a few of the fungus diseases of man which might be cited, but they will serve to show that many

---

[1] 1490 B.C., *Leviticus*, xiii and xiv.

of these plants affect mankind a little more intimately than is generally supposed.

The fungus diseases of animals only tend to become obvious to man when they appear on animals of economic importance to him. It is for this reason that, except in the case of those infecting domestic animals, they are in general little known. Many of these fungi are the same as, or similar to, those which attack man. For example, Favus (*Achorion Schonleinii*) occurs also in rabbits, cats, fowls, and other birds and mammals. Ringworm (*Trichophyton tonsurans*, etc.) is common to man, oxen, horses, dogs and rabbits. Thrush (*Oidium albicans*) attacks young herbivora and birds as well as children ; while ergotism is of course produced in any animals which are fed on grain containing ergots.

A disease of cattle, sheep, and pigs, which has at times had very serious consequences in this and other countries, is " Lumpy Jaw " or " Hard Tongue," due to *Actinomyces bovis*. This fungus grows on many grasses, and, when eaten with these foods, attacks the animal, forming ulcerating tumours, which seriously interfere with the functions of the organs affected. The chief seat of the trouble is the mouth, where are developed the symptoms suggested by the name of the disease, which runs a chronic course and is very often fatal. In 1907 it was ascertained that on various farms in Norfolk this disease affected from two per cent. to as much as thirty per cent. of the cattle kept. Lumpy Jaw occasionally appears in man, such cases usually arising from chewing grain, or blades of grass—a habit often practised by country people.

A number of gastric diseases of herbivorous animals

are due to the eating of fodder, the component plants of which are infected with various parasitic fungi. The symptoms vary, but they are usually akin to those of gastro-enteritis. Various bronchial troubles in animals may also be traced to the action of fungi, arising from the inhalation of spores. Of this type is aspergillosis, caused by species of *Aspergillus*. This disease, which is especially common in birds, is accompanied by such pneumonia-like symptoms as purulent inflammation of the lungs, etc.

Fishes and other amphibians are very liable to attack from various of the water-moulds (*Saprolegnieae*), of which the effects on goldfish, etc., are quite familiar to breeders of such creatures. From an economic standpoint, the most destructive member is *Saprolegnia ferax*, which has been responsible for a number of serious epidemics among adult salmon in Scottish and English rivers.

Insects, of all animals, are the favourite hosts of parasitic fungi. In one sense this is very fortunate, for in this way are destroyed millions of insects noxious to mankind. The " cholera " of the common house-fly, due to *Empusa Muscae*, is a case in point. An insect disease which has, however, led to serious financial losses is the " muscardine " disease of silkworms, caused by *Botrytis Bassiana*. First discovered in 1835, this affection has on several occasions been so wide-spread as to threaten the existence of the French silk industry.

An enormous number of other animal diseases of various kinds caused by fungi could be detailed, if space permitted ; but enough have been cited to demonstrate that many of the fungi concern mankind more closely than is often realised, and these certainly cannot be dismissed, as many would the "toadstools," with a shrug of the shoulders or a kick of the boot.

THE FUNGUS DISEASES OF PLANTS.

Turning to the parasitic fungi, which are either the primary or secondary cause of disease in plants, we find that they are so multitudinous in number and so far-reaching in effect that it is difficult to decide how much or how little to discuss them. It is scarcely an exaggeration to say that there is no plant of any description which is not a potential victim ; while it is in no way wide of the mark to assert that no cultivated crop, no forest, no similar collection of plants in bulk, escapes their ravages. This is undoubtedly by far the most serious aspect of fungus depredation, for the *direct* attacks of fungi on mankind and the domestic animals are somewhat isolated and sporadic, while the march of modern civilisation has naturally diminished enormously the effects of ergotism and other food-transmitted diseases. On the other hand, the fungus diseases of plants, particularly of the various crops on which mankind is so dependent, have, owing to a variety of reasons, considerably increased. This aspect of the matter, therefore, deserves a more detailed consideration, which may first be given from the historical stand-point.[1]

There is no reasonable doubt that fungus diseases attacked plants long before the advent of plant cultivation—an art which was certainly acquired at a

---

[1] Those desiring fuller information on the history of plant diseases are referred to Whetzel, *An Outline of the History of Phytopathology*, 1918, Philadelphia and London.

very early stage in man's most primitive evolution, and which, indeed, was one of the first things which differentiated him from his simian forerunners. It is hardly to be expected, however, that these plant diseases should impress themselves upon him at that early stage. There are few records of early husbandry and agriculture, and the extent to which these were affected by parasitic fungi must remain a matter for conjecture. As, however, these arts came more and more into being, improved cultivated varieties were developed from the more useful of the wild plants—a process which incidentally has given us the bulk of the vegetable necessities and luxuries which we enjoy to-day—and collaterally with this process, the respective fungi which were originally harboured by the wild plants adapted *themselves*, and continued to affect these cultivated forms. But, as the latter, by means of intensive cultivation, were gradually relieved of the need of battling for their existence, a battle which their wild confrères are facing daily, and in which the power of resisting disease plays no small part, they have naturally become more vulnerable, and the attacks of the parasitic fungi have, therefore, gained in intensity. In addition, the cultivated plants have become liable to infection by new fungi, whose attacks they had formerly successfully withstood, the damage wrought being thus correspondingly augmented. The history of the evolution of plant diseases is, therefore, in a measure coincident with that of the development of agriculture in its numerous forms.

Early References to Plant Diseases. The first written records of plant diseases which have come down to us occur in early Hebraic writings, where they are treated as if they were then of almost every-day occurrence. The first reference to a disease of crops is found in Genesis,[1] and, if the usual Biblical chronology be accepted, dates back to about the year 1715 B.C. Here the disease is ascribed to the evil effects of the east wind. In various other books of the Bible, " blasting " and " mildew " of the crops, which were certainly caused by the attacks of parasitic fungi, are referred to in very familiar fashion.[2] As with all scourges, then strange and inexplicable, these pests were considered to be expressions of the wrath and dis-favour of the Deity, and this rôle they filled for many centuries.

Classical References to Plant Diseases. The next large group of citations relating to crop diseases is to be found in classical writings. The early Greeks and Romans had unpleasant practical experience of the evils wrought by these pests, particularly by the red rust of wheat, but were certainly quite unaware as to the cause. If Pliny is correct, the losses caused by the wheat rust induced Numa Pompilius, the second king of Rome, some six centuries before the coming of the Christian era, to appoint a special day of intercession to, and propitiation of the Corn God, to avert the possible ravages. Whether this is correct or not, we have more definite evidence as to crop diseases from Aristotle, who was born in 384 B.C., and a little later from the writings of his famous pupil, Theophrastus. The latter, who flourished about 322 B.C., appears to

---

[1] 1715 B.C., *Genesis* xli. 23.
[2] See : 1451 B.C., *Deuteronomy* xxviii. 22 ; 1004 B.C., *I. Kings* viii. 37 ; 1004 B.C., *II. Chronicles* vi. 28 ; 787 B.C., *Amos* iv. 9 ; 520 B.C., *Haggai* ii. 17.

have made a special study of them, for in his celebrated
history of plants, which appeared a little later than
307 B.C., he remarks :

> " As to diseases—they say that wild trees are not liable to
> diseases which destroy them.   Cultivated kinds, however, are
> subject to various diseases, some of which are, one may say,
> common to all or to most, while others are special to particular
> kinds. . . . Generally speaking, cereals are more liable to rust
> than pulses, and among these barley is more liable to it than
> wheat ; while of barleys, some are more liable than others, and
> most of all, it may be said, the kind called ' Achillean.'   Moreover,
> the position and character of the land make no small difference
> in this respect ; for lands which are exposed to wind and elevated
> are not liable to rust, or less so, while those that lie low and are
> not exposed to wind are more so.   And rust occurs chiefly at
> full moon."

It may be noted that the remarks on the effect of the
situation of the land are as true to-day as when they
were written.   Here, then, are the first speculations as
to the origin of the crop diseases, and although the
ancients made much conjecture concerning this, little
real progress was made in the elucidation of the matter
for many centuries, indeed until comparatively recent
times.   Some account should, however, be given as to
classical belief on these points.   In ancient Greece, half
a century before the Christian era, so destructive were
the diseases of the staple crops of the country that
libations were offered regularly to Apollo or to some
other god, to gain relief.   Pliny, that prodigious compiler
of miscellaneous data upon natural history, who lived
from 23 to 79 A.D., thought that rust, which he describes
as " the greatest pest of the crops " [1] was due to frost,
although others considered that it was caused by the

---

[1] Pliny, *Nat. Hist.*, XVIII., 46.

sun heating the dew.[1] It was to be guarded against
" by fixing branches of laurel in the fields, for then the
rust passes over into the laurel leaves," [2] this practice
being of course of no efficacy in reality.

The Rubigalia. The same author relates that :

> " the ancients feared three periods of the year for their crops,
> on account of which they instituted feasts, the Rubigalia, the
> Floralia and the Vinalia. The Rubigalia were instituted by Numa
> in the eleventh year of his reign, and they are now celebrated on
> the 25th of April, since at that time the Rust generally attacks
> the corn." [3]

On the day in question, a procession took place to the
sacred grove of the Corn God, Robigus, five miles out
of Rome along the Claudian way. This powerful deity,
created by the Romans, was named after the disease,
which they called the *robigo* (from *robus = ruber*, red)
and probably represented Mars Rusticus. Those taking
part in the ceremony wore white togas, and on arriving
at the sacred spot, an offering of wine was poured over
the altar, incense was burnt, and a sheep and dog were
sacrificed by the Flamen Quirinalis, this being considered
to avert danger to the crops from the dog-star. The
dog was of a reddish colour, in symbolical allusion to
the colour of the rust.[4] On one occasion, Ovid (43 B.C.-
18 A.D.), while journeying from Nomentum to Rome,
encountered the Rubigalian procession accidentally, and
has described the rites which accompanied the ceremony
in question.[5] There is no doubt that the *Robigo veris*

---

[1] *Ibid.*, 68.

[2] *Ibid.*, 46.

[3] Pliny, *Nat. Hist.*, XVIII., 69.

[4] 1899, A. W. Fowler, *The Roman Festivals of the Period of the Republic*, p. 91.

[5] Ovid, *Fasti*, IV., 905.

of Pliny, Ovid and others, is the modern *Puccinia graminis*. It should be noted that Pliny does not agree with Theophrastus and considers wheat to be the cereal most severely affected.

Mediaeval References to Plant Diseases. From the time of the final passing of the Roman Empire, in 476 A.D., until the classical revival of the fourteenth and fifteenth centuries, there is an almost complete absence of records of plant diseases. There is, however, one bright light which suddenly shines out in these dark ages, in the writings of Ibn-al-Awam, an Arabian country gentleman, who lived at Seville in Spain during the tenth century.[1] He wrote on agriculture and appears to have been quite conversant with the works of Theophrastus and Pliny, but was also a critical and independent observer of plant diseases, who writes with accuracy and gives much consideration to their control.

In the fourteenth century began in Europe a great recrudescence of interest in Greek and Roman literature, which continued during the next century, and this brought to the attention of the naturalists and agriculturists of that day, the data supplied by the two classical authors in question on plant diseases. It is, however, to be regretted, that the few writers on agriculture in this era of darkness contented themselves with merely repeating in blind acceptance the statements of the Greek and Roman philosophers, no attempts being made to confirm or refute them by actual experiment.

---

[1] See Clement-Müllet. *Le livre de l'agriculture d'Ibn-al-Awam* (*Kitab-al-Felahah.*) Traduit de l'Arabe. Vol. I. (1864): Vol. II., part 1 (1866): Vol. II., part 2 (1867). For his treatment of the diseases of trees and other plants, see Vol. I., ch. 14, pp. 543–597.

Even so much later as the year 1600, Coler in his
Oeconomia[1] includes information on plant diseases which
is merely a rehash of the views of ancient writers ; and
a few years later Lauremberg expressed the opinion
that the so-called secret evils, among which he included
rust, mildew and carbuncle, were due to the evil
influence of certain stars, such as Orion, the Pleiades
and others.[2]

The seventeenth century certainly showed the arising
of a new spirit, and, among other contributions to
scientific thought, numerous references to plant diseases
are to be found in the agricultural literature of this
period, although the views of most writers who dealt
with their supposed causes were still dominated by the
classical legend. It was the agriculturists and gardeners,
rather than the botanists, who led the way in this revival,
and, in addition to descriptions of the symptoms of
various diseases, there are given empirical, but often
original, methods by which these might be controlled.
As an example, we may refer to Parkinson's advocacy of
the use of vinegar against canker on fruit trees. This
century is also noteworthy for the promulgation at
Rouen, in 1660, of the first legal enactment aimed at
the prevention of a plant disease. This directed the
grubbing-up and destruction of all barberry bushes, as
they were held, as we now know rightly, to have some
mysterious influence on the distribution of wheat rust.
There is little doubt that this deduction was in the
first case due to the practical observation of farmers,
and there were probably scientific men in that day who

---

[1] 1600, Johannis Coler, *Oeconomia oder Hausbuch*.
[2] 1631, Petrus Lauremberg, *Rostochiensis Horticultura*, Frankfort.

were amused at such superstitious beliefs.[1] Towards the end of this century, Heinrich Hesse stated the three chief causes of the blighting of trees to be as follows :

(1) Superfluous sap with inflammation of the same. (2) Transplanting a tree so as to give it an orientation differing from its original one. (He says that such trees may be preserved from attack by coating the south side of the trunk with a mixture of cow manure, oat chaff, glue and ashes.)   (3) Using a breadknife in grafting a tree.

With further reference to grafting, he believed that cankers on trees were the result of performing this operation at a time when the moon lies in the sign of the crab or scorpion.[2]

The Study of Plant Diseases in the Eighteenth Century showed further development.   The causes were still generally considered to be various occult influences, such as winds, low temperatures, unfavourable soils and the like, but there were seen the beginnings of the theory that these were autogenetic, i.e., that they arose from an unhealthy condition of the affected individuals rather than from any outside influence.   Some attempts at classification, based on the supposed causes, were made, and further efforts at control are to be noted.

---

[1] In this connection, it has been shown by Broadbent that black rust on wheat is scarce in all parts of the British Isles, except in the counties of Carmarthenshire, Cardiganshire and Pembrokeshire, where the barberry is also common ; while, according to Lind and Güssow, the gradual extermination of barberry since 1903 has led to a great decrease in the extent of this disease in Denmark.

[2] 1690, Heinrich Hesse, *Neue Gartenlust d.i. gründliche Vorstellung wie ein Lust, Küchen- und Baumgarten unter unsern Climate füglich anzurichten*, Leipzig.

Thus, in 1755, the state legislature of Massachusetts passed an Act compelling the inhabitants to extirpate all Barberry bushes.[1] In 1790 Forsyth recommended the following mixture " to cure disease, defects, and injuries of plants."

> " Take one bushel fresh cow dung, one half bushel lime rubbish from old buildings, one half bushel wood ashes, one-sixteenth bushel pit or river sand.   The last three are to be sifted fine before they are mixed.   Then work them well together with a spade, and afterward with a wooden beater until the stuff is very smooth, like fine plaster used for the ceilings of rooms."

Soap-suds or urine was employed so as to give the material the consistency of plaster or paint, and after application it was to be covered with a sifting of fine powder, made of " dry powder of wood ashes, mixed with the sixth part of the same quantity of the ashes of burnt bones." [2]

Modern Developments in the Study of Plant Diseases. During the first quarter of the nineteenth century, the classification of plant diseases was still

---

[1] THE BARBERRY LAW OF MASSACHUSETTS. Anno Regni Regis Georgii II., Vicesimo Octavo, Chapter X. (published Jan. 13, 1755).

An Act to prevent Damage to English Grain arising from Barberry bushes.

Whereas it has been found by experience, that the Blasting of Wheat and other English grain is often occasioned by Barberry bushes, to the great loss and damage of the inhabitants of the Province :

Be it therefore enacted by the Governour, Council, and House of Representatives, that whoever, whether community or private person, hath any Barberry bushes growing in his or their Land, within any of the Towns in this Province, he or they shall cause the same to be extirpated or destroyed on or before the thirteenth Day of June, Anno Domini One Thousand Seven Hundred and Sixty.   And so forth.

[2] E. G. Lodeman, *The Spraying of Plants*, p. 6.

based on their supposed causes, while the autogenetic theory of their origins received general support. As early as 1807, the efficacy of copper salts as a preventive of smut was discussed by Prévost; while in 1821, Robertson first recommended sulphur as " the only specific that can be named for the treatment of mildew in peaches. It should be mixed with soap-suds and then applied by dashing it violently against the trees by means of a rose syringe." A variety of this remedy is still widely used against the attacks of the powdery mildews, e.g., of the grape. Towards the middle of the century the autogenetic theory of plant diseases was shown to be entirely fallacious by the work of Fries, Berkeley, Tulasne, de Bary and others, and it became recognised that the causal agents of disease were certain classes of fungi. This demonstration of the true relation of fungi to plant diseases gradually enabled the methods of prevention to be established on a sound basis, and heralded the dawn of the modern era of disease control. The years between 1878 and 1882 were noteworthy for severe epidemics of plant diseases in Europe, especially in the case of the downy mildew of the vine, caused by *Plasmopara viticola*, which appears to have invaded Europe from America in the first of these years. The European vines were found to be more liable to attack than the American varieties. These epidemics led to the inauguration of an extensive campaign to discover the most effective remedies, and many experiments were made. We may associate with this new era the name of Millardet, who was responsible for the introduction of the now-celebrated Bordeaux Mixture. The original discovery was the result of a happy chance, and arose from the practice, obtaining in some vineyards,

Photo by A. E. Peck, Scarborough

Fig. 42.—A typical fungus gall, produced by *Frankiella alni*, on alder roots.

Photo by W. A. Millard, Leeds

Fig. 43.—Corky Scab of Potatoes (*Spongospora subterranea*). This disease often causes serious losses.

Photo by A. F. Buckhurst

Fig. 44.—Brown Rot (*Monilia fructigena*) of fruit. It quickly spreads from fruit to fruit, causing rapid decay.

Courtesy of The Fruit Grower

Fig. 45.—Treating fruit trees by means of a modern spraying machine, to inhibit fungus attack. The cloud of fungicide, at the left of the picture, obscures the trees.

of sprinkling a few rows of vines, adjoining the road, with a mixture of milk of lime and blue vitriol (copper sulphate), in order to give them a poisonous appearance, and thus avert the inroads of the hungry wayfarer. It was observed by Prillieux and Millardet, in 1882, that the vines which had been thus treated were less attacked by the mildew than were the others, which fact they naturally ascribed to the treatment. As a result of further experiments with varying mixtures, the efficacy of the lime-bluestone wash was demonstrated by Millardet, who published, in 1885, the following recipe :

BORDEAUX MIXTURE.
Water—130 litres (34 gallons)
Bluestone—8 kilos (17·6 lb.)
Lime—15 kilos (33 lb.)

This was to be shaken on the plants with a broom. Later tests have shown that much weaker solutions are quite effective. The last forty years have seen steady progress in means of inhibition and control, particularly in the development of methods of spraying much more effective in distribution than was Millardet's somewhat primitive broom, in the devising of special washes for particular diseases, and in the production of disease-resisting varieties.

The Effects of Plant Diseases on Mankind. It might not at first be supposed that these depredations of parasitic fungi would be on sufficiently large a scale to imperil human life. Yet such has too often been the result, and a vivid example is to be found no further away than Ireland. In that country, in 1846, the potato crop was devastated by a severe epidemic of the Blight or Downy Mildew (*Phytophthora infestans*), the results of which can have no more graphic description than that of an eye-witness, one Father Mathew, who wrote :

> " On July 27 I passed from Cork to Dublin, and the doomed plant bloomed in all the luxuriance of an abundant harvest. Returning on August 3rd, I beheld with sorrow mere wastes of putrefying vegetation."

In those seven days the stage had been set for one of the most appalling famines which that country has ever known—a famine which cost the inhabitants tens of thousands of lives, and brought misery and privation to millions more.

Epidemics of such devastating proportions are of course infrequent, but, nevertheless, every season in every country witnesses the exaction by plant diseases of a toll on the food crops of the people which, in the aggregate, is exceedingly heavy. Some slight impression of the extent of this spoliation is gained from the fact that in the United States alone, in the year 1919—a season which was by no means exceptional—plant diseases were responsible for the loss of 190,000,000 bushels of wheat, of 78,000,000 bushels of oats, of 200,000,000 bushels of maize, of 86,000,000 bushels of potatoes, of 58,000,000 bushels of sweet potatoes, and of 18,000,000 bushels of apples ; quantities which represent from two per cent. to as much as fifty per cent. of the individual harvests. When such losses, even in normal years, are possible, it will be readily understood that after really adverse seasons—especially when they are experienced in several countries simultaneously—a condition of scarcity may, and frequently does, arise, so as to place many of the common necessities of life almost beyond the reach of those people whose purchasing powers are limited, and may in extreme cases even lead to that state of semi-starvation which paves the way for so many further ills.

The Monetary Losses occasioned by Plant Diseases. Turning to the financial aspect of the matter, and extending our field so as to include other than food crops, we are brought face to face with a situation which is staggering in its immensity. Thus, considering a few particular crops in one country, the United States, the ravages, measured by a monetary standard, perpetrated in different years by parasitic fungi, are given below, the authority responsible for each estimate being also cited :

The California vine disease in 1892	$10,000,000	Pierce
Wheat rust in the United States, 1898	$67,000,000	Galloway
Wheat rust in Illinois, 1885	$1,875,000	Burrill
Violet leaf spot in the United States, 1900	$200,000	Dorsett
Peach leaf curl in the United States, 1900	$2,335,000	Pierce
Potato late blight in New York, 1904	$10,000,000	Stewart
Oat smut in the United States, annual	$6,500,000	Orton
Wheat loose smut, United States, annual	$3,000,000	Orton
Wheat bunt in the United States, annual	$11,000,000	Orton
Potato blight in the United States, annual	$36,000,000	Orton

Taking cereal crops alone, the Prussian Statistics Bureau estimated the losses in Prussia, during the year 1891, from grain rust attacking wheat, oats and rye, at £20,628,147. In Australia in the same year, the loss to the wheat harvest caused by rust was estimated at £2,500,000. In New South Wales, in 1916, stem rust (*Puccinia graminis*) alone accounted for damage exceeding two millions sterling. Other crops in various parts of the world exhibit similar losses. Data concerning the ravages perpetrated in this manner in our own country are not available, but would probably be of the same order of magnitude.

Over the crops of the whole world, we envisage damage which can only be reckoned in hundreds of millions sterling. In 1912, no less an authority than the late George Massee stated that "the annual loss throughout the world due to injury caused by parasitic fungi exceeds £150,000,000," and then, as if fearing to underestimate, he adds "*Probably double this amount would be nearer the truth.*" Such stupendous totals represent, of course, the activities of very many different species of fungi and are, therefore, a little difficult to visualize ; but the losses, as a whole, undoubtedly constitute a drain upon the world's vegetable resources which is very disquieting. Nor is this feeling materially relieved by the additional information that plant diseases " are increasing by importation from other countries and other states ; that diseases formerly insignificant are, in many cases, becoming serious ; and that long intensive culture of one crop in a locality permits new diseases to develop." In this factor alone we can find evidence of the destructive capabilities of fungi which demands the most earnest attention of every citizen.

The Control of Plant Diseases. A question which naturally arises is, whether many of these losses are preventible ; and the answer must be emphatically in the affirmative. Unfortunately, the spirit of apathy, which so long has dogged the footsteps of the fungi, is still abroad, and it is this spirit which, to a large extent, is nullifying the efforts of scientific men. Agriculturists are a notoriously conservative race and do not take over kindly to new methods. There is, however, now no doubt as to the efficacy of many methods of disease control, some of which may be briefly indicated.

It is, of course, of the utmost importance to investigate the life history of the parasite (so as to be able to know when to catch the fungus " napping "), for by such knowledge one is enabled to institute preventive, rather than curative, measures, and it should be hardly necessary to state that the former methods are the only useful ones, the value of an infected individual being generally too small to permit of the labour and expense involved in the latter. On the other hand, many diseases can largely be prevented by spraying the plants, at suitable times, with the wash found most efficacious for the particular disease ; while the cost of so spraying the whole of the crop may be only a small fraction of the loss involved if the plants later on become seriously blighted. This practice is, therefore, very generally adopted with certain crops, e.g., potatoes, apples, grapes, gooseberries, and fruit of various kinds. The question as to the compounds best suited for the individual crops, their strengths, and the times of application, are matters which are too complex to describe here, but are fully dealt with in special treatises.[1]   As a typical example of the increased yields obtainable by treatment, we may cite, however, those obtained with apples by the use of ordinary 5—5—50 Bordeaux mixture of the following formula :

ORDINARY BORDEAUX MIXTURE
5—5—50

Copper Sulphate (bluestone)	5 pounds
Quicklime	5 pounds
Water	50 gallons

(This strength is suitable for most plants, whose foliage is not specially sensitive to copper salts.)

---

[1] An excellent example is Stevens and Hall's *Diseases of Economic Plants*, New York, The MacMillan Co., 1910.

SPRAYING AT AVON, VA., DURING THE SEASON OF 1905, AND ITS RESULTS.[1]

Plot Numbers (2 trees to each plot)	TREATMENT WITH BORDEAUX MIXTURE. (5—5—50 FORMULA.)										PICKED SEPT. 19 TO 23.		
	April 8	May 1	May 9	June 12	June 27	July 10	July 25	Aug. 7	Aug. 22	Sept. 4	Sound Fruit.	Rotten Fruit.	Percentage of Sound Fruit.
											Bushels	Bushels	
1	"	"	"	—	—	—	—	—	—	—	18·50	30·25	37·9
2	"	"	"	"	"	—	—	—	—	—	47·50	22·50	67·8
3	"	"	"	"	"	"	"	—	—	—	56·00	2·00	96·5
4	"	"	"	"	"	"	"	"	—	—	54.00	1·75	96·8
5	"	"	"	"	"	"	"	"	"	—	32·75	1·15	96·6
6	"	"	"	"	"	"	"	"	"	"	68·50	0·70	98·9
A	Check-one untreated tree										·00	10·00	00·0[2]
7	"	"	"	—	—	—	"	"	"	"	56·50	14·00	80·1
8	"	"	"	—	—	—	—	"	"	"	7·00	6·50	51·8
9	—	—	—	—	"	"	"	—	"	—	28·50	6·00	82·6
B	Check-one untreated tree										·00	17·00	00·0[2]
10	—	—	—	—	"	"	"	"	"	"	59·00	6·50	90·0
11	—	—	—	—	—	"	"	"	"	"	42·25	6·50	86·6
12	—	—	—	—	—	—	"	"	"	"	28·50	24·75	53·5
C	Check-one untreated tree										·00	13·00	00·0
D	Check-one untreated tree										·00	20·75	00·0[2]
15	—	—	—	—	—	"	"	"	"	—	52·25	5·25	90·8
16	—	—	—	—	"	"	"	"	—	—	52·50	3·75	93·3
17	—	—	—	"	"	"	"	—	—	—	40·00	5·00	88·8
E	Check-one untreated tree										·25	16·25	1·5

These results are sufficiently striking. The two following quotations show a comparison between the improved yields obtainable by spraying, and the cost of the operations :

" The return per acre from unsprayed area (grapes) is calculated at 316 baskets per acre, worth less than $10 per acre, while from

---

[1] Scott, W. M., *U.S. Dept. Agr. Bur. Plant Indus. Bul.* 93, p. 23.
[2] Of the check trees, A had one sound apple, B six, and D two, but the percentages were too small to show in the table.

the sprayed areas the average yield was 1252 baskets per acre, worth $125·20 per acre, secured at a cost of $7·50 per acre." [1]

" In New York (Geneva) in one case spraying for pear scab, at a total cost of 55 cents per tree, increased the average yield from 45 cents to $6·55 per tree, a net profit of $6·10 per tree." [2]

Other methods of control involve the destruction of the fungus on the seed (smuts of oats and wheat, or the black rot of cabbage); the grubbing-up of complementary hosts (wheat rust); the avoidance of the use of infected hay or manure (black scab of potato) or of methods which will distribute the disease (e.g., unsuitable location, ground being already invaded by infecting organism); the arranging of a proper rotation of crops, the use of disease-resisting strains, and so on. By these means, many diseases, which have in the past committed extensive ravages, have been very considerably diminished in extent, and there is little doubt that, in the future, practically all diseases of cultivated crops due to fungi will, if the proper methods be employed, be very largely subjugated.

THE DEPREDATIONS OF SAPROPHYTIC FUNGI.

The activities of saprophytic fungi in causing damage of various kinds is the aspect most obvious to the layman, but even these are considerably greater, and cover an even wider range, than he would probably imagine, for between such widely-separated items as the expenditure of the thousands of pounds required to renew the woodwork of some public building attacked by dry rot, and the merely nominal loss involved in the discarding of a mouldy crust of bread, occur an enormous number

---

[1] *Ohio Bulletin*, 130, p. 46.
[2] 1910, Stevens and Hall, *Diseases of Economic Plants*, p. 52.

of deteriorations, the variety of which is too great to tabulate, and the value impossible to compute. It is thus idle to attempt any full description of the machinations of the thousands of fungi which in this way are working adversely to man's interests, but a consideration of some of them will serve to show that their effects are more serious than would generally be considered possible. One or two of the main classes of saprophytic fungi are, therefore, dealt with briefly below :

The Wood Rots are responsible for enormous damage to stored timber, the wood of buildings, etc. The "leprosy of the house" referred to in some detail in Leviticus, ch. xiv., is probably one of these, although there is not sufficient evidence to identify it with any species that we now know. The extent of the damage that may be done is well illustrated in the case of the old Louis XIII Wing of the Palace of Versailles. Here the oak beams of the roof were recently found to be attacked by the polypore, *Polyporus cryptarum*. The conditions for the development of this fungus, which generally occurs in cellars and mines, were singularly favourable, for the beams in question had been embedded in plaster, thus excluding light and air. The attacked timbers, especially the ends fixed in the masonry, were reduced almost to the consistency of lint, and were easily crushed by slight pressure, but did not crumble.

There are two main classes of fungi which affect timber, differing in their manner of attack :

(*a*) In the first class, spores coming in contact with the outside of the timber, germinate and give rise to minute thread-like hyphae, which grow into and spread through the wood, always keeping at some distance from the exterior, The wood may thus show no external sign of attack, except when broken, or when a fruiting body emerges.

(*b*) In the second class, the attacks of which are more severe, the hyphae grow not only into the wood, but also develop rapidly on the outside, forming matted masses, skins or long strings (*rhizomorphs*), from all of which are developed other hyphae which penetrate in their turn into the wood.

By means of the rhizomorphs, these fungi are enabled to climb over brick, stone or metal, in their apparent search for more distant woodwork. Their development, for which water is necessary, sometimes proceeds at an extraordinarily rapid rate. Some, e.g., *Coniophora cerebella*, cannot flourish except in really damp wood, and can thus readily be destroyed, even when they have gained a footing, by drying the wood and ensuring a good ventilation for the future. Others, although requiring moisture for the germination of their spores, can, when established, produce the necessary water themselves. This is the case with *Merulius lacrymans* (Fig. 46), the fungus responsible for " dry-rot." [1] This requires air for respiration, during which process it takes up oxygen and gives out water, which may thus be produced to the extent of half as much by weight as the original wood. The presence of these drops of water on the hyphae have been responsible for its name of *lacrymans* = " weeping." This faculty, in conjunction with its frequency of occurrence, and its habit of growth, renders *Merulius lacrymans* probably

---

[1] It should be noted that the terms " dry-rot " and " wet-rot " may only represent different aspects of the results of the same fungus.

the most dangerous of any timber-rot, for it can attack the driest wood, and cannot be eradicated by drying or ventilation, unless heat is applied. It affects not only soft woods but also hard woods, including teak, oak and mahogany, which in the space of a few years, or under exceptional circumstances in a much shorter time, may be practically destroyed. The woody tissue permeated by mycelium is left as a spongy mass of brownish material, which absorbs water so as largely to retain its original dimensions while wet. The drying-up of the material produces, however, the well-known " dry-rot " effect, showing a multiplicity of cracks often disposed more or less at right angles to each other (Fig. 47). The power of " locomotion " of this fungus is really remarkable, for it has been known to travel for yards along thin tubes containing bell-wire ; it can climb up a wall from one floor of a building to the next, and it can even penetrate brickwork through the mortar, involving in a common disintegration the walls no less than the woodwork. *Merulius lacrymans* appears to be almost always found in buildings, and very rarely in woods, for which reason it is known to the Germans as " haus-schwamm," or house-fungus.

Among other fungi of the same type are *Polyporus vaporarius* and *Coniophora cerebella*. The first is a dangerous enemy to the woodwork of dwellings, having effects very similar to those of *Merulius*. It, however, is frequently found in woods, both on the roots and stems, gaining a footing by means of a wound. It attacks chiefly soft coniferous woods. The second has already been mentioned as more amenable to treatment than *Merulius*. As the latter, it produces water in respiration, but to a lesser degree.

Courtesy of H.M. Office of Works

Fig. 46.—An example of the damage caused to the woodwork of a building by ' Dry rot ' (*Merulius lacrymans*).

Courtesy of H.M. Office of Works

Fig. 47.—Examples of woodwork totally destroyed by the same fungus. The right-angled cracking is characteristic.

Photo by A. E. Peck, Scarborough

Fig. 48.—*Fomes fomentarius*, a fungus formerly employed as a counter-irritant and styptic, and still used in the manufacture of tinder.

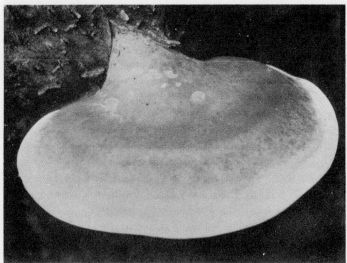

Photo by A. E. Peck, Scarborough

Fig. 49.—*Polyporus betulinus*, occasionally used by apiarists as an anaesthetic for bees, preparatory to clearing out hives.

Since the most effective method of prevention of dry-rot differs with the species responsible for it, it is necessary to identify the individual accurately, and in the case of the three species in question, this is best accomplished by a comparison of their fruiting bodies or sporophores, which are characterised as follows :

(a) That of *Merulius* is rusty, with irregular furrows and ridges.

(b) That of *Polyporus* is white, with regular and definite pores.

(c) That of *Coniophora* is brown, with the surface embossed all over with small pimple-like lumps.

As it is obviously not always a satisfactory procedure to wait for the appearance of fruiting bodies, the strands are also used for this purpose.

As counter measures, the timber used should first be thoroughly seasoned so as to render it as dry as possible, and an effective circulation of air should also be arranged within the structure, so as to prevent the conditions from becoming suitable for the development of these fungi. A counsel of perfection, where dry-rot is feared, is to soak the wood, before use, in a solution of creosote or a derivative, or other solution of a fungicidal nature. Affected wood should be removed and replaced by treated wood, and the adjoining portions must also be treated by coating with creosote or other suitable compound, of which a large number are employed. In addition to coating, drilling and injection is also practised. The adjoining brickwork, etc., should also be sterilised. This may be accomplished by spraying with a creosote derivative heated to 140–160° F., or with formalin diluted with water. The brickwork should be allowed to dry, and sprayed again as before. It should be noted that some wood-destroying fungi only attack particular timbers, while others are quite immune, and another method is to replace the wood infested by one of these " specialists " by another wood, not subject to attack by the particular fungus. The question of the method of infection, often brought about by the use of timber already affected before felling, must perforce be passed over.

In view of the dangerous consequences entailed in the case of the attack of mine timbers, railway sleepers, etc., the importance of the subject can hardly be exaggerated, while the question of the annual cost of replacing the rotten timber is a most serious one. Thus in the United States alone, about the year 1909, some 110,000,000 ties were being used by the railroads annually; while to maintain 4,000,000,000 posts in use, an annual replacement of 500,000,000 was necessary. In contrast with U.S. practice, in which the ties are not treated, they are in this country creosoted under pressure, and data as to the comparative " tie mortality " would be of interest. Other factors, besides fungus attacks, play a part in the deterioration of timber, but fungi are responsible for no small proportion of the damage. In view of the enormous annual charge thus involved, the question of the prevention of these fungus depredations by impregnation has become of the first importance, and, as with the ravages of the parasitic fungi, increasing attention is being devoted to the subject.

The Meat-Moulds. These have frequently been responsible for considerable damage to imported meat kept in cold storage, this being particularly the case in the year 1918, when, owing to war conditions, the normal length of time during which the meat was in transit was often considerably increased. These moulds are quite common on vegetable débris and animal excreta in the southern hemisphere, where they are found around abattoirs. Air-borne spores are deposited on the carcasses before and during storage, and under favourable conditions develop into the moulds in question. The spores retain their vitality for extended periods, e.g., for as long as two years at a temperature of – 6° C., or 21° F., in the case of several species.

Much investigation on the nature of these fungi has been carried out for the Food Investigation Board of the Department of Scientific and Industrial Research.[1] The fungus most commonly found on cold-store meat is *Sporotrichum carnis*, which occurs in the form of a large number of small white somewhat-woolly patches, which are entirely superficial, and apparently require a temperature not sensibly lower than about freezing-point for effective development. The same temperature is required for the profuse greyish-white growths, known in the meat-trade as "whiskers," due to species of *Thamnidium* and *Mucor*, which grow very little below the temperature of 0° C. These patches do not penetrate into the flesh at all, do no harm to it, and can readily be removed by means of a cloth.

A very common mould found on chilled meat gives rise to " Black Spot," caused by the ramification in the

---

[1] See Special Report No. 6, Food Investigation Board, published in 1921, upon the " Black Spot " of chilled and frozen meat ; also *Mould-Growths on Cold-Store Meat*, Brooks and Hansford, Trans. Brit. Myc. Soc. 1923, Vol. VIII., p. 113, from which the above data have largely been obtained.

tissues of the dark hyphae of *Cladosporium herbarum*, which possesses the somewhat remarkable power of growth at a temperature of – 6° C. The germination of its spores can also take place at this low temperature, but subsequent growth is more rapid if germination has taken place at the ordinary temperature.

Several other species also occur on cold-store meat, of which fungi *Penicillium expansum* and *Torula botryoides* will also grow slightly at – 6° C., but readily at freezing-point, and possibly to an intermediate degree between these temperatures. When profuse growths of any of these fungi are found on meat, it usually indicates that the temperature has been raised to 0° C., or slightly higher, at some time or other during storage—for example, by a temporary breakdown of the refrigerating system. All the growths are merely superficial, the maximum recorded penetration, in the case of " Black Spot," being 4 mm. Further, no poisonous properties are imparted to the meat, which, unless the fungi are associated, as sometimes, with putrefactive bacteria, is quite fit for human consumption. Such meat, however, has frequently been condemned. In this connection, it should be remembered that at temperatures a few degrees above freezing-point, bacterial growth may proceed so vigorously that the development of moulds is prevented. Such conditions, however, can very seldom occur. The occurrence of the moulds can be prevented by a proper control of humidity and temperature, and by avoiding too long a period of storage, for " Black Spot " may occur with prolonged storage at a temperature several degrees below zero. It is note-worthy that similar moulds are found on meat coming from widely-separated countries, this being evidence of the very cosmopolitan nature of the fungi, which is referred to later.[1]

The Fruit Moulds.   The effects of these are familiar to everyone, although the extent of the losses that they occasion is probably not always so well-known.   In the case of " Bitter rot," or " ripe rot," of apples, due to *Glomerella rufomaculans*, it was estimated by the president of the National Apple Shippers Association that a loss of $10,000,000 was caused to the U.S. apple crop in the year 1900, while there is frequently in certain localities a loss of from 50 to 75 per cent. of the crop.

The most prevalent apple rot, however, is that which attacks stored apples late in the year, caused by a species of *Penicillium*, and known as " soft rot " or " blue mould."   This requires a bruise or fracture of the skin before it can gain a foothold, uninjured fruit being never affected.   The means of prevention are thus obvious.   The result of infection is a light tan-coloured rotten area, which is soft and watery, and which spreads rapidly over the whole fruit ; in the case of apples in store or in transit, which are in contact with one another, throughout the whole mass of fruit.   Later appear delicate tufts of hyphae, breaking through cracks in the skin over the diseased tissue, and finally growing over the whole mass.   These hyphae are at first white, and later bluish green, owing to the development of large numbers of the coloured spores.

A most destructive fungus on European apples and other fruits is *Monilia fructigena* (Fig. 44), responsible for " Brown rot," which rapidly causes an entire decay of the whole fruit, which becomes brown, soft and wrinkled,

---

[1] See ch. ix. : The Uses of Fungi, as Foods.

and shows the usual tufts of hyphae. The fruit finally
dries up to a hard mass, which may remain on the tree
or fall to the ground, and in which the spores winter.
The " Brown rot " of plums, cherries, and peaches is
caused by the same fungus, which does enormous damage
to these crops in the United States, where, however, it
appears to affect apples, pears and quinces in a decidedly
less degree. This variability of attack of the same
species in different countries is by no means uncommon.
The estimated damage inflicted by " Brown rot " on
the Ohio peach crop alone in one year was $250,000;
while in one year, in Pennsylvania, twenty car-loads of
fruit were ruined. It is frequently the case that fruit
which appears quite sound on picking becomes seriously
damaged in a day or two during transport to market.
This disease is often to be seen on cherries on sale in the
shops. As protective measures, spraying at intervals
with lime-sulphur wash is of great service, although the
injury of fruit by insects will permit the entry of " Brown
rot," even when spraying is carried out quite effectively.
In addition, all affected fruit must be removed and
destroyed, so as to prevent further infection in the
following spring. Warm damp weather appears to
provide the best conditions for development of this
disease, the ravages of which have been so severe in the
United States that many peach and plum cultivators
have had to give up growing these fruits. Among other
fruits liable to be seriously damaged by fungus attack
during transport is the tomato, which is affected by the
dreaded potato blight or downy mildew (*Phytophthora
infestans*), and where, as frequently, no indication of
unsoundness may have been seen on packing. The
whole plant is often destroyed by this fungus, which

has been responsible for much damage. It should be noted that two other species of *Phytophthora* also attack the tomato. Another disease of the tomato, anthracnose, caused by *Colletotrichum phomoides*, occurs chiefly on the ripe fruit, as sunken, discoloured and wrinkled areas, with black specks.

Other Saprophytic Fungi. Probably the most obvious, and, therefore, best known forms of fungus depredation, are the various kinds of " mouldiness " which attack foods of every description when left too long exposed to the air. The blue moulds of bread are familiar to all, as also are those of cheese. In the case of the latter is found one of the few cases where such fungi are not only tolerated, but even encouraged, for, as is well known, special cheeses are deliberately inoculated with special species of *Penicillium*, the consumption of which appears to lead to no ill-effects. The ordinary species *attack* any cheese, when their inroads are not regarded with the same favour. In certain cases of the consumption of mouldy provisions, serious effects have ensued ; whether due to fungus poisoning, or to the products of decomposition of the matrix, it is impossible to say. In the case of bread, the development of *Penicillium* has been known to take place within a few hours, the mould being in active growth almost before the bread was cold.[1] Among other saprophytes which are the bane of the house-wife are those moulds which attack jams, books, linen, silk, and, in fact, any organic material when stored under damp conditions. It is unnecessary to discuss these in detail ; enough having already been given to show that the depredations, of

[1] 1857, Berkeley, *Introduction to Cryptogamic Botany*, p. 298.

which fungi are the prime or secondary cause, are of an extensive and far-reaching character. The need for dealing more thoroughly with these various depredations in their multitudinous forms—a need even now evident to many—must become more and more pressing as time goes on, with its resultant steady increase of population. It is admitted generally by those who are in a position to judge, that the world's supply of foods, and of the other necessities of life, cannot be extended, nor even augmented, at a rate commensurate with that of man's increasing needs. The conservation of existing supplies must, therefore, be pressed to its limits, and consequently, there must inevitably come a time when fungus inroads upon staple products can no longer be tolerated.

In view of these facts—even if these plants themselves have no attractions for the layman—the damage which they do to him and his possessions should be sufficient inducement for him to learn more of their life habits. For only in this way can he hope to apply intelligently the various preventive and remedial measures, the devising of which is absorbing the whole energies of numerous investigators in various parts of the world, and which constitute the sole means of reducing the losses which we have indicated.

CHAPTER VII

The Uses of Fungi : In Medicine

" Larche tre . . . giueth also . . .
ye famus medicine called . . .
Agarick."
1551 TURNER, *Herbal* II., 29.

" One dramme of Agaryke and half a
dramme of fine Reubarbe."
—1533 ELYOT, *Castel of Helth*
(1541), 79.

THE fungi have only a very restricted application in modern *materia medica*, but in bygone days they had a much greater vogue. The reasons for their gradual desuetude are exactly parallel with those obtaining in the case of the medicinal herbs, formerly so extensively used in " simples," [1] but nowadays replaced by the purer and stronger drugs extracted from the plants, or, as is more frequently the case, prepared synthetically by a chemical process.

Nor must this former larger use in medicine be considered as contradictory to the undoubtedly great popular repugnance to the fungi in nearly all their aspects, for those who employed them in this manner were the physicians and astrologers, who were not only accustomed to surround themselves with skulls, toads, serpents and suchlike objects of horror and loathing, as emblems of their craft, but some of which they used

---

[1] For examples of this use, see Cockayne's *Leechdoms, Wortcunning and Starcraft of Early England*, 1864–6.

in the preparation of potions of supposed medicinal value. The ingredients of the " hell-broth " that the three witches were concocting in *Macbeth* [1] may be referred to in this connection. The various medicinal purposes for which fungi have at different times been employed are legion.

Counter-Irritants. The earliest mention of the employment of a fungus in this manner is found, in the fifth century B.C., in the writings of Hippocrates, who recommends that cauterization should be made, by means of a fungus, in order to cure certain complaints :

> " One should cauterize the osseous and nervous parts with *fungi (mukes)* " ; " Quickly cauterize in eight places so as to intercept the extremities of the spleen " ;

and again,

> " When the liver has attained its greatest volume, one should cauterize with fungi." [2]

The fungi here indicated are probably some of those used in the manufacture of *amadou,* or German tinder, and were possibly either *Polyporus officinalis,* the " Female Agarick " of the old Pharmacopoeias, or *Fomes fomentarius* (Fig. 48), which was later used on a very large scale for the production of tinder ; while the treatment, after the fungus had been softened, immersed in a solution of saltpetre, and dried, so as to increase its inflammability, would simply involve lighting it, and then, as it smouldered, applying it to the affected part. In the early practice of surgery, while frequently a really remarkable knowledge of anatomy was displayed, the methods of treatment were of a rudimentary and drastic

---

[1] 1606, W. Shakespeare, *Macbeth*, Act IV., Scene 1.
[2] 1888, Richon et Roze, *Atlas des Champignons*, Paris, Part I., p. 3.

nature ; and these, among which may be numbered bleeding and cauterization, find only a very restricted use in modern practice.

It is of interest to note that cauterization by means of fungi appears to have survived among uncivilised races almost to the present day, and it is quite possible that it may still be employed. According to Rees,

> "the Laplanders have a way of using funguses, or common toadstools, as we call them, as the Chinese and Japanese do the moxa, to cure pains. They collect the large funguses which they find on the bark of beech and other large trees, and dry them for use. Whenever they have pains in their limbs, they bruise some of this dried matter, and pulling it to pieces with their fingers, they lay a small heap of it on the part nearest to where the pain is situated, and set it on fire. In burning away, it blisters up the part, and the water discharged by this means generally carries off the pain. It is a coarse and rough method, but generally a very successful one, especially when the patient has prudence enough to apply it in time, and resolution enough to bear the burning to the necessary degree." [1]

Hooker found the same use being made of puffballs in Sikkim in 1850, and relates :

> "My servant having severely sprained his wrist by a fall, the Lepchas wanted to apply a moxa, which they do by lighting a piece of puff ball, or Nepal paper that burns like tinder, laying it on the skin, and blowing it till a large open sore is produced ; they shook their heads at my treatment, which consisted in transferring some of the leeches from our persons to the inflamed part." [2]

It is difficult to see how such cauterization can be of any real efficacy, and when successful appears only to demonstrate that the complaint was amenable to a kind of faith-cure. It would, however, have much to recommend it in the eyes of the primitive medical practitioner, for its failure must naturally always be

---

[1] 1819, Rees, *Cyclopaedia*, Vol. 24, under " Mushroom."
[2] 1854, J. D. Hooker, *Himalayan Journals* (1891), ch. xviii., p. 297.

due entirely to a lack, on the part of the patient, of the necessary degree of fortitude.

Universal Medicines.   Such a use, however, is not that for which *Polyporus officinalis* was once held in such high repute, for, under the name " agarick," it was taken internally as a sort of universal remedy for all complaints and disorders.   The belief in a universal remedy was held to some extent by the Greeks and Romans ; while, in a later day, it allured many of the alchemists, and stimulated them in their assiduous search for the Elixir of Life.   To Dioscorides, who flourished about 200 A.D., *agaricum* was certainly little removed from being the universal remedy, and in his book *De Medicina*, he expatiates upon its virtues as follows :

" Its properties are styptic and heat-producing, efficacious against colic (*strophous*) and sores, fractured limbs, and bruises from falls : the dose is two obols [1] weight with wine and honey to those who have no fever ; in fever cases with honeyed water ; it is given in liver complaints, asthma, jaundice, dysentery, kidney diseases where there is difficulty in passing water, in cases of hysteria, and to those of a sallow complexion, in doses of one drachma ; in cases of phthisis it is administered in raisin-wine, in affections of the spleen with honey and vinegar.   By persons troubled with pains in the stomach and by those who suffer from acid eructations, the root is chewed and swallowed by itself without any liquid ; it stops bleeding when taken with water in three-obol doses ; it is good for pains in the loins and joints, in epilepsy when taken with an equal quantity of honey and vinegar. It prevents rigor if taken before the attack ; in one- and two-drachma doses, it acts as a purgative when taken with honeyed water ; it is an antidote in poisons in one-drachma doses with dilute wine.   In three-obol doses with wine it is a relief in cases of bites and wounds caused by serpents.   On the whole it is serviceable in all internal complaints when taken according to the age and strength of the patient ; some should take it with water, others

---

[1] 1 obol $=\frac{1}{6}$ of a drachma ; 1 drachma = about 66 gr. avdp

with wine, and others with vinegar and honey, or with water and honey." [1]

Another fungus, not so famous as " agarick," was regarded by the Romans, if not as a universal remedy, certainly as a cure for a number of different complaints. This was *Boletus edulis* (Fig. 82), which by all authorities is considered to be the *suillus* (or hog-fungus) of Pliny and Martial, of which the former states :

> " Suilli are dried and hung up, being transfixed with a rush, as in those which come from Bithynia. These are good as a remedy in fluxes from the bowels which are called *rheumatismi*, and for fleshy excrescences of the anus, which they diminish and in time remove ; they remove freckles (*lentiginem*) and blemishes on women's faces ; a healing lotion is also made of them, as of lead, for sore eyes ; soaked in water they are applied as a salve to foul ulcers and eruptions of the head and to bites inflicted by dogs." [2]

The attitude of the ancients towards nature was somewhat careless and entirely empirical, and even the careful observer of natural objects preferred rather to indulge in wild speculation than to carry out a simple experiment that might have demonstrated the falsity of his hypothesis. It therefore followed that many opinions were based on very slight evidence or were simply pure conjecture. Yet such an opinion, when expressed by a high authority, became a creed which it was heresy to doubt.

The dogmas, many erroneous, of the classical writers undoubtedly held ground for a very lengthy period, and, in fact, found no opposition until the alchemistic period ended with the coming of Paracelsus in the sixteenth century. Thus the herbalists of the Middle Ages used

---

[1] Dioscorides, *loc. cit.*, III., 1.
[2] Pliny, *Nat. Hist.*, XXII., 47.

the axioms and doctrines of such Arabian physicians as Geber and his pupils Rhazes, Avicenna, and others ; and the latter prepared their medicines, which were almost entirely of vegetable origin, according to the original receipts of Galen, Andromachus and others, these having been transmitted to them by the Nestorians. The apothecaries' shops before the advent of Paracelsus were, therefore, nothing more than stores for roots, herbs, and syrups and confections of all kinds, the latter being prepared exclusively by the pharmacists.

The extent to which these still relied, for their knowledge of materia medica, upon classical sources, is quite evident from a study of the famous herbal of Gerard, which was first published in the year 1597. To Gerard, " agaricke " was still a universal remedy, and he thus describes its applications :

> " Agaricke is hot in the first degree and dry in the second, according to the old writers. It cutteth, maketh thin, clenseth, taketh away obstructions or stoppings of the intrailes, and purgeth also by stoole.
> " Agaricke cureth the yellow jaundise proceeding of obstructions, and is a sure remedy for cold shakings, which are caused by thicke and cold humors.
> " The same being inwardly taken and outwardly applied, is good for those that are bit of venomous beasts which hurt with their cold poison.
> " It provoketh urine and bringeth downe the menses : it maketh the body well coloured, driveth forth wormes, cureth agues, especially quotidians and wandering feavers, and others that are of long continuance, if it be mixed with fit things that serve for the disease : and these things it performes by drawing forth and purging away grosse, cold and flegmaticke humours, which cause the diseases.
> " From a dram weight, or a dram and a halfe, to two, it is given at once in substance or in pouder : the weight of it in an infusion or decoction is from two drams to five.
> " But it purgeth slowly, and doth somewhat trouble the stomacke ; and therefore it is appointed that Ginger should

be mixed with it, or wilde Carrot seed, or Lovage seed, or Sal gem, in Latine, *Sal fossilis*.

" *Galen*, as *Mesue* reporteth, gave it with wine wherein Ginger was infused : some use to give it with Oxymel, otherwise called syrrup of vineger, which is the safest way of all.

" Agaricke is good against the paines and swimming in the head, or the falling Evill, being taken with syrrup of vineger.

" It is good against the shortnesse of breath, called Asthma, the inveterate cough of the lungs, the ptysicke, consumption, and those that spet bloud : it comforteth the weake and feeble stomacke, causeth good digestion, and is good against wormes." [1]

Many of these virtues are probably quite imaginary.

Even when Agarick was not prescribed as a universal remedy in itself, it was still an essential constituent of any of these panaceas, and, in particular, of perhaps the most famous of them, that known as " Mithridate." This preparation, which was formerly one of the capital medicines of the apothecaries' shops, was named after Mithridates VI., or Eupator, who was king of Pontus from about 120 to 63 B.C., and who was much skilled in poisons, for which he was in the habit of concocting antidotes, by the aid of which he could take the poisons with impunity. His reputation was, therefore, commemorated by the term " Mithridate," which was composed of a very large number of ingredients in the form of an electuary, regarded as a universal antidote or preservative against poisons or infectious diseases, being also considered a cordial, opiate, sudorific and alexipharmic. One recipe for it reads as follows :

" ' Take of cinnamon, fourteen drachms ; of myrrh, eleven drachms ; *agarick*, spikenard, ginger, saffron, seeds of treacle-mustard, frankincense, Chio turpentine, of each ten drachms ; camel's hay, costus, Indian leaf, French lavender, long pepper, seeds of hartwort, juice of the rape of cistus, strained storax, opopanax, strained galbanum, balsam of Gilead, or in its stead,

---

[1] 1597, Gerard, *Herbal*, 2nd ed., reprinted 1636, lib. 3, pp. 1366–7.

expressed oil of nutmegs, Russian castor, of each an ounce ; poly-mountain, water germander, the fruit of the balsam tree, seeds of the carrot of Crete, bdellium strained, of each seven drachms ; Celtic nard, gentian root, leaves of dittany of Crete, red roses, seed of Macedonian parsley, the lesser Cardanum seeds freed from their husks, sweet fennel seeds, gum Arabic, opium strained, of each five drachms ; root of the sweet flag, root of wild valerian, anise-seed, sagapenum strained, of each three drachms ; spignel, St. John's wort, juice of acacia, the bellies of scinks, of each two drachms and a half ; of clarified honey, thrice the weight of all the rest : dissolve the opium first in a little wine, and then mix it with the honey made hot.   In the meantime, melt together, in another vessel, the galbanum, storax, turpentine, and the balsam of Gilead, or the expressed oil of nutmeg ' (I have no doubt that one will do quite as well as the other ; and this must be highly satisfactory for sufferers to know), ' continually stirring them round, that they may not burn, and, as soon as these are melted, add to them the hot honey, first by spoonful, and afterwards more freely.   Lastly, when this mixture is nearly cold, add by degrees the rest of the spices reduced to powder,' *and*, as the French quack used to say of his specific for the toothache, if it does you no good, it will certainly do you no harm.   For my own part, I think the remedy worse than the disease ; but a gentleman just poisoned may be of another opinion ; and I can only say, that if with prussic acid knocking at his pylorus, he has leisure to wait till the above prescription is made up for him—till the bellies of scinks and the camel's hay are procured, and till the ingredients are amalgamated ' by degrees '—he will, *if* he survive the poison, the waiting, and the remedy, have deserved to be called . . . ' the patient.' " [1]

From the end of the sixteenth century, after Paracelsus had enunciated the doctrine that the object of chemistry (e.g., of alchemy) was not to make gold, but to prepare medicines, officinal preparations other than those of vegetable origin, i.e., metallic salts and the like, came more and more into use, and there gradually developed the more enlightened practice of medicine based on actual physiological tests on the human organism rather than on conjecture. With the advance of

---

[1] 1854, Dr. Doran, *Table Traits*, p. 202.

scientific pharmacy, the empirical remedies in general, and the vegetable simples in particular, gradually lost favour, although still surviving in some degree even to the present day. Examples of this survival are the herbalist shops still occasionally to be met with, and the herbal remedies still employed in rural households, and by some of the less civilised races of mankind. Some of these remedies naturally possess some therapeutic virtue, while others are of doubtful or of no efficacy. We are naturally only concerned with those vegetable recipes in which fungi are employed.

Cathartics. From the nature of some of the complaints for which *agarick* was regarded as a specific remedy, it is obvious that it must have some definite physiological effects, and if there is one instance where it found proper application, it is for the purpose in question, where, however, it has also been superseded in modern times by other less empirical drugs, the effects of measured doses of which are subject to no such variability as probably characterized those of the more primitive remedy. When, however, its use was in favour, it was considered that "agaric . . . purgeth phlegm, and opens obstructions in the Liver."[1] This use has to a large extent been already dealt with in the last section, and needs no further elaboration here. It may, however, be mentioned that various other fungi, not possessing definitely poisonous principles, have an emetic or purgative value. Among these may be mentioned *Hypholoma fasciculare* (Fig. 13), *H. elaeodes*, *H. sublateritium* and *Hirneola Auricula-Judae* (Fig. 8).

Styptics. Either agaric, or frequently any of the

---

[1] 1657, *Phys. Dict.*

large fleshy puffballs, were formerly extensively used, in a dried condition, in the treatment of wounds, being applied in order to stop the bleeding. Thus *The Gentleman's Magazine* for 1756 refers to " the agaric sent from France, and applied as a styptic after amputations," [1] while a few years later, Gooch, in his work on the treatment of wounds, describes the same application as follows : " Over which . . . it will still be right to apply Puff-ball, . . . or some such substance, . . . to retard the fall of the eschar as long as possible." [2] Nearly a century later, the same use of agaric was still being made, and Todd indicates the mechanism of its action when he says that " agaric and sponge entangled the blood and retained a coagulum on the spot." [3] *Fomes igniarius* and *F. fomentarius* (Fig. 48) were formerly known as " surgeon's agaric " on this account, the latter being more frequently employed. The method of preparation is somewhat similar to that used in the making of *amadou*, but much more care is naturally necessary. Young specimens are selected, and the rind and tubes are removed. The remainder is softened by storing for some time in a cool place, and is then cut into thin slices and well beaten with a mallet ; being damped from time to time and beaten again. After further rubbing with the hands, the material acquires finally a certain softness and laxity, and is suitable for styptic use. The same fungi could, like *Polyporus officinalis*, be impregnated with saltpetre to produce *amadou* for cauterization or other purposes, and they have frequently been so employed.

---

[1] 1756, *loc. cit.* XXVI., 352.
[2] 1767, Gooch, *Treatment of Wounds*, I., 173.
[3] 1836, Todd, *Cycl. Anat. and Phys.*, I., 229/1.

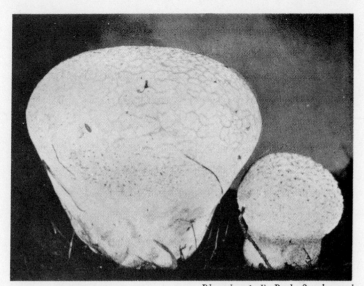

Photo by A. E. Peck, Scarborough

Fig. 50.—*Lycoperdon caelatum*, one of the larger puffballs, still occasionally in use as a household remedy in cases of bleeding.

Photo by A. E. Peck, Scarborough

Fig. 51.—"Cramp Balls" (*Daldinia concentrica*). In rural districts, these have often been carried in the pocket as a charm against cramp.

Photo by Authors

Fig. 53.—Ergot (*Claviceps purpurea*). Ears of rye, showing the ergots *in situ*, and a small heap of medicinal ergots.

Photo by Authors

Fig. 52.—*Hirneola polytricha* (sun-dried), as exported from New Zealand and the South Sea Islands to China, where it is used both as a food and in " medicine."

The employment of agaric has now been almost entirely abandoned in surgery, as indeed was inevitable, when its qualities are contrasted with those of the perfectly aseptic and antiseptic materials with which the resources of modern science has furnished us. It is interesting to note, however, that as recently as 1910 a reference is made by Whitla to *Lycoperdon giganteum* (= *L. Bovista*) (Fig. 78), as forming "a soft and comfortable surgical dressing. The dusty powder is a powerful haemostat." [1] Locally, however, puffballs are apparently still used as a household remedy, and Swanton states that " *Calvatia gigantea* (=*Lycoperdon Bovista*), *C. caelata* (=*L. caelatum*), *Lycoperdon gemmatum* and apparently any other species of Puffball, though the larger kinds were always given preference, were at one time kept in the farmhouses and cottages of West Sussex for use as styptics. The custom still lingers but is rapidly dying out." [2] There is, however, one styptic use of a fungus still remaining, for *amadou*, of course in its natural or unimpregnated condition, but after the usual preparation, is sometimes used by dentists as an absorbent for drying cavities in teeth before filling them.

Anaesthetics. Since the fumes given off by the larger puffballs in burning have properties resembling those of chloroform, they have in bygone days been even used in surgical operations, but more frequently by bee-keepers, who, when they wish to clear a hive, are in the habit of " intoxicating the bees .   .   . by filling

---

[1] 1910, Whitla, *Pharmacy, Materia Medica and Therapeutics*, 9th ed., p. 827. This would appear to be a quotation from some earlier work.

[2] 1916, Swanton, Economic and Folk-Lore Notes, *Trans. Brit. Myc. Soc.*, Vol. V., pp. 408–409.

the hive with the smoke of an ignited puffball." [1]
Swanton mentions *Calvatia gigantea* (= *Lycoperdon
Bovista*) as being thus still in use in West Sussex " and
at the present time bee-keepers in the Godalming
district occasionally employ smouldering *Polyporus
betulinus* and *Daedalea quercina* for that purpose." [2]

Miscellaneous Medicinal Uses. A variety of other
therapeutic applications of fungi have at different times
been made. Of uses favoured in mediaeval times, but
which have now disappeared, some were derived from
classical sources ; while others were of later mediaeval
origin, arising for example from the superstitious beliefs
relating the appearance of a particular fungus to some
purpose for which it was supposed to be suitable. In
quite recent times, one may note the recommendations
that have been made, by some qualified practitioners,
as to the use of certain fungi for special diseases, but
the value of which is exceedingly problematical. At the
present day, we have, on the one hand, those few fungi
which still find place in the pharmacopoeias, and as to
whose efficacy for certain purposes there is no doubt ;
and on the other, those used by the " medicine-man,"
or his equivalent, among races whose therapeutic practice
is still in a rudimentary state, which fungi it would be
rash to condemn as having no specific value, but whose
virtues may sometimes appear a little obscure. As
related to the last, we may refer also to the few cases of
household remedies in which fungi are used, of which
some survived up till recently in rural districts in this
country.

---

[1] 1843, *Zoologist*, I., 25.
[2] *Loc. cit.*, pp. 408-409.

Among fungi whose employment was based entirely upon superstition, and which use has naturally been abandoned, may be mentioned the Jew's Ear, *Hirneola Auricula-Judae* (Fig. 8), which, according to Berkeley, " owed its reputation in throat cases, probably to the fancied resemblance of its hymenial surface to the fauces." [1] Gerard says it " is much used against the inflammations and all other sorenesses of the throat, being boyled in milk, steeped in beere, vineger, or any other convenient liquor." [2] It was doubtless more efficacious when the second most " convenient liquor " was employed. In a similar manner, *Elaphomyces granulatus* was formerly regarded as an aphrodisiac, being known as *Fungi cervini* and used in the preparation of love potions. [3] A curious household specific, which again is of entirely superstitious origin, is mentioned by Swanton, who says :

" *Daldinia concentrica* [Fig. 51] was carried until quite recently by old men in the ' fold ' district of West Surrey and Sussex as a charm against cramp. At Haslemere the little spherical tumours so frequently seen on beech and oak trunks were carried instead and were considered equally efficacious. Specimens of these ' cramp-balls,' as they were called, given me by old villagers, have been placed in the Haslemere museum." [4]

Their efficacy would appear to be entirely imaginary. The same writer mentions another interesting surviving application of a fungus in this locality. It is that of *Fomes pomaceus*, which has a great reputation as a dressing

---

[1] 1857, Berkeley, *Introduction to Cryptogamic Botany*, p. 255.
[2] 1597, Gerard, *Herbal*, 2nd ed. (reprinted 1636), lib. 3, p. 1584.
[3] Vide Cordus, *Annotationes*, 1540, pub. 1561 ; also J. Bauhin's *Historia*, 1651, lib. XL.
[4] 1916, Swanton, Economic and Folk-Lore Notes, *Trans. Brit. Myc. Soc.*, Vol. V., pp. 408–409.

for a swollen face, the fungus being ground down on a nutmeg grater and heated in an oven before application.

Considering now some of the cases in which the use of a particular fungus has been advocated, we find in comparatively recent times Badham speaking of the value of *Trametes suaveolens* in the cure of consumption ; [1] while as recently as 1884, Gautier deprecates the employment of *Lactarius piperatus* and *L. torminosus*, which had recently been recommended for the same purpose, but which gave no results of any value. The same writer mentions other medicinal applications. Several species of the same genus have been considered as diuretic against gravel, and their juice has also been vaunted as of great efficacy in the removal of warts, but would appear to be less successful than that of the wall celandine, well known for this use.* *Amanita muscaria*, the Fly Agaric (Fig. 15), has been strongly recommended as a remedy for epilepsy and other nervous maladies, scrofula, etc. The lotion made from it has been applied externally, and even internally, against ringworm and skin eruptions. It has also been proposed as a narcotic, but there are other more active and more easily administered agents. This fungus yields the uncrystallis-able alkaloid, muscarine, the nitrate of which was formerly used in medicine for purposes similar to those of pilocarpine, but which appears not now to be in general use. Another *Amanita* is referred to by Gautier, who says : " Fairly recently Dr. Curtis has recommended a tincture of *A. phalloides* (Fig. 72) in use against cholera, Bright's disease and intermittent fevers, conduct

[1] 1847, Badham, *Esculent Funguses of England*, ed. II. (1863), p. 25.
* See footnote [1] p. 141.

which can only be described as an 'haute fantaisie therapeutique.' " [1]

At the present day, a number of fungi are used by less civilised people. One of the most celebrated Chinese medicines, " Tong-chong-ha-cho," consists of a fungus, *Cordyceps sinensis*, which is parasitic upon a species of caterpillar, these being finally killed by its effects. The dead caterpillars, with the fungus attached to them, are made up into bundles and sold and consumed as an invaluable specific, the caterpillar being thus an integral part of the dose. The approved method of administration is to place a bundle of the necessary dimensions in the stomach of a duck, which is roasted, and consumed by the patient. Analogous methods of disguising the " medicine " will doubtless be recalled by the reader. The remedy in question has probably been in use in China for thousands of years, and is much praised by Du Halde,[2] but probably on somewhat scanty evidence, and Berkeley describes it as " a drug of doubtful virtues." [3] However, to this day, it holds, together with " Toad-spittle cakes " and " Powdered tiger's bones," a worthy place in the ranks of that heterogeneous and mysterious medley which comprises Chinese materia medica. *Lysurus Mokusin* is another fungus used by the Chinese, in the treatment of gangrenous ulcers.

In India, the common mushroom is official in the Punjáb. The young dried specimens are known as " Mokshai " and sold in the bazaars, being regarded as

---

[1] 1884, Gautier, *Les Champignons considérés dans leurs rapports avec la médecine, etc.*, p. 56.

[2] 1735, Du Halde, *Description historique, géographique et physique de l'Empire de la Chine, et de la Tartarie Chinoise*, Paris, 4 vols. folio.

[3] 1857, Berkeley, *Introduction to Cryptogamic Botany*, p. 283.

alteratives.[1]   In the same bazaars are found on sale the spores of a puffball, probably *Lycoperdon gemmatum* (Fig. 6), which are used for " expelling cold and bilious humours." [2]   In Burma, *Polyporus anthelminticus* grows at the roots of old bamboos, and is employed as an anthelmintic.[3]   In the Malay States, *Polyporus sacer*, under the name " Susu Rimau " or " Tiger's Milk," is used for treating consumption and colds, the whole plant being utilised ; while *P. sanguineus*, known as " Chendawan Merah " or " Red Fungus," is employed in cases of dysentery.[4]

The Fungi in Modern Pharmacology.   In modern pharmacology, which may be considered to date from the beginning of the nineteenth century, to include any still more recent uses, and being not necessarily restricted rigidly to present-day practice, only four fungi are admitted to the ranks of drugs possessing undoubted therapeutic value.   These are *Claviceps purpurea* (Fig. 53), *Ustilago Maydis*, *Saccharomyces cerevisiae* and *Polyporus officinalis*, which are dealt with separately below, and of which only the first appears in the British Pharmacopoeia at the present day.

Claviceps purpurea.   This, under the name of Ergot of Rye, has long been used as a drug of the first importance for obstetric purposes.   It is not mentioned by classical writers as being so employed, although it was presumably as wide-spread in its distribution as it is to-day.   The earliest specific reference to this application is made

---

[1] 1889, Watt, *Dict. of Econ. Prod. of India*, I., p. 131.
[2] *Loc. cit.*, III. (1890), p. 455.
[3] *Ibid.*, p. 456.
[4] 1922, Foxworthy, *Minor Forest Products of the Malay Peninsula*, Malayan Forest Records No. 2, p. 190.

towards the middle of the sixteenth century by Adam
Loricer of Frankfort, who describes the appearance of
the ears of rye on which the ergot parasitically occurs,
and relates that it is considered by women to be of
sovereign efficacy. Johannes Kalius in 1588 also describes
its appearance and effects. " Rathlaw, a Dutch
accoucheur, employed ergot in 1747. Thirty years later,
Desgranges of Lyons prescribed it with success, but its
peculiar and important properties were hardly allowed
until the commencement of the present century, when
Dr. Stearns of New York succeeded in gaining for them
fuller recognition. Ergot of rye was not, however,
admitted into the London Pharmacopoeia until 1836."[1]

Ergot is the sclerotium of this fungus, and originates
in the ovary of rye (*Secale cereale*) by the absorption of
the ovarian tissues ; rye which has been so attacked,
being sometimes known as " spurred " rye. The fungus
is found all over Europe and gives rise commercially to
Spanish, Russian and German ergots, of which the first
is the boldest and is usually considered the best ; but
physiological experiments have demonstrated that the
Russian variety is generally more active. In appearance,
the sclerotium is generally from $\frac{5}{8}$ to $1\frac{5}{8}$ inches in length,
in section roughly cylindrical or somewhat triangular,
longitudinally furrowed on each side, and curved and
tapering towards the ends ; dark or violet-black externally
and pinkish white inside, with a characteristic and
disagreeable smell and taste. It is used in cases where
active contraction of the muscles of the uterus is necessary,
the dose varying between 15 and 60 grains. Ergot
deteriorates with time, and therefore requires to be kept

---

[1] 187*, Flückiger and Hanbury, *Pharmacographia*, p. 673.

whole, not in a powdered condition, and dry, while the official requirement is that it shall not be used if more than a year old. It is a complex substance, containing many different constituents, and published analyses differ considerably; but there is no doubt that its chief alkaloidal principles are ergotoxine and ergotinine, of which the former is definitely most active. Its B.P. preparations are :

Extractum Ergotae, used in the preparation of Injectio Ergotae Hypodermica, one part in three.

Extractum Ergotae Liquidum, 1 part in 1.

Infusum Ergotae, 1 part in 20.

Tinctura Ergotae Ammoniota, 1 part in 4 of a mixture of 60 per cent. alcohol and ammonia solution.

Martindale and Westcott [1] quote " one authority " as recommending the use of ergot in all diseases in which a drug inducing muscular contractions is required, e.g., in disturbances of the circulatory system, skin affections, in nervous complaints (caused, for example, by excessive smoking), and in cases of surgical shock. It has also been recommended by some of the faculty in typhoid and intermittent fevers. The application that has been made of ergot for various forms of internal hemorrhage is entirely incorrect, for, by increasing the blood pressure, it may cause the bleeding of a wound which had stopped, to start again, thus acting in a manner precisely contrary to that for which it had been prescribed.

Ergots from other graminaceous plants are also used instead of rye ergot. Among these may be mentioned *ergot of wheat*, which is shorter and thicker than the official kind ; *ergot of oat*, which is much more slender ;

---

[1] 1912, *The Extra Pharmacopoeia*, I., p. 352.

and *ergot of diss* (*Arundo ampelodesmus*, a North African grass), which is said to be twice as active as rye ergot.

Ustilago Maydis. This fungus, parasitic upon maize (*Zea Mays*) in the United States, is known as Corn Smut, Corn Ergot or Maize Ergot. It occurs on the Continent and is also recorded for this country, and is used in parturition instead of rye ergot.

It is found in commerce as an irregular globose mass, sometimes six inches thick, consisting of a blackish membrane, enclosing a large number of brownish black nodules, and has an unpleasant smell and taste. As with rye ergot, it should be kept whole and dry, and must not be stored for longer than one year. It is stated to increase the force without increasing the duration of uterine contractions. The dose consists of from 15 to 60 grains, or from ½ to 2 drachms of the fluid extract.

Saccharomyces cerevisiae. The ferment produced by brewing beer is known medicinally as Cerevisiae Fermentum, or Faex Medicinalis. In character it is viscid, frothy, flocculent and semi-fluid, and in the compressed pasty form shows under microscopic examination numerous rounded or oval cells, either separate or arranged in clusters, sometimes in branching chains. It has a characteristic and peculiar smell and a bitter taste.

It is used as an antiseptic in poultices for application to ulcers. Internally it is used for various purposes, in cases of boils ; as a remedy for diabetes, enabling the patient to take more carbohydrates ; for septic endocarditis ; while it is also said to increase the opsonic power of the blood to an invading organism. In acne, fresh yeast, in doses of from half a teaspoonful to a tablespoonful, may be taken with a little water at meals.

Yeast dried at 30° C. is a light grey powder, which is used in half-gramme doses for constipation, being injected per rectum to break up the faeces. It has recently been employed in tuberculous affections and in dysentery. By extracting fresh yeast with alcohol is obtained Extractum Cerevisiae Fermenti, or Faexin Extract, which has also been employed for all the purposes for which fresh yeast has been used, viz., in acne, erysipelas, furunculosis, folliculitis, leucorrhoea, diabetes, typhoid, rheumatoid arthritis and other complaints. It is interesting to note that yeast enters into the composition of several present-day patent medicines.

Polyporus officinalis. This, the most famous fungus used in medicine, is known as Agaricus albus, White Agaric or Purging Agaric. Its earlier reputation and applications have already been dealt with, and, although fallen from its high estate, it is still found in the pharmacopoeias.[1] For officinal purposes, the outer skin is removed, only the inner portions being utilised. These are found in commerce in irregular pieces, about six inches broad, and hoof-shaped or conical. They are white, light, somewhat fibrous, spongy and friable ; having a faint smell and a sweetish taste, with a bitter pungent after-taste.

The active principle is agaricic acid, known alternatively as agaric or laricic acid, which is obtained in minute silvery plates or prisms by the extraction of the fungus, either with dry ether or with 90 per cent. alcohol. The alcoholic extraction is sometimes known as *agaricin.*

---

[1] See Martindale & Westcott, *The Extra Pharmacopoeia,* 1912, London, I., p. 795 ; and Southall, *Organic Materia Medica,* 1915 (8th ed.) London, p. 215.

As its name would imply, the fungus in a powdered state is a powerful purgative. The dose in this form is from 5 to 30 grains, but it is usually administered in the form of agaricic acid, of which the dose is ¼ to 1 grain. In too large quantities it causes diarrhoea, sickness and even death, though central paralysis. In small doses it is used in the form of agaricin in diarrhoea ; to diminish bronchial secretion and to inhibit night sweats in phthisis. There is thus no doubt as to its specific utility in certain cases. Since for those cases, however, results similar to those produced by agaricum and its extract, can be obtained from atropine and other drugs, which are stronger in their effects, it is not surprising that this once-famous remedy is now little used. Its employment as a purge may be regarded as quite extinct, but for other purposes it still has a limited application.

Conclusion. Although, for reasons we have detailed, the uses of fungi in medicine have now been largely abandoned, it is clear that they have in their time played a not unworthy part, but one which is, perhaps, in some danger of being forgotten in this more scientific age. If we have helped to preserve from a premature oblivion some small account of their activities, and if this relation is found of some general interest, we shall be content enough.

CHAPTER VIII

The Uses of Fungi: In Industry

" The Dorians . . . us'd to write upon Toad-stools."
—1707, Hearne, *Collect.*, 29 Nov. (O.H.S.), II, 76.

" Nor may we here omit to mention the . . . fungus's
to make Tinder."
—1664, Evelyn, *Sylva*, (1679), 27.

THE number of specific fungi that have been harnessed for the use of man in the arts and manufactures is not so large as the numerical strength of this enormous group of plants would have led one to suppose, but, of this very limited number, some have been utilised on so great a scale as to lead to the development of industries of paramount importance to humanity and of gigantic commercial value.

Fermentation. Probably the most notable application of the fungi is in those various processes of fermentation involved in bread-making and in the production of wines and other fermented liquors. From the earliest recorded times, these arts have been universally practised, and their attendant phenomena —the rising of the dough in bread-making, and the frothing and effervescence of the *must* in the manufacture of wine—have been well known ; but only quite recently has it been demonstrated that these fermentation processes are brought about by fungi.

Yeasts. Although Leeuwenhoek had microscopically observed the granular appearance of yeast in the year 1680, the means by which it found its way into sugary

148

solutions was a profound mystery, and its true nature and function remained unknown until early in the nineteenth century. Prior to the discoveries of 1836, it was generally believed that the organisms responsible for the causing of putrefaction and fermentation, in various animal and vegetable materials and infusions, were spontaneously generated in the solid or liquid undergoing the change. In 1836, Schulz demonstrated, however, that in the case of such organic infusions, putrefaction did not occur, if, after they had been well boiled, they were allowed to remain in air which had been purified by being passed through sulphuric acid. Schwann showed that the same remarks applied, even if the air were heated, and the same thing was found to hold good for alcoholic fermentation. Both these investigators came to the conclusion that the processes in question were brought about by living germs present in the air, which developed in the liquid and were responsible for the phenomena in question. The search for the causal organism led speedily to a result, for in the same year (1836) Schwann, Kützing and Cagniard de Latour made simultaneously and independently the discovery that yeast was a low organism, which is self-propagating. Schwann ascribed to this living organism, which he called " Zuckerpilz " (sugar fungus) the responsibility for alcoholic fermentation. This view, although strongly contested by Berzelius and Liebig, was clearly shown to be correct by the researches in 1857 of Pasteur, who demonstrated that every fermentation was produced by a specific organism.

As with the spores of other fungi, the minute cells of yeasts are always present in the air. On being deposited in a suitable medium, these propagate themselves, indefinitely under suitable conditions, by a method of "budding." In this process an outgrowth forms on the surface of the yeast cell, gradually increases in size and ultimately splits off to become a separate rounded or oval cell. Occasionally groups of cells are produced, sometimes in chains. The required medium is one containing sugar, which by an enzyme action set up during the growth of the fungus is converted finally into alcohol and carbon dioxide (carbonic acid gas). The ferment, zymase, can be isolated from yeast and used to bring about the same change.

From the industrial standpoint, the most important of the yeasts, of which a great number of species, races, and strains have now been isolated, are :

Beer Yeast (*Saccharomyces cerevisiae*), forms of which are employed in beer brewing and bread making, and for the fermentation of cereals, potato mash, etc., for distillery purposes.

Wine Yeasts (*S. ellipsoideus and its allies*), of great importance in the fermentation of various fruit juices or wine, cider, vinegar, and alcohol manufacture.

Apple Cider Yeast (*S. mali*), which is useful in the manufacture of sparkling hard cider.

Saké Yeast (*S. sake*), used principally in Japan for the fermentation of rice wort for saké and brandy manufacture.

For our purpose, it is perhaps unnecessary to differentiate between the various yeasts, and in the following account of their industrial applications, the term 'yeast' is used in its wider sense.

Bread Making. In the usual process of bread making, the necessary sponginess is imparted to the dough by the addition of a little yeast, afterwards allowing the whole to stand for some hours at a temperature of about 70° F., when the dough increases largely in bulk, and *rises*, owing to the fermentation of the sugar contained in the flour, with the consequent evolution of the gas in question in the form of a multitude of small bubbles scattered through the mass of the dough. It should be remarked that the sugar is one of the constituents of the wheaten flour generally used in bread making, which flour consists of starch and gluten, with a little dextrin and sugar. On mixing the flour with a little water, the tenacity of the dough so produced is due to the gluten, but if baked in this condition, it would yield a very indigestible food. By the process of aeration described, however, aided by the fact that the gas bubbles are considerably expanded by the heat of the oven in baking, the porosity of the bread being thereby greatly increased, a perfectly digestible product is obtained.

There are of course other means by which gases can be generated in the dough, by the admixture of suitable chemicals, which are innocuous as regards the consumption of the bread. By such means what is known as aerated or unfermented bread can be obtained, but the usual process involves the use of yeast and is substantially as we have described.

Wine. Turning to the manufacture of wines, it should in the first place be made clear that it is the small air-borne cells of the fungus which settle on the skin of the grape, and finding there suitable food, develop as stated, giving rise to the bloom of the ripe fruit. For this reason, the juice obtained by expressing the grapes will ferment spontaneously, no addition of yeast being absolutely necessary.

In the production of white wines, the grapes are picked in an unripe condition, and after crushing and pressing, the juice is allowed to ferment at a temperature of about 50° F., in barrels, of which the bunghole is left open for the escape of the gas.   In the case of red wines the characteristic colour is obtained by stirring the ripe grape husks in the fermented liquor, so that the necessary amount of the colouring matter is dissolved. The greater bulk due to the husks, and the need for stirring, necessitates the fermentation in this case being performed in open vats. Yeast will not grow and propagate in pure sugar solution, because this does not contain the necessary nutritive albuminous matter and phosphates, but in grape juice or infusion of malt (sweet wort) the action takes place freely, with the production of wine and beer respectively. By this means, the grape sugar is partly converted into alcohol and carbon dioxide, the latter giving the usual effervescence. It should be noted that fermentation can only take place within a certain temperature range, being inhibited below 32 or above 95 degrees F. " Dry " wines are those in which all the sugar has been converted to alcohol, while " fruity " wines still contain some varying proportion of their original sugar. Other phenomena attending the fermentation are the evolution of heat, and a decrease in the specific gravity of the solution, alcohol being lighter than water. When the alcohol produced by the reaction amounts to about one-sixth by weight of the liquid, the action automatically ceases, owing to the killing of the yeast plant, so that no fermented drink can contain more than about seventeen per cent. by weight of alcohol. The strongest wine is port, and the approximate alcoholic percentages by weight of some typical wines are given below :

						Alcohol per cent.
Port	...	...	...	...	...	15—17
Sherry	...	...	...	...	...	14—16
Burgundy...	...	...	...	...	...	13
Champagne	...	...	...	...	...	11·5
Hock	...	...	...	...	...	9
Claret	...	...	...	...	...	8

Cider. In cider making the general principles are similar to those which govern the production of wines. The apples are crushed or grated, and the resultant pulp ("pomace") is pressed to extract the juice. The latter is allowed to stand until all solid particles have risen to the surface and have been skimmed off; the clear liquid being then transferred to the fermenting casks. If a sweet cider is required, the liquor is removed and filtered before all the sugar has been converted into alcohol; while for a "dry" cider, fermentation is allowed to proceed further. The sweet ciders usually preferred in this country contain less than four per cent. of alcohol, but many of the French "dry" ciders contain as much as seven per cent.

Beer. In the production of beer, barley grain is used. This contains diastase, an enzyme or ferment that has the power of converting starch into sugar. Diastase is found in small quantity in the raw grain before germination, but as germination proceeds the quantity of diastase increases enormously. The production in the grain of the maximum quantity of diastase is accomplished by malting, which consists in steeping the grain in water, draining off the water, and then spreading the grain out in a layer a few inches deep on the floor of a chamber, allowing it to remain for several days at a suitable temperature, turning it and moistening it from time to time. When germination has proceeded sufficiently, the germinated grain is heated to stop the process, to improve the flavour of the beer finally brewed from it, to arrest all fungus growths that would be inimical to it, and thus to render it capable of lengthened storage. The dried and germinated grain so produced is termed *malt*. After a period of storage, the malt is ground up and mashed with hot water, the aqueous extract (or sweet wort), containing the fermentable matter in the malt, being finally drawn off. During the mashing, the remaining starch of the malt is gelatinised and is finally converted by the diastase into sugar (maltose). The wort is next boiled with hops to impart the desirable bitter flavour, and is finally caused to ferment by the addition of yeast. In this process, the quantity of yeast may increase to six or eight times its original weight. It occurs partly as a scum and partly as a sediment, and when removed is capable of setting up fermentation in other saccharine solutions, being produced in this manner for bread making, and known as " brewers' yeast." After fermentation is complete the yeast is separated, and the beer run into casks ready for consumption. The approximate pre-war alcohol content of ale was from 6 to 7 per cent.; of porter from 5 to 6, and of Munich beer from 4 to 5 per cent.

Bee Wine. We may here refer to " Bee Wine," a curious concoction, which is brewed in country households, and which has come into considerable favour during the last few years. The active principles in the brew are known variously as Balm of Gilead, Wine Bees, Water Bees, Californian Bees, Macedonian or Salonika Bees, Mesopotamian Bees, Jerusalem and Palestine Bees ;

and, in fact, as bees of almost any locality sufficiently remote to render verification difficult. The brew is produced by the fermentation of sugar by means of a yeast, *Saccharomyces pyriformis*. A curious effect is obtained in the jars of sugary solution being fermented, by reason of the yeasty lumps being constantly carried up to the top of the brew by the rising of bubbles of gas, and then sinking to the bottom again as soon as the bubbles have been liberated. The lumps are composed of the yeast in question, in combination with a bacterium, *Bacterium vermiforme*, and are the " bees " of popular estimation. A dear old lady of our acquaintance solemnly asseverates that they are " alive " in every meaning of the term, and says that if she does not give them their spoonful of sugar every morning, they will surely die. The " wine " resembles cider, but is sweeter and more intoxicating.

Spirits. Alcohol on the larger scale is obtained by the fermentation of potatoes, rice, barley and other materials, the weak alcoholic solution so produced being then distilled and redistilled, to remove water and yield a rich alcoholic concentrate or *spirit*. Yeasts are by no means the only fungi which take part in fermentation processes, and " raggi," used in the manufacture of arrack, contains *Mucor Oryzae*, which transforms rice starch into dextrose, the latter being then fermented by yeasts. A similar change is brought about in rice by *Mucor Rouxii*, found on rice husks in China, which has been also used, to some extent, in the manufacture of alcoholic liquors, and by *Aspergillus Oryzae*, used in saké brewing. Many other examples could be given.

Power Alcohol. In years to come, the use of alcohol in its numerous beverage forms will probably be completely overshadowed by its utilisation for power purposes. At present, the employment of alcohol as a fuel for internal combustion engines is receiving considerable attention, and this is bound to extend as preliminary difficulties are overcome. The advantage of alcohol over petrol for this purpose lies principally in the fact that whereas the world's supplies of petroleum, and therefore of petrol, are being gradually exhausted, the supply of Power Alcohol is practically inexhaustible. It is only limited by the earth's capacity of producing plant growths whose products are amenable to the fermentative processes which yield alcohol—processes in which, as we have shown, the fungi play no inconsiderable part.

Vinegar. It is well known that weak fermented liquors, such as beer, cider, and the lighter wines, may turn sour, and this again is due to the action of a fungus, *Mycoderma aceti*, the minute cells of which, as in the case of yeast, are always present in the air, and germinate and develop as soon as they are deposited in any suitable medium. For growth, a weak alcoholic solution, and the presence of air, are required, the reaction being more vigorous when the alcohol content of the liquor is low and the surface exposed to the air is large. If the proportion of alcohol, however, falls below 3 per cent., the fermentation is more slowly accomplished. In this process, the action of the fungus is to convey the oxygen of the air to the alcohol, the oxidation of which yields a weak solution of acetic acid, known as vinegar. This process is used commercially in several slightly different ways, a brief description of one of which should be of interest.

The Quick Vinegar Process. In this process, a

suitable tall cask is employed, having a tray perforated with small holes near the top, and a similar one near the bottom, the space between being packed with a quantity of beech shavings, previously soaked with vinegar to cover the whole of the surface of the shavings. Holes are drilled in the side of the cask to permit the free entry of air. Weak spirit, such as fermented wort or cider, previously heated to about 80° F., is allowed to trickle slowly down short lengths of wick, fixed in the perforations of the upper tray, and percolate slowly through the bed of shavings, finally collecting in the bottom compartment. The oxidation of the alcohol rapidly raises the temperature to about 100° F., which causes a free circulation of air among the shavings. If the supply of air is insufficient, the action is incomplete, an intermediate oxidation product being formed instead. By allowing the liquor to pass three or four times through the cask, the whole process taking from one to two days, the action is complete.

Tinder. While there is thus no need to emphasize the vast importance of some fungi in industry, their uses, apart from those of fermentation, are nowadays of a secondary nature. A number of minor applications have, however, been made of them. Some of the polypores, when dried, have long been employed as tinder, this use being apparently first recorded by Pliny (23–79 A.D.), who says: "One piece of wood is rubbed against another, and the friction sets them on fire, which is augmented by dry tinder (*aridi fomitis*), especially that of fungi and leaves."[1] This is considered to refer to the fungus now known as the Amadou Polypore

---

[1] Pliny, *Nat. Hist.*, XVI., 77.

(*Fomes fomentarius*) (Figs. 48 and 54), which was later used on a large scale in Europe to supply the amadou of commerce, although other polypores have frequently been used for the same purpose. About the year 1398, Trevisa [1] mentions the employment of " drye tadstoles " for this purpose, and in the same connection Turner, in his *Herbal*, relates of the larch agaric (*Polyporus officinalis*) that " some make tunder both in England and Germany for their gunnes."[2]   Turner also speaks of " a todstole . . . in a birche or walnut tre, where of som make tunder,"[3] which from its habitat would more probably be either *Fomes fomentarius* or *F. igniarius.*

The former is certainly the polypore chiefly used in the manufacture of German tinder, the method employed being to cut slices of the fungus, which in its older state is hard and corky, and pound them until quite soft and flexible, after which they are dipped in a $2\frac{1}{2}$ per cent. solution of saltpetre and allowed to dry in the shade, being afterwards beaten again.   Buller states, in reference to this use :

> " I find by enquiry that in the East of Canada, about fifty years ago, before the introduction of matches, it was quite usual in country places to make fire with the help of *punkwood*, i.e., very rotten wood rich in the brown mycelium of a fungus which appears to have been *Fomes fomentarius*. I myself have learned the art of making fire in this way. One takes a piece of flint and holds just below one of its sharp edges a small piece of the punk-wood. Then one strikes the edge of the flint smartly with a pocket-knife or a small steel file. Sparks are made and soon one falls upon the punkwood, which immediately begins to smoulder. One then judiciously blows on the punkwood, and places around it some pieces of the shreddy bark of the White Cedar (*Thuja*

---

[1] 1398, Trevisa, *Barth. De P. R.*, xvi., xxxi. (Tollem. MS.)
[2] 1551, Turner, *Herbal* II. (1562), 29 b.
[3] *Loc. cit.*

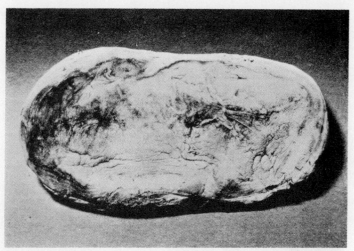

Photo by Authors

Fig. 54.—" German Tinder," as prepared from *Fomes fomentarius*. This, used in conjunction with a flint and steel, was the forerunner of matches.

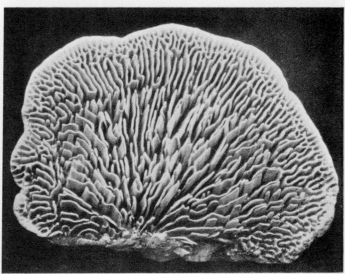

Photo by A. E. Peck, Scarborough

Fig. 55.—*Daedalea quercina*, a natural curry-comb, occasionally employed for cleaning down horses which have tender skins.

Photo by A. E. Peck, Scarborough

Fig. 56.—The Champignon (*Marasmius oreades*), a mushroom of delicious flavour, but which is something of an acquired taste.

Photo by A. E. Peck, Scarborough

Fig. 57.—The Horse Mushroom (*Psalliota arvensis*) is closely allied to the Common Mushroom (*P. campestris*) for which it is often sold.

occidentalis L.). In a few seconds a flame is produced. I have been told by one who regularly used punkwood that he always carried a piece of it with him in a pouch, as it was an admirable means of lighting his pipe. Thus the use of fungi for tinder, instead of rags, by civilised people, has persisted almost to the present day." [1]

In this connection some interesting details as to the use of *amadou* in the Godalming district are given by Swanton, from which the following extract has been made :

"*Polyporus betulinus* [Fig. 49] is still used for various economic purposes by cottagers in the villages near Godalming. In the days of flint and steel it held a very important place in household economy, because of the persistent way in which it slowly smoulders if placed in a tin with restricted ventilation. It was so kept and used for renewing or duplicating fires, thus saving the bother of making fresh ignition by flint, steel and tinder. In windy and wet weather the labourer carried a tin of smouldering amadou to the fields and woods to enable him to make a fire to eat his lunch . . . Strips of the size and shape of a lead pencil are used as fuses for firing the charge when blowing up timber. In the raw state they are called ' slow torch ' ; those that have been steeped in saltpetre are known as ' quick torch.' " [2]

Other species which can be put to the same use are *Polyporus lucidus, Daedalea quercina* (Fig. 55), *Trametes betulina* and any of the larger puffballs. It is a noteworthy fact that this earliest industrial use of fungi still exists, and in Messrs. F. E. Becker & Co.'s current list of Physical Apparatus, we find German tinder advertised at 6d. per box, for use with pneumatic fire syringes (in which the tinder is ignited by the heat generated by the compression of air), with an illustration showing pieces of a polypore.

---

[1] 1914, Buller, The Fungus Lore of the Greeks and Romans, *Trans. Brit. Myc. Soc.*, Vol. V., p. 46.

[2] 1916, Swanton, Economic and Folk-Lore Notes, *Trans. Brit. Myc. Soc.*, Vol. V., pp. 408–409.

Uses of Phosphorescent Fungi. In logical sequence to their employment in making fire, fungi have also been used for producing light, although of a somewhat feeble variety. Cooke thus refers to the practice :

> " In our schoolboy days we remember to have often carried home in our pockets a piece of *touchwood*, to be taken to bed with us on account of the little light it afforded. What we, in common with our elders and betters, termed touchwood, was merely the light, white decaying wood of an old stump, entirely permeated with the minute mycelium of a fungus, and which exhibited phosphorescence in the dark. The fact was well enough known to us, but the cause was a mystery ; the remotest idea of its being due to the presence of a fungoid growth, never entered our boyish heads." [1]

In the same connection, Mark Twain, in " The Adventures of Huckleberry Finn " refers to " them rotten chunks that's called fox-fire and just makes a soft kind of glow when you lay them in a dark place." [2] Although this illustration occurs in fiction, it was such a common fact in that time and country that no apology should be necessary for introducing it here. Cooke says, further, that, in the tropics, it is not at all uncommon to encounter fungi which glow so brightly as to enable the traveller to write up his journal by their light, but we are not able to vouch for this statement.

This useful property of light without fire has naturally had various applications, in cases where many artificial lights would be inadmissible. Thus the women of New Caledonia gather a phosphorescent fungus as an ornament for their hair ; while " punkwood," etc., has often been used as a kind of " safety-lamp " in barns of ripe corn, hay and similar crops, where, for example, a torch would

---

[1] 1862, Cooke, *British Fungi*, p. 8.
[2] 1884, Twain, *loc. cit.*, ch. xxxv.

be dangerous. Magnus in 1652 relates that in far northern countries, the inhabitants collect luminous pieces of rotten oak-bark for marking out a path through woods which they wish to traverse in the dark, an early and more literal method of " blazing " the trail ; while Rumphius [1] refers to a *Fungus igneus*, which shines like stars with a bluish light, and which is carried at night as a sort of lamp to show the way. Very recently, luminous wood was employed by the British troops on the Western front during the War, for putting on the straps of their steel helmets, and on the fore-sights of rifles.

Tunbridge Ware. The so-called " Green Oak " is simply the common oak which has been attacked by the mycelium of a fungus, *Chlorosplenium aeruginosum*, when the tissues become stained with green, giving a very pleasing effect. Wood so affected is used in the manufacture of Tunbridge Ware and fancy work. Owing, however, to its comparative scarcity and the great demand, substitutes obtained by staining the wood artificially have been much used instead.

Razor Strops. Some species of *Polyporus* have been used for this purpose, for which their close texture serves admirably. Cooke cites *P. squamosus* (Frontispiece) and *P. betulinus* (Fig. 49) as being equally suitable for the purpose, and " a person who has had one in use for many years, says that it is far superior to the majority of those offered for sale."[2] Swanton records that, in the Godalming district,

" in the early part of the past century razor strops were commonly made of *Polyporus betulinus*. Mr. J. Denyer of Eashing has kindly

---

[1] *c.* 1680, Rumphius, *Herbarium Amboinense.*
[2] 1862, Cooke, *British Fungi,* p. 78.

made for the Haselmere Museum collection a replica of the strop as used in his parish. A piece of the fungus, about 6 × 2 × 1 inches, is nailed to a piece of wood, the spore-bearing surface making the stropping surface, which was dusted with siliceous earth. Canadian soldiers who have seen this strop tell me that similar ones are made by lumbermen in British Columbia, but the stropping surface is never powdered." [1]

Curry-combs. *Daedalea quercina* (Fig. 55), whose use for tinder has already been mentioned, is sometimes employed to clean down horses, particularly those whose skin is too tender for an ordinary curry-comb ; and it has similarly been used by man for cleaning the hair.

Snuff. Berkeley records that " a species of *Polyporus* growing upon the birch, and probably a state of *P. igniarius* or *fomentarius*, or possibly *P. nigricans*, without specimens it is uncertain which, is used when dried and pounded as an ingredient in snuff, by the Ostyacks on the Obi,"[2] the narcotic properties of the preparation being thereby improved.

Dyeing. Various fungi have been, and may still be employed by dyers, leather-dressers and cabinet-makers, for the colours which they produce, and some interesting information on this point is given by Gautier.[3] Thus an excellent brown is obtained from *Polysaccum crassipes* or *tinctorium*, the colour, which is contained chiefly in the spores, being used in the Canaries, in Italy and also round Nice, for the dyeing of silks.

Another brown dye, coming from *Polyporus hispidus*, finds application in the colouring of silk, cotton and

---

[1] 1916, Swanton, Economic and Folk-Lore Notes, *Trans. Brit. Myc. Soc.*, Vol. V., pp. 408-409.

[2] 1857, Berkeley, *Introduction to Cryptogamic Botany*, p. 255.

[3] 1884, Gautier, *Les Champignons considérés dans leurs rapports avec la médecine, etc.*, p. 50.

wool, being used also by cabinet-makers and joiners, to give certain woods the same colour ; while it is also employed by leather-dressers for skins, a fawn-chestnut colour being the result. Two allies of the last species are also used in dyeing, *P. sulphureus* to give a yellow, and *Fomes igniarius* a brown-black. It was possibly the latter which the celebrated Doctor Johnson meant, when he referred to " male agarick " as used in " dying " [*sic*].[1] He distinguishes the male as growing on oaks ; the female on larches. The terms " male agaric " and " female agaric " have, however, been very loosely understood by different writers, and the latter (*P. officinalis*) was certainly similarly employed at times. *Hexagona mori* serves in Italy for dyeing various fabrics, and according to the proportions used and the length of immersion, different shades, such as a very solid yellowish green, " jaune chamois " and " jonquille," may be obtained. Among other dyes may be mentioned a very fine red, obtained at Toulouse from several different species of *Russula* having red caps, while Bulliard has produced a beautiful reddish bistre from the violet variety of *Tremella lutescens*.

Writing Materials. When, as Hearne tells us, the Dorians wrote on toadstools, we are not informed what ink, if any, they employed, but this could equally well have been obtained from a toadstool, for the common Shaggy-cap (*Coprinus comatus*) (Figs. 60 and 76) " is so rapidly deliquescent, that while standing, or more speedily if gathered, it melts away drop by drop, and is soon converted into a black fluid resembling ink ; and

---

[1] 1785, Samuel Johnson, *A Dictionary of the English Language*, under " agarick."

indeed this resemblance is so complete, that it may readily be employed as a substitute; all that is required being to boil and strain it, and add a small quantity of corrosive sublimate to prevent its turning mouldy."[1] By a similar means, Bulliard was able to manufacture an ink, which he describes as very suitable for tinting, from a *Coprinus* in its old stage, to which in consequence he gave the name of *atramentarius*.

Hygrometers. An unusual application of a fungus is found in the case of *Geaster hygrometricus*, the radiating segments of which become bent back in dry weather and straighten out when wet, thus constituting a moderately sensitive hygrometer, of much the same efficiency as the well-known "Darby and Joan" instrument.

Miscellaneous Uses. *Polyporus nidulans* has been used in Sweden for the manufacture of bottle corks; while amadou (*Fomes fomentarius*) (Fig. 48) finds in various parts of the Continent, particularly in Bohemia, a variety of employment in addition to the usual one. Thus, not only are caps, aprons and various articles of dress made from it, but also chest protectors, picture frames, ornaments and other articles. We may mention finally the employment of the Fly Agaric (*Amanita muscaria*) (Fig. 15) for killing flies, after first sprinkling it with sugar to attract them; or sometimes in the form of a decoction, to which Albertus Magnus refers in a quotation which is cited later.[2] Although this use has now been replaced by the ubiquitous "fly-paper" in its numerous forms, it is said to be still used, in the form of the extract, for

---

[1] 1862, M. C. Cooke, *British Fungi*, p. 51.
[2] See ch. XV. : The Derivation of Fungus Names.

the eradication of those insects which are abhorred by good housewives, for their unpleasant habits of residing in beds and on furniture, the affected parts being sprinkled or rubbed with the infusion.

The fungi have doubtless found industrial or domestic employment in ways other than those we have dealt with, and we should be glad of any information as to such uses.

CHAPTER IX

The Uses of Fungi : As Foods

" Todestolys that be gethered from
the tree be good to eate."
—1519, HORMAN, *Vulg.*, 101 b.

" Some of these penny-reading toad-
stool-eaters would even turn a toad
off its stool to eat its seat."
—1886, P. S. ROBINSON, *Valley Teet. Trees*, 137.

THE employment of fungi as food is a very ancient
practice, whose beginnings are lost in the mists
of antiquity, and which is probably as old as man
himself. Could we go back as far as the palaeolithic age,
when times of scarcity may have been the rule rather
than the exception, it is certainly probable that hunger
must at times have driven our early ancestors to sample
almost anything of a biteable nature. Thus we should
probably find them including these plants in their
dietary, and also, occasionally, paying in no uncertain
manner for their ignorance of the poisonous kinds. It
may then be surmised that a certain amount of knowledge
of these plants would here and there be accumulated by
experience, and handed on ; of which, of course, no
records now exist.

Classical Use as Foods. For their earliest mention
as esculents, we must have recourse to classical references.
There is thus no doubt that they were so used by the
Greeks in the fifth century B.C., probably, of course,
very much earlier. About that time, however, both

Hippocrates and Euripides refer to cases of fungus poisoning. From the writings of Theophrastus, about 300 B.C., it is clear, not only that they were eaten on a fairly large scale, but that some of them, particularly truffles, were articles of commerce and export.[1] There is no doubt, however, that in the later years of the Roman Republic and under the regime of the Empire, their consumption had much increased, some of them being regarded as very great luxuries. When the sterner virtues of the Romans had decayed, and they had acquired many luxurious tastes, one of the most significant was that for the pleasures of the table, in which it is to be regretted that the fungi played no small part.

The Sumptuary Laws of the Romans. To check these self-indulgent habits, at different times a number of sumptuary laws were enacted, each framed so as to check some definite and growing evil. Most of them were apparently very little observed and quickly fell into disuse. They were naturally very difficult to enforce, and even when the letter of any particular one of them was observed, it led to a fresh excess in other directions.

The first laws to prescribe the nature of the foods and liquors consumed at private dinners were the Lex Fannia in 161 B.C. and the Lex Didia in 143 B.C.; while the Lex Licinia, promulgated about 103 B.C., limited the amounts of meat and fish that were to be consumed on ordinary occasions, and encouraged the consumption of vegetables.

Increased use of Fungi by the Romans. Among the vegetable foods which thus came into greater favour

---

[1] See ch. XIV. : Some Further Historical Aspects of the Fungi.

were the fungi, in regard to which Cicero says : "While these elegant eaters wish to bring into high repute the products of the soil which are not included in the Act, they prepare their fungi, helvellae, and all vegetables with such highly-seasoned condiments that it is impossible to conceive anything more delicious." [1] In effect, they were so treated as to resemble animal foods, while the same extravagance continued. The most celebrated mushroom that was so employed was " the imperial mushroom, which the Romans of the Empire, past-masters in gluttony, called the food of the gods, *cibus deorum*, the agaric of the Caesars." [2] This is undoubtedly the *Amanita Caesarea* of modern mycologists, known to the French to-day as the *oronge*, and termed by the Romans *boletus*. Pliny (23–79 A.D.) paints a vivid picture of the manner in which boleti and some other fungi were regarded, and in his remarks on the cooking of fungi, he says that these were "the only food which dainty voluptuaries themselves prepare with their own hands, and thus, as it were, by anticipation feed on them, using amber knives and silver service." [3] Juvenal, who flourished towards the close of the first century A.D., regretfully says : "Nor will that youth allow any relative to hope better of him who has learnt to peel truffles and to pickle boleti." [4]

Fungus Luxuries of the Romans. In the cooking of boleti, special vessels, called *boletaria*, were used, and these were not to be employed for more ignoble purposes.

---

[1] Cicero, *Ad. Fam.*, VII., 26.   Letter to Gallus.
[2] 1913, J. H. Fabre, *The Life of the Fly*, English Translation by A. T. de Mattos, ch. xviii. : " Insects and Mushrooms."
[3] Pliny, *Nat. Hist.*, Delphin. ed., XXII., 47.
[4] Juvenal, *Sat.*, XIV., 6–8.

Martial (43–104 A.D.), in an Epigram, depicts one of these vessels as bewailing its fallen state in the functions of a Roman kitchen : " Although boleti have given me so noble a name, I am now used, I am ashamed to say, for Brussels sprouts." [1] In another Epigram of Martial, there appears a certain host, Caecilianus, who invites various friends to dinner and then eats all the boleti himself, upon which one of the guests protests as follows :

> " What brutishness is this ?   When friends you treat,
> They looking on, alone you mushrooms eat,
> What on such gluttony shall I implore ?
> May'st Claudius' mushroom eat, and ne'er eat more ! " [2]

The reference is to the death of the emperor Claudius through eating a dish of poisoned mushrooms. In the opinion of Martial, boleti were very great delicacies, which, if sent as a gift to a friend, should never be entrusted to a slave, for he would most certainly devour them on the way, although gold and silver might safely be committed to his care :

> " Argentum atque aurum facile est, laenamque togamque
> Mittere : boletos mittere difficile est." [3]

Juvenal refers specifically only to the boleti and describes all other fungi as " ancipites."

> " Vilibus ancipites fungi ponentus amicis, Boletus domino."[4]

> " Doubtful fungi shall be served to his clients, the boletus to the lordly patron."

As further evidence of the madness which had befallen the Romans, Suetonius relates [5] that the

---

1 Martial, *Ep.* XIV., 101.
2 Martial, *Ep.* I., 21.
3 Martial, *Ep.* XIII., 48.
4 Juvenal, *Sat.* V, 146.
5 Suetonius, *Tiberius*, ch. xlii.

Emperor Tiberius (14–37 A.D.) awarded the sum of 200,000 sesterces (about £2,000) to Asellius Sabinus for a Dialogue he had written, in which boleti, beccaficos,[1] oysters and thrushes were depicted as contending for the honour of being considered the choicest fare.

Divided Opinions of Romans as to the Food Value of the Fungi. It would appear, however, that the Romans were by no means unanimous as to the virtues of the fungi, and Seneca thus delivers himself : " Good gods ! how many men does one belly engage ! What ! Do you think that those boleti—a pleasant poison—albeit they hurt not now, conceal within them no hidden mischief," [2] and again : " For they are not food, they serve only to tickle the appetite, constraining those that are full to eat more ; a very gratifying amusement to such persons as stuff themselves with such things as readily go down and as readily return." [3] Cicero (106–143 A.D.) had previously contributed some evidence in agreement with that of Seneca, and relates in a letter to Gallus how he had attended a banquet given by the augurs at the house of Lentulus, where, being unable to indulge in such delicacies as oysters and eels, because of the sumptuary law forbidding them, he had instead eaten various dishes of highly-seasoned fungi, with the result that he was seized with a violent attack of diarrhoea, so as to be hardly able to stand up for about ten days. He says plaintively : " I who willingly abstained from delicate fishes, found myself taken in by

---

[1] Beccaficos were small birds much esteemed by the Romans in the autumn, when they had become fattened on figs and grapes.

[2] Seneca, *Ep.* XCV.

[3] Seneca, *Ep.* CVIII.

vulgar herbs." [1] He finishes his letter by saying that in future, he will be " more careful," which recalls the old proverb, " The devil was ill," etc.

Deprecation of their Use. Galen (130–218 A.D.), whose fame in medicine lasted for many centuries, also threw the weight of his authority against the fungi. He says : " Of fungi, the boletus, when well boiled, must be counted among insipid things ; it is generally eaten with various kinds of spices, as is done with other insipid food. These fungi, after being eaten in large quantities, yield cold, clammy, noxious juices as their nourishing qualities ; the boleti are the most harmless, and after them the amanitae ; as for the rest, it is far safer to have nothing to do with them," [2] and elsewhere : " Of all such kinds of food, fungi have the coldest, most viscid, and thickest juice ; however, among them the boleti have never been known to cause anyone's death ; still, to some persons, even they cause cholera and indigestion." [3] As would, however, be expected, the populace were not to be deterred by the efforts of the " reformers," from indulging in their favourite fungi, and they continued, in general, to eat heartily, and occasionally, to suffer dreadfully.

Fungi used by the Romans. The reasons for the identification of the boletus with the modern *Amanita Caesarea* can more appropriately be discussed in a later section, and the same remark applies to the other species in which the Romans indulged. It should be remarked

---

[1] Cicero, *Ad. Fam.*, VII., 26. Letter to Gallus.

[2] Galen, *De Aliment. Facult.*, lib. II., 69.

[3] Galen, *De Probis Pravisque Alimentorum Succis* (" The Good and Bad Juices of Foods "), cap. IV., p. 770.

that the *amanitae* of Galen were almost certainly the Common Mushroom, *Psalliota campestris*, and not representatives of the modern genus of *Amanita*. It is a matter of history that the emperor Claudius was poisoned in 54 A.D. by a dish of boleti, of which he was very fond, but it is quite clear, from the writings of Tacitus,[1] Suetonius,[2] and Pliny,[3] that the fungi were only the means, and that a poison was added to the dish, either by, or at the instigation of Agrippina, the wife of Claudius.

Besides boleti, Roman writers also frequently mention *fungi* and *suilli* (" hog-fungi "), so called because swine were fond of them. The latter have been identified as *Boletus edulis* (Fig. 82), a fungus belonging to a genus of an entirely different character, whose members are characterized by having the hymenium covering tubes or pores, and not gills, as with the genus *Amanita*. Suilli were often contrasted unfavourably with boleti by the Romans, and Martial in an Epigram complains to Ponticus that when he was invited to a banquet, Ponticus had boleti, but *he* had to be content with suilli.

" Sunt tibi boleti : fungos ego sumo suillos." [4]

The Romans also used as foods, several kinds of truffles, puffballs, morels, the Common Mushroom, and a variety of other fungi, whose identifications with modern species have been more or less surely arrived at.[5]

---

[1] Tacitus, *An.*, XII., 66.
[2] Suetonius, *Nero*, 33.
[3] Pliny, *Nat. Hist.*, XXII., 22.
[4] Martial, *Ep.* III., 60.
[5] For further consideration of this question, see ch. XIV. : Some Further Historical Aspects of the Fungi.

Use by the Greeks. Not only were the Romans addicted to luxury and extravagance, but also the Greeks, and Plutarch, the Greek writer contemporary with the Roman Juvenal, speaks of the folly of indulging in costly foods and liquors, merely because they *are* so, and therefore accessible only to the rich. Among such he mentions Italian mushrooms,[1] which were evidently an article of import into Greece, the latter country being notoriously poor in mushrooms to the present day.

Classical Recipes for Preparation of Fungi. A large number of recipes for the preparation of fungi in different ways for the table are given in the work De Re Coquinaria,[2] ascribed to Caelius Apicius, and written in the third century A.D. Apicius is the name of no fewer than three famous Roman epicures, of whom the best known was M. Gavius Apicius, who lived under Tiberius,[3] and who is said to have written on cookery, but the work in question appears to be based on earlier Greek writings.

Apicius refers to four kinds of fungi in his recipes : boleti, tubera (truffles), fungi farnei (thought to be *Boletus edulis*) and Sfonduli, Funguli or Spongioli (believed to be the same as the *spongiole* of Porta, 1592, and the modern Italian *spugnola*, the morel). Houghton has translated these recipes,[4] of which those for the preparation of truffles may be given.

---

[1] Plutarch, *De Tuenda Sanitate Praecepta* (" Rules for the Preservation of Health "), Vol. II., p. 124, F. ed. Xylander.

[2] Caelius Apicius, *De Opsoniis et Condimentis, sive de Arte Coquinaria Libri Decem*, ed. 2, by Martin Lister, 1719, pp. 208–211.

[3] See Seneca, *Consol. ad. Helviam*, 10.

[4] 1885, W. Houghton, Notices of Fungi in Greek and Latin Authors, *Annals and Magazine of Natural History*, Series 5, Vol. 15, pp. 22–49. See p. 47.

" For *Tubera :* (1) Slice, boil, sprinkle with salt, and transfix
with a twig (surculo infigis) ; partly roast, and place in a cooking
vessel with oil, liquor, sweet boiled wine (caroenum), unmixed
wine, pepper and honey ; while boiling, beat up with fine flour,
take out the twigs and serve. (2) Another recipe : Boil and
sprinkle salt, transfix with twigs, partly roast, place in a cooking
vessel with liquor, oil, greens, sweet boiled wine, a small quantity
of unmixed wine, pepper, and a little honey, and let it boil ; while
boiling beat up with fine flour ; prick the tubers that they may
absorb, take out the twigs and serve. If you like you may surround
the tubers with the omentum of a pig, then roast and serve."

Other recipes are given for cooking truffles and the
other fungi in question, and among other ingredients
occur green coriander and pounded coriander seeds,
cummin, echinus eggs (?) (uvam), leeks, lovage, mint,
parsley, rue and seseli. It is probable that the
recipes of Apicius closely resemble those in use by the
Romans.

Mediaeval use as Foods. In times more recent,
one may find many references by our own writers to the
use of fungi as foods, with, at times, warnings as to the
attendant dangers, and a description of the methods of
discrimination between the edible and poisonous kinds.
It is of interest to learn, from the few monastic diet rolls
that have come down to us, that the consumption of
mushrooms, both in summer and winter, was certainly
enormous ; while, on the other hand, there are no
records relating to vegetables. Many religious houses
certainly had herb-gardens, in which were cultivated the
plants used in simples, and also, presumably, pot-herbs
for domestic use ; but to what extent they cultivated
the ordinary vegetables remains a matter of conjecture.

The culinary use of fungi is mentioned by King
Richard II's chief cook, whose name is forgotten, but
whose initials, C.S.S., survive, for over them he wrote

one of the first Cookery Books in English, " On the
Forme of Cury," which was published about the year
1390. Here one is told to " take funges and pare hem
clene, and dyce [= dice] hem." [1]   What the " funges "
were, we do not know, but they were most likely the
Common Mushroom. Horman, whose reference we
have cited at the head of this chapter, must, however,
have had something quite different in mind, for the
Common Mushroom never grows on trees, although
quite a large number of edible kinds are found so
growing.

Half a century or so later, Maplet emphasizes the
need for care in collecting them for food, and says :

" The Mushrom or Toadstoole . . hath two sundrie kinds, . . .
for the one may be eaten : the other is not to be eaten." [2]

Gerard, in his Herbal, thought even less of the fungi
from the gastronomic standpoint, for he divides them
into two classes " whereof some are very venomous and
full of poyson, others not so noisome ; and neither of
them very wholesome meate." [3]   He quotes Galen to
the effect that they " ingender a clammy, pituitous and
cold nutriment if they be eaten," [4] and he clearly thought
that a liking for them was strongly to be deprecated, as
indicating a depraved taste.   He concludes by saying :
" Therefore I give my advice unto those that love such
strange and new-fangled meates, to beware of licking
honey among thornes, lest the sweetnesse of the one do
not countervaile the sharpness and pricking of the

---

[1] 1791, R. Warner, *Antiquitates Culin.*, 5.
[2] 1567, Maplet, *Gr. Forest*, 52.
[3] 1597, Gerard, *Herbal*, 2nd ed. (reprinted 1636), lib. 3, p. 1578.
[4] *Loc. cit.*, p. 1584.

other." [1] The epicures of that day paid doubtless as little attention to his strictures as did the Romans the earlier condemnation of the fungi by Seneca and other writers.

At the beginning of the next century, Topsell speaks of a curious natural phenomenon as follows :

> " Hermolaus also writeth this of the Lycurium, that it groweth in a certaine stone, and that it is a kind of mushrom, or padstoole, which is cut off yearly, and that another groweth in the room of it, a parte of the roote or foot being left in the stone, groweth as hard as a flint, and thus doth the stone encrease with a naturall fecundity ; which admirable thing (saith he) I could never be brought to beleeve, untill I did eate thereof in myne owne house." [2]

This irresistibly reminds us of the story told by that entertaining voyager, Sir John Mandeville, who, writing of course much earlier,[3] relates that " in that vale [of Ebron or Hebron] is the felde where men draw out of the earth a thinge the which men in that countrey call Chambell and they eate that thinge in the stede of spyce, and they beare it to sell, and men may not grave [i.e., dig] there so deepe ne so wyde, but it is at the yeeres ende full againe to the sydes through the grace of God." [4] But whether there is any etymological connection between " chambell " and " champignon " we will not venture to say. However, it certainly appears not impossible, in view of the collateral evidence of Topsell, that this " thinge " was a fungus, and there was of

---

[1] *Loc. cit.*, p. 584.

[2] 1607, Topsell, *History of Four-footed Beasts*, p. 494.

[3] He is supposed to have left England on his travels on Sept. 29th, 1322.

[4] *circa* 1355–1371, *The Voiage and Travayle of Sir John Maundeville, Knight*, 1887 ed., p. 42.

course often some substratum of truth in Mandeville's stories.

A little later than Topsell, Francis Bacon, in his "Naturall Historie," written about the year 1624, but not published until 1627, the year after Bacon's death, writes :

> "The mushrooms have two strange properties ; the one that they yeeld so delicious a meat ; the other, that they come up so hastily, as in a night, and yet they are unsown." [1]

The Truffles and Morels. These historical references to the uses of fungi as foods would hardly be complete without some mention of those justly-celebrated delicacies, the truffles and morels, and an early reference to the former is made by Evelyn, who relates in his diary for the year 1644 : "We got to Vienne in Dauphine . . . here we supped and lay, having amongst other dainties, a dish of Trufles, an earth-nut found out by an hogg train'd to it, and for which those animals are sold at a great price." [2] This statement is of some interest, for Evelyn moved in "the best circles" and would not have so phrased his description, if truffles had been used as a luxury in England in his day. They do occur in this country, but were not commonly found or eaten until later. Evelyn writes elsewhere "concerning Morilles and Truffs : (the first whereof is a certain delicate red mushroom.") [3]

A few years later, Sorbière says, in relation to the Londoners, "as that for Champignons, and Moriglio's,

---

[1] 1627, Bacon, *Sylva Sylvarum, or a Naturall Historie in Ten Centuries*, § 546.

[2] 1644, Evelyn, *Diary*, 30 Sept.

[3] 1672, Evelyn, *Fr. Gard.* (1675), 260.

they were as great strangers to 'em as if they had been bred in Japan," [1] and we are not so sure that he would have much better to say about the Londoners of to-day. Sorbière betrays, however, a lamentable ignorance of the use, centuries old, made of fungi as foods by the Japanese, for this, in the light of the evidence given a little later in this chapter, is not only extensive, but even remarkable.

More Recent Uses as Foods. Turning from the historical side of the matter to consider the modern utilisation of the different fungi as foods, it is of interest to note that the savage and more primitive races of the present day make a much greater use of them than do their more civilised brothers. This is not surprising, in that the regular cultivation of staple foods renders unnecessary the casual gathering of a very variable crop of nature's own providing, and one, moreover, of decidedly inferior food value.

Uses by Savage Races. The staple edible of the Fuegians is a *Cyttaria*, which grows freely on living twigs of the evergreen beech during a considerable portion of the year. Under the name of " Thunder dirt," the Maories of New Zealand used formerly, because of the lack of better food, the gelatinous volva of *Ileodictyon*, which Berkeley describes as " an execrable article of diet." The " native bread " of the Australians is also a fungus, *Polyporus Mylittae* (Fig. 65), said to be considerably better than the last, and " when dry in some conditions looks like hard compacted lumps of sago." [2] According to Guppy, fungi are often cooked

---

[1] 1698, W. King, tr. *Sorbière's Journ. Lond.*, 32.
[2] 1857, Berkeley, *Introduction to Cryptogamic Botany*, p. 254.

and eaten by the natives of the Solomons, being
known as "magu," but the author cannot give the
species.[1]

Recourse is had to fungi as food in Central Africa,
and H.M. Stanley, on his third journey to the Nyanza
in 1888, in describing the privations endured by his
column on the Ihuru river, relates that "our Nyanza
people were provident and eked out their stores with
mushrooms and wild fruit."[2] Apparently, however,
not all of the natives knew how to distinguish poisonous
kinds, perhaps in their desperation being impelled to
try some whose properties were unknown to them, for
on returning to camp on Nov. 12th, Stanley found that
"six people had succumbed, a Madi from a poisonous
fungus."[3]

Uses Among More Civilised Races. Passing on
to the more civilised races of the world, one is immediately
struck by the varying degree in which edible fungi enter
into their dietary; a variability which, indeed, is almost
national. We have seen that fungi are extremely
cosmopolitan in their distribution, and thus the same or
a similar group of esculent species can be found in
almost every temperate country. Yet it does not follow
that they are used to the same extent in all these countries.
For example, our own countrymen exhibit a preference
for the Common Mushroom, and, save for a small band
of enthusiastic mycophagists, regard with indifference or
contempt a number of other species of equal or superior
esculence; species which the French seek with eagerness

---

[1] 1887, Guppy, *The Solomon Islands and their natives*, p. 84.
[2] 1890, H. M. Stanley, *In Darkest Africa*, II., 47.
[3] *Ibid.*, p. 50.

and devour with avidity. It would, therefore, be of interest to consider briefly the chief countries of the world in which edible fungi are consumed to any appreciable degree, and to trace the extent to which the best-known esculents are used.

France. In the markets of Paris, before about the year 1876, only the Common Mushroom and certain truffles were allowed to be exposed for sale, although doubtless many other kinds were collected and eaten privately. Even the morel was at this time forbidden. At Nantes, however, the right of entry was not so restricted, and Génevier, writing in 1876 of this market, calculated the quantity of wild mushrooms sold each year as about 30,000 kilos (or, roughly, 66,000 lbs.), which he considered might approximately be subdivided into three parts of about 10,000 kilos each ; one third being *Psalliota campestris ;* another third composed of three edible kinds very common locally, namely, *Boletus edulis*, *B. aereus* and *Lepiota procera ;* while the third part consisted of some ten or more common kinds, among which were several species of *Lepiota*, *Morchella* and *Amanita*. Probably much the same obtains to-day, when, however, a very different state of affairs is found in Paris than that existing before 1876, for the market has now been extended so as to include commonly some thirty kinds, while others would be permitted, if they were forthcoming. In addition to the truffle and the Common Mushroom, the two species which are dried or preserved in other ways are *Boletus edulis* (la cèpe) and *Amanita Caesarea* (l'oronge), the annual value of all kinds preserved being some 250,000 francs. The inspection of the edible fungi entering the markets of St. Etienne in the Department of the Loire began in 1897, in which year

Photo by A. E. Peck, Scarborough

Fig. 58.—*Helvella crispa*, a fungus whose unappetising appearance belies its undoubted gastronomic qualities.

Photo by A. E. Peck, Scarborough

Fig. 59.—*Gyromitra esculenta*, which, in spite of its specific name, should be regarded with suspicion.

Photo by A. E. Peck, Scarborough

Fig. 60.—The "Shaggy Cap" (*Coprinus comatus*). This species provides
a succulent dish if gathered young, and has the additional
advantage of being unmistakeable.

Photo by A. E. Peck, Scarborough

Fig. 61.—The "Blewitt" (*Tricholoma personatum*) makes excellent
eating. Mr. Peck informs us that "Sheffield anglers who visit
Lincolnshire in vast numbers at week-ends, often return with
more blewitts than fish."

an ordinance was promulgated by the mayor permitting
the sale of the following species :

1. L'agaric champêtre (*Psalliota campestris*).
2. L'agaric élevé (*Lepiota procera*).
3. L'agaric faux mousseron (*Psalliota arvensis*).
4. La chanterelle (*Cantharellus cibarius*).
5. Le bolet bronzé (*Boletus aereus*).
6. La cèpe (*Boletus edulis*).
7. La langue de boeuf (*Fistulina hepatica*).
8. L'hydne sinué (*Hydnum repandum*).
9. L'hydne écailleux (*Hydnum imbricatum*).
10. Clavaires.
11. Helvelles.
12. Morilles.
13. Truffes.

In 1912 and 1921, new regulations were made, the
latter permitting the sale of a larger number of species,
which are detailed below :

Boletus aereus.
Boletus edulis.
Boletus scaber.
Cantharellus cibarius.
Clitocybe laccata.
Coprinus comatus.
Fistulina hepatica.
Hydnum imbricatum.
Hydnum repandum.
Hygrophorus niveus.
Lactarius deliciosus.
Lepiota procera.
Marasmius oreades.
Psalliota campestris.
Psalliota arvensis.
Tricholoma equestre.
Tricholoma nudum.
Tricholoma portentosum.
Clavaria.   All species.
Helvella.   „
Morchella.   „
Tuber.   „

All the above occur in this region, but those most abundant on the market, in order of decreasing importance, are as follows :

> *Cantharellus cibarius.*
> *Boletus edulis.*
> *Hydnum repandum.*
> *Hydnum imbricatum.*
> *Lepiota procera.*
> *Tricholoma equestre.*
> *Tricholoma portentosum.*
> Clavarias, various.

In France there is scarcely any city near to a woody region which has not become an important market for many kinds of wild mushrooms in their season, the chief species sold varying with the locality. Thus, in Lyons, in 1907, about 26,000 lbs. of different kinds were so disposed of, the greater part of which consisted of the chanterelle (*Cantharellus cibarius*), with *Tricholoma terreum* second in amount ; while in other markets *Boletus edulis* and *B. granulatus* are often the species sold in greatest quantity. Besides these " wild " mushrooms, there appear in almost all markets the products respectively of the great mushroom-growing industry of Paris and of the truffle industry of Southern France, both of which are of such magnitude as to require separate consideration.

Switzerland. In Switzerland, both Lausanne and Geneva are notable markets. Thus, in the former town, no fewer than seventy-eight different kinds are allowed to be sold, to the amount of some 60,000 lbs. annually ; while in the latter, a particular portion of the market is allocated solely for their sale, and during the season constitutes a veritable fungus exhibition. These are all very carefully inspected, in order that they may be passed as wholesome before being sold, and even those who gather wild fungi for their own use are invited to submit their spoils to be thus certified.

Italy. With regard to Italy, it is of interest to note that, as early as the year 1820, the Government of Milan published a list of about half a dozen species as being edible, but provided for the varying kinds to be found in different localities, by decreeing, that each district should similarly issue its own local list of wholesome fungi. These were even then of some economic importance. The varieties sold in Italian markets to-day are naturally the lineal descendants of those known to the Romans and some account of them is given later in this connection.[1]

Germany. According to Duggar,[2] who visited Berlin and Leipzig in 1899, these markets were at that time not well organized to encourage the sale of any large number of different species, and only about a dozen common kinds were represented, this being, possibly, partly the result of a Prussian law passed early in 1812, restricting the sale of wild mushrooms to the following species :

> *Morchella esculenta.*
> *M. conica.*
> *Psalliota campestris.*
> *Lactarius deliciosus.*
> *Agaricus cebaceus* (=*Hygrophorus ceraceus*).
> *Merulius cantharellus* (=*Cantharellus cibarius*).
> *Boletus edulis.*
> *Clavaria flava.*

All other species were to be rejected, some as being poisonous themselves, and others as being liable to be confused with deadly kinds.

---

[1] See ch. XIV. : *Some Further Historical Aspects of the Fungi.*
[2] 1920, Duggar, *Mushroom Growing*, p. 228.

In Bavaria, however, possibly because the moist woods of the southern portion of this state are climatically very favourable for their growth, a very different state of affairs is found, and Duggar says that the city of Munich is the largest market in the world for wild mushrooms. According to Prof. Giesenhagen, the quantity sold in the provision market of that city in the summer and autumn of 1901 was about 850,000 kilos. (about 1,850,000 pounds), distributed as shown in the following table :

		Kilos.
1. *Clavaria aurea* ...		
2. *Clavaria botrytis*		10,000— 12,000
3. *Clavaria flava* ...		
4. *Craterellus clavatus*	...	500— 600
5. *Sparassis crispa* ...		——
6. *Cantharellus cibarius*	...	70,000— 90,000
7. *Boletus edulis* ...	...	300,000—350,000
8. *Boletus granulatus*	...	1,000— 1,500
9. *Boletus scaber* ...	...	150,000—180,000
10. *Polyporus confluens*	...	500— 600
11. *Polyporus ovinus*	...	15,000— 20,000
12. *Hydnum imbricatum*	...	13,000— 15,000
13. *Armillaria mellea*	...	600— 800
14. *Clitocybe nebularis*	...	50,000— 60,000
15. *Lactarius deliciosus*	...	200— 300
16. *Lactarius volemus*	...	8,000— 10,000
17. *Lepiota procera* ...	...	12,000— 13,000
18. *Pleurotus ostreatus*	...	1,000— 2,000
19. *Russula alutacea*		
20. *Russula cyanoxantha*		
21. *Russula vesca* ...		30,000— 35,000
22. *Russula virescens*		
23. *Tricholoma gambosum*	...	10,000— 12,000
24. *Pholiota mutabilis*	...	5,000— 6,000
25. *Psalliota campestris*	...	80,000—100,000
26. *Morchella bohemica*		
27. *Morchella conica*		
28. *Morchella esculenta*		5,000— 8,000
29. *Morchella patula*		
30. *Gyromitra esculenta*		2,000— 3,000
31. *Gyromitra gigas*		

The sale of thirty-one species, therefore, occurred on this market. Doubtless this number would be somewhat increased by the fact that several species may be included under *Psalliota campestris*, and the same may be true of some other forms. Aside from this, it is to be noted that this list is a local one and that many fairly common edible fungi are not included.[1]

India. In Asia, as in Europe, the Common Mushroom does not belie its name, and it is abundant in many parts of India, being found particularly in cattle-fields in many parts of the Central Panjáb after the rains, in the desert tracts of Central and Southern Panjáb, and also in Afghanistan. It is consumed extensively by the natives, either fresh or after drying in the sun. It is described by Europeans as excellent, and equal in quality to the English variety.

The morel (*Morchella esculenta*), which also closely resembles the European form (Fig. 85), is found in abundance locally, and, according to Troup, is exported in large quantities from Kashmir and elsewhere in the Himalayas to the plains. They " are collected in April and strung up on a string to dry in the sun previous to export."[2] It is of interest to note that the Mahommedans will only eat morels, as they consider other kinds to be impure food. On the other hand, the Hindoos will eat any mushroom having an agreeable taste and smell. Besides the two species in question, the other chief edible fungi of India are *Helvella crispa* (Fig. 58) and *Hydnum coralloides*.

" Edible truffles, known in Burma as ' kaing-u,' are

---

[1] Duggar, *loc. cit.*, p. 226.
[2] 1913, Troup, *Indian Forest Utilisation*, ed. 2 (revised) 1913, p. 204.

obtained in the rainy season from the roots of the 'kaing' (elephant-grass); while another form of edible truffle grows on the roots of *Pinus khasya.*" [1] Stewart mentions [2] an " underground mushroom," which may possibly be a truffle, and which is found in cultivated ground near Multan and known in the vernacular as " boenphal." This, he says, is also eaten by the natives. Balfour refers [3] to an underground fungus, *Mylitta,* found in the Nilgiri hills, which he considers to be closely allied to the so-called " native bread " of the Tasmanians, *Polyporus Mylittae* (Fig. 65). He does not say, however, whether the Indian species is eaten by the natives.

Another doubtful species mentioned by Stewart is known as " shírian " in the Jhelam, and " bat-bakri " in the Kair valley. Stewart describes this as " a thin flat ragged-looking fungus, yellow above and with white gills below, which is found on dead trees in various parts of the Panjáb Himalaya at 8,000 to 8,500 feet. The natives slice and cook it either fresh or dry, and eat it as a relish with bread. I have tried this species in stews, etc., but found it leathery and flavourless." [4] A *Lepiota,* of which the species is not stated, is referred to by Gibbon " as being found in the nests of white ants and eaten with relish by the natives," [5] while Berkeley states that " *Hypoxylon vernicosum* is consumed by the Bhoteans in the Himalayas." [6]

---

[1] Troup, *loc. cit.*

[2] 1869, Stewart, *Punjab Plants,* p. 269.

[3] Balfour, *Agricultural Pests of India,* p. 61.

[4] Stewart, *loc. cit.,* p. 267.

[5] Gibbon, *Journal of the Agri-Horticultural Society of India* (N.S.), Vol. V., pp. 51–53.

[6] 1857, Berkeley, *Introduction to Cryptogamic Botany,* p. 271.

Tibet. In the pinewoods of Tibet, Hooker records that a large mushroom, known by the natives as " Onglau," is abundant, and constitutes a favourite article of food. This species, which was afterwards named and described by Berkeley as *Cortinarius emodensis*, is also called by the Tibetans " Yungla tchamo," the latter word signifying a toadstool.[1] Doubtless many other fungi are also eaten by the natives of different parts of India, but the literature of the subject is scanty and a complete list cannot be given.

Japan. This country has been called " the land of mushrooms." With its humid climate and large extent of forest, it certainly possesses great natural advantages for their production, and the total annual crop exceeds 5,000 tons. Of the dozen or more species in general use, the " shii-take " (*Armillaria Shiitake*) and the " matsu-take " (*A. edodes*) are by far the most important, and their huge production may well be compared with the mushroom and truffle industries of France, with which they have received detailed consideration.[2]

The chanterelle (*Cantharellus cibarius*), held in high repute in our own country, is also known in Japan, as " shiba-take," for Rein tells us that " under that name, persons were offering for sale by the basketful our well-known egg-mushroom, in September, 1874, in the village at the foot of Fugi-san. I saw it in other places, too, but cannot find it anywhere mentioned as growing in Japan." [3] In the forests of Fugi-san there occurs

---

[1] 1854, J. D. Hooker, *Himalayan Journals* (1891), ch. xix., p. 320.

[2] See ch. X.: The Cultivated Fungi, and other Fungus Foods of Commerce.

[3] 1889, Rein, *The Industries of Japan*, p. 59.

also another British species, *Clavaria botrytis*, known as "nedzumi-take," with an ally, *C. flava*, both being mentioned by Rein as sold in the neighbouring villages.

In sandy localities, where the pines grow, is found in spring the " shoro," the name being derived from " sho," for " matsu," a pine ; and " ro-tsuyu," dew. The name is applied equally to three allied species, *Rhizopogon aestivus*, *R. rubescens* (Fig. 41) and *R. virens*, of which the second occurs also in this country. The members of this genus, although quite distinct, resemble truffles, and the species in question are highly prized in Japan as ingredients in soups and also as separate dishes. They are said to be very tender and of a delicate flavour, and are often dried for future use. The same method of preserving is followed in the case of the " kikurage " (*Hirneola polytricha*), which grows on the mulberry and elm, and the " kawa-take " (*Hydnum olidum*), found in the dense parts of forests, and having a pleasant smell and exquisite taste. According to an official Japanese publication, both of these are " very nice food." [1]

Among mushrooms also eaten by the Japanese may be mentioned the " hara-take " (*Psalliota campestris*), the " hira-take " (*Pleurotus ostreatus*), the " shiba-take " (*Boletus subtomentosus*), the " amigasa-take " (*Morchella conica*), and the " hatsudake " (*Lactarius Hatsudake*), the last-named growing in the forests and having two varieties, one brown and the other green. There are also the " ko-take," " shimeji-take " and " tsuga-take," the botanical names of which we have not yet been able

---

[1] 1910, *Forestry of Japan*, Bureau of Forestry, Dept. of Agriculture and Commerce, Tokyo, p. 70.

to trace ; while probably still other fungi are used on a smaller scale. At the present day, the rapid " westernization " of the Japanese, with its concomitants in the form of new habits of eating, does not appear to have led to any falling-away in this notable industry, which does not fear comparison with that carried on by any other country.

China. The Chinese mushroom trade is remarkable by reason of the scale on which the so-called " Jew's Ear " (which, however, is not *Hirneola Auricula-Judae* (Fig. 8), but its ally, *H. polytricha* (Fig. 52), is cultivated. This subject, however, is dealt with later.[1] In addition, the Chinese use as food a number of other kinds, those gathered on the largest scale being *Cantharellus cibarius*, *Lactarius deliciosus*, *Psalliota campestris* and *Tricholoma gambosum*.

Australasia. *Hirneola polytricha*, which we have just referred to, is of decided economic importance in New Zealand and the South Sea Islands, particularly Tonga ; from both of which localities it is exported in a dry state to China. The New Zealand trade does not seem so flourishing as formerly, but the fungus is still regularly collected in the northern forests, three to sixpence a pound being given for the dried material. The trade apparently began in 1871, and increased rapidly. During 1918, 2,054 cwt. of the fungus, of an estimated value of £5,784, were exported, mainly to Hong-Kong. We note further, from a Blue Book, that in 1921 a rather smaller quantity, 1,616 cwt., was exported from New Zealand, but this had a much enhanced value, recorded as £12,852.

---

[1] See the following chapter.

United States. Fungi are plentiful in the United States, but those sold in the local markets are restricted to a few species. Thus, of the thirty or so good-sized edible species that are to be found in the District of Columbia, only four kinds are sold in any abundance in the Washington markets. These, which will be seen on almost any market day in autumn and sometimes under favourable conditions in spring and summer, are the Common Mushroom (*Psalliota campestris*), the Horse Mushroom (*Psalliota arvensis*), which is not always distinguished by the market people from the first ; the Shaggy-cap (*Coprinus comatus*), incorrectly called " French mushroom " by the market women ; and the puffball (*Lycoperdon Bovista*). Some of the other edible species of this district are occasionally brought to market, generally to fill some particular order, but they are slow to find a buyer in the open market, since even those who bring them are a little doubtful as to their wholesomeness, and progress towards their coming into general use is very tardy.

Great Britain. Returning to our country, we find that the market is almost entirely confined to wild and cultivated forms of the Common Mushroom (*Psalliota campestris*) or of its ally, the Horse Mushroom (*P. arvenis*) (Fig. 57). The trade in such wild mushrooms as the blewitt (*Tricholoma personatum*) (Fig. 61), the Common Parasol (*Lepiota procera*) (Figs. 74, 75 and 81), the so-called "Summer Truffle" (*Tuber aestivum*), *Craterellus cornucopioides* (Fig. 33) and others, which was formerly a feature of Covent Garden and of some provincial markets, has fallen away or entirely disappeared. This is doubtless primarily due to the more extensive supplies of the Common Mushroom which are now

Photo by Authors

Fig. 62.—*Sparassis crispa* has something of the appearance of a cauliflower, and, like it, is perfectly edible.

Photo by A. E. Peck, Scarborough

Fig. 63.—*Clavaria abietina*, found in fir woods, is edible when young and is frequently sold in Continental markets.

Fig. 64.—" Spongy morells in rich ragousts are found." A dish of Morels (*Morchella esculenta*).

Photo by Authors

Fig. 65.—" Black-fellow's Bread." The sclerotium of *Polyporus Mylittae*, formerly used for food by the Australian aboriginals.

available ; but a further factor, that the collection and marketing of these other edible fungi never received official encouragement in the form of the appointment of referees, who could, as in some other countries, vouch for the authenticity of species offered for sale, should not be overlooked. This economic neglect of practically all species but the Common Mushroom is doubtless also due in a measure to the occasional cases of poisoning which have from time to time occurred through the eating of kinds other than this species. The ill-repute into which the fungi have thus fallen has seriously detracted from their more general employment in this capacity.

The need for a greater encouragement of their use as Foods. In this connection we would most strongly urge that some serious attempt should be made to encourage the use of the other edible fungi on a scale comparable with that of France and Germany, for most of the species which are employed so extensively in these countries are available in Britain, and a livelier interest in them would not only afford supplies of cheap and agreeable food, but would also tend to the development of an industry among our country folk which would stand them in good stead at a time when farmers' work is none too plentiful.

We need not tabulate the many species which might be used. It should be sufficient to say that for those enthusiastic enough and sufficiently well-versed in their identification, *some* edible species are furnished by most months of the year.

Discrimination between Edible and Poisonous Fungi. The eating of fungi, apart from the well-known cultivated form, has always been attended by the danger of using poisonous kinds, for there are no general rules by which to tell one from the other. Various empirical methods have at different times received popular support, but all of these are utterly untrustworthy, for not only would a reliance on any one of them rule out many edible species, but it would *not* exclude many poisonous ones. Some of these beliefs are first recorded by Greek and Roman writers. Thus Horace (65–8 B.C.) says that "fungi which grow in meadows are the best ; it is not well to trust others." [1] Many growing in the open, however, are deadly, while some of those found on or under trees are quite harmless and also most excellent. Like Horace, Pliny (23–79 A.D.) refers to the method of distinguishing harmful kinds by their situation, but also judges from their general appearance. He records that " some persons have discriminated the kinds of fungi from the kinds of trees on which they grow, such as those found on the fig, the fennel (ferula) and gummiferous trees. We have already spoken of those which are produced on the beech, the oak, or the cypress . . . All the poisonous fungi have a livid colour." [2] He says also that " those kinds which remain hard after cooking are injurious, while those which admit of being thoroughly well cooked, when eaten with saltpetre are harmless," [3] while in Holland's edition of his works, we read that " the nearer that a Mushrome or Toadstoole commeth to the color of a fig hanging upon the tree, the lesse presumption there is that it is venomous." [4]

Dioscorides, a century or so later, tells us that poisonous fungi " have a thick coating of mucus, and when laid by after being gathered, quickly become

---

[1] Horace, *Sat.*, II., 4, 20.
[2] Pliny, *Nat. Hist.*, XXII., 47.
[3] *Loc. cit.*
[4] 1601, Holland, *Pliny* (1634) II., 133.

putrid, but others not of this kind impart a sweet taste to sauces." [1] A few years later, Athenaeus, in his *Deipnosophistae* ("Banquet of the Learned") quotes from a much earlier writer, Diphilus, a Greek physician, who wrote a book on *Diets Suitable for Persons in Good and Bad Health*, the following passage : " The wholesome kinds appear to be those which are easily peeled, are smooth and readily broken, such as grow on elms and pines ; the unwholesome kinds are black, livid and hard, and such as remain hard after boiling ; such when eaten produce deadly effects." [2] The general appearance is of course no guide, for a toadstool of vivid hue, red or blue in colour, may be not only innocuous but also pleasant to the palate ; while in another, snow-white and of fair outward seeming, may lie hid the promise of an unhappy fate for the unwary gatherer.

The empirical " tests " which have been advanced from time to time, are well tabulated by Ramsbottom, as follows :

(1) " Poisonous fungi have either a repugnant appearance ; are viscid ; do not 'peel' ; are green, red or white in colour ; have a foetid odour ; have a sharp bitter taste ; exude a milky fluid when broken ; have their flesh rapidly turning colour when broken. *Every one of these characters occurs in both poisonous and edible species.*

(2) " A fungus which has been nibbled by rabbits, squirrels, etc., or which is slug-eaten, is edible. *Slugs thrive on Amanita phalloides, the most poisonous fungus known.* (It may be added that the experimental evidence

---

[1] Dioscorides, *Mat. Med.*, IV., 83.
[2] Athenaeus, *Deipnosophistae*, II., 61 d.

acquired by feeding domestic animals on doubtful species is not absolutely trustworthy).

(3) " Fungi which blacken a silver coin or silver spoon when cooking ; which coagulate milk ; which turn an onion bluish or brown, or which make parsley leaves yellow, are poisonous. *This is not true : and, further, fungi which do not act in any of these ways are not necessarily edible.*

(4) " Fungi which grow on highly manured places are poisonous. *Such fungi may be either poisonous or edible,* e.g., *the common mushroom.*" [1]

With regard to the second, a widely-held presumption, there is perhaps a little to be said for it, for, although rabbits and squirrels are less discriminating than man in their selection of species on which to feed, they appear, on the whole, to avoid those kinds which *he* considers poisonous. Slugs, snails and insects, however, show a much greater catholicity of taste, and in regard to the relation of the last to the belief in question, the great French naturalist, J. H. Fabre, says :

> " The insect which feeds on one sort of mushroom and refuses others, cannot tell us anything about the kinds that are good or bad for us. Its stomach is not ours. It pronounces excellent what we find poisonous ; it pronounces poisonous what we think excellent. That being so, when we are lacking in the botanical knowledge which most of us have neither time nor inclination to acquire, what course are we to take. The course is extremely simple." [2]

There is, of course, only one sure method of discrimination. It is to know one kind from another, as surely as one can distinguish between a carrot, a parsnip

---

[1] 1923, Ramsbottom, *Handbook of the Larger British Fungi*, p. 12.
[2] 1913, Fabre, *The Life of the Fly*, English translation by A. T. de Mattos, ch. xviii. " Insects and Mushrooms," p. 402.

and a beetroot; to restrict one's choice rigidly to those recognised with certainty, and not to add any to the number without independent and unchallengeable authority. Furthermore, it is advisable, in one's first essays, to exclude certain edible ones, because others, which are most toxic in their effects, resemble them, more or less closely, according to the variability of the species and the knowledge of the gatherer. Thus the Blusher (*Amanita rubescens*) should be rigidly avoided on principle, not that the expert would be misled for a moment, but the deadly *A. pantherina* is often mistaken for it by the novice. Thus, under the name " Golmotte," large quantities of *A. rubescens* are annually eaten in Lorraine and the Ardennes, where every year *A. pantherina*, the " Fausse Golmotte," is frequently collected instead, with unhappy consequences. In the same country there is a similar and most deplorable confusion between the delicious *A. Caesarea* (l'Oronge), which is common in the departments of the Midi and the Centre, and the poisonous Fly Agaric, *A. muscaria* (Fig. 15), known as the " Fausse Oronge." It is therefore better to avoid those esculents in which such possibilities of confusion occur. It is of course not the student who suffers, but the imitator.

It is, naturally, inadvisable to eat any which have begun to change colour and decay, for they are then just as apt to produce toxins as is meat or fish in a similar condition, and this has led on various occasions to the improper condemnation of quite harmless varieties. It is also advisable to make sure that the fungi are not already tenanted by any of the various grubs which may infest them. These often seem to appreciate the fungi quite as well as does man, and when *he* comes second, the flavour may be the worse. Their presence, however, can be ascertained by first examining the top of the cap to see that there are no holes in it, and then by cutting cleanly across the stalk, near to the gills, when, if again no holes are found, it is clear that no grubs have penetrated into the cap from the ground. The stalk is usually rejected, being tougher, but can again be cut across, and used.

We must not metamorphose into a Cookery Book, having no space for the multifarious recipes which have been concocted for the preparation of fungi for the table. As with other foods, however, a good cook can serve up one of indifferent flavour as an appetising dish ; while, contrariwise, an excellent variety may be quite spoilt by unsuitable cooking. In concluding the con-sideration of the wild fungi as foods, it may be remarked that their greater use has been retarded, not only by the difficulty, to the layman, of identifying them, with the consequent danger of confusing edible and poisonous kinds, but also to the fact that the wild fungi are much more frequently grub and rabbit-eaten, and generally to the precarious and uncertain nature of the " crop."

CHAPTER X

The Cultivated Fungi, and other Fungus Foods of Commerce

" By tying a Cord to the hind-leg of a Pig, and driving him before them . . . observing where he stops and begins to root, . . . they are sure to find a Trufle."

1691, RAY, *Creation*, II. (1692), 99.

WHEN one considers the gastronomic excellence of many of the fungi, and the total disadvantages of utilising those occurring naturally, it is not surprising that early attempts should have been made to cultivate some of the more esculent kinds ; but of the many species available, few have passed into general cultivation. The most important of these is the Common Mushroom (*Psalliota campestris*), which is now grown to such a degree as to provide a livelihood for large numbers of people in many different countries.

Early Attempts at Cultivation. Many sporadic attempts have been made to cultivate other species, but, with one or two exceptions, the results obtained do not appear on the whole to have warranted the labour involved, and the ancients certainly went to considerable trouble for this end. The earliest endeavours appear to have had, for their purpose, an artificial reproduction of the natural conditions under which the particular fungus grows, in the hope that, on creating the former, the latter would make its appearance.

The Poplar Fungus. Thus, Dioscorides, in writing of the Poplar Fungus (? *Pholiota aegerita*), remarks : " Some people say that the bark of the white and black poplar cut into small pieces and scattered over dunged spaces will produce edible fungi at all seasons," [1] while in the *Geoponica,* an anonymous work on rural economy, possibly published about 900 A.D., it is recorded of the same species that " in order to make fungi grow one must saw off the stump of a black poplar and pour sour dough dissolved in water upon the cut pieces. Black-poplar fungi soon appear." [2] Even if success attended these experiments, it is not surprising that the methods have rather fallen into disuse, for *Pholiota aegerita* is not considered a delicacy by modern standards.

Cultural Methods Involving Burning. The preference for charred spots exhibited by some fungi is made use of in another method recommended in the *Geoponica.* " If you would have fungi to grow from the ground, you must select a spot of light soil on a hill where reeds grow ; there you must collect together twigs and other inflammable materials, and set all on fire just before rain is expected ; if rain does not come you must sprinkle the spot with pure water ; but the fungi thus produced are of inferior quality." [3] Presumably the vegetable was supposed to spring incontinently from the earth with the first shower, but the fungus cultivator of old was doubtless as used to disappointments as are our agriculturists of to-day.

Some modern methods involving a preliminary

---

[1] Dioscorides, *Mat. Med.* i., 109.

[2] *Geoponica,* xii., 31.

[3] *Loc. cit.,* xii., 36.

burning, by which it is attempted to stimulate the natural production of fungi, are of interest.   Thus in the Roman Campagna, a local delicacy, *Polyporus corylinus*, appears freely on charred stumps of hazel and cob-nut trees.   Its growth is therefore artificially accelerated by heating the stumps and logs of the trees over burning straw, and in this charred condition the stumps are sold in the markets.   By keeping them in a warm cellar, watering freely, and leaving for a time undisturbed, a plentiful crop, of excellent quality, is obtained.   In the same connection, a curious custom, which formerly for a considerable time had vogue in Germany, should be referred to.   It was long ago noticed by the peasants that morels often came up abundantly where woods had accidentally been burnt, whereupon, inspired by a motive similar to that which animated the Chinaman, after his first discovery of the virtues of roast pork,[1] they proceeded to stimulate the activities of Nature by firing the woods on purpose.   Although the extent to which this was practised leaves us in no doubt as to the success of the scheme, an unsympathetic Government later suppressed the practice by penal legislation.

Cultivation of the Common Mushroom.   Such empirical, casual and even reprehensible methods can, however, hardly be recommended, and those who would cultivate their own fungi will be well advised to limit their activities to the Common Mushroom (*Psalliota campestris*), for here they are on sure ground, and most other efforts pale into insignificance when compared with the enormous French production of this species at the present day.   The Common Mushroom has

---

[1] 1823, C. Lamb, *Essays of Elia :*   A Dissertation on Roast Pig.

been esteemed as an article of diet from very early times, but its cultivation from spawn probably did not take place before the beginning of the seventeenth century. The results of investigations appear to show that the art first arose in France, probably near Paris, the first scientific description of it being given by Tournefort in 1707.[1]

The French Industry.   At the present day, Paris is still the seat of one of the most extensive and intensive mushroom-growing industries in the world, and some account of it should be given.[2]   The industry is carried on in disused quarries and mines, from which stone was formerly extracted.   There are, in the Department of the Seine, about 3,000 of these excavations, of which those no longer used for their original purpose, and almost all of which are quite close to Paris (at Montrouge, Bagneux, Vaugirard, Châtillon, Ivry, Vitry, Houilles, and Saint-Denis) are occupied by the two hundred and fifty to three hundred mushroom growers of the Department.[3]   Some of these excavations are quarries, approached by adits on the ground level, but most of them are mines, with access by a vertical shaft, usually varying between one hundred and one hundred and thirty feet in depth.   The quarry entrances are often practicable for carts, when the transport question presents no difficulties.   The shafts of the mines are fitted with vertical ladders, with steps over eighteen inches apart, for the workmen ; new manure is

---

[1] Tournefort, *Mém. de l'Acad. Sci. de Paris*, 1707, pp. 58–66.

[2] Further details are given in Lachaume, *Le Champignon de Couche*, 6th ed., Paris, 1918 (Librairie Agricole de la Maison Rustique).

[3] These and other figures and prices refer, when not otherwise stated, to the year 1918.

simply thrown down, while spent manure, and mushrooms, are hauled up in baskets, by means of a hand-operated winch. The interiors of these excavations consist of a number of winding corridors, varying very much in size, particularly as to height, which generally ranges from about 2ft. 6in. to 6ft. 6in. One of the most spacious is at Méry, and has a total length of nearly two miles, with an average height of about thirteen feet. The principal entrance is at Méry, and there is another at Saint-Ouen-l'Aumone, near to the station to which manure is sent from Paris. It is quite often the case that manure has to be wheeled a distance of several hundred yards from the shaft, or entrance, and this becomes an irksome task when the roof is low, and the workman has to proceed in a bent position, or even on his knees, guided by a lamp fixed in the front of his barrow. To facilitate transport, a system of relays is used, long or short, according to the difficulties of the course.

Ventilation. In the quarries, with the entrance on the ground level, no special means of ventilation are usually necessary; but in the mines, the breathing of men, the burning of lamps, and the emanations from the beds, would soon render these untenable, were not some definite method of ventilation in force. For this purpose, shafts of small diameter are carried up to the ground level at intervals, according to the needs of each gallery, and a small conical wooden chimney is built over each, the top of this being closed by a sort of cowl, pointing towards the north. The top of this chimney should preferably be higher than the top of the main shaft. In many cases, the ventilation shafts are those left by the stone-miners, but occasionally additional shafts have been drilled. The excavations sometimes communicate with each other, when the ventilation problem becomes simplified, but too violent draughts may result, and doors have sometimes to be installed. This varying facility or difficulty of ventilation, conjoined with the extent, the height of the galleries, and so forth, causes a considerable difference in the annual rent, which may range from one hundred and fifty to six hundred francs.

Water Supply. Some of the excavations are more favoured than others, by a regular infiltration of water, which is collected in reservoirs constructed for the purpose. Where such natural supply is not forthcoming, and where, as is usually the case, the shaft is far from buildings or wells, large barrels on wheels, holding about 132 gallons, are used for the transport, and from these the water is run down a pipe, into small wheeled buckets or tubs below. The beds are generally supplied by an ordinary watering can, or sometimes by means of a wheeled tub, fitted with a fine "rose." The latter method is of course only suitable where the necessary roof height obtains. The whole business is thus of a somewhat laborious nature.

The Beds. As in this country, the beds are composed of stable manure, of which the kind and quality are of the first importance. The beds are smaller than is customary with us, while fresh spawn is constantly being brought in from outside, because the continual use of spawn taken from mushroom-bearing beds leads gradually to a diminution in the yield obtained. The spawn does not take the form of the compact " bricks " used in England, but of much smaller flakes of dry manure containing mycelium, and after " sowing," the surface of the bed is covered to a depth of about one inch with a layer of fine white stony soil. By keeping moist with water, mushrooms are obtained about six weeks after sowing, and the beds remain in bearing for a period of six to eight months, after which the spent material is returned to the surface for ordinary manurial purposes in agriculture. By sowing in rotation, a succession of crops is obtained. The mushrooms are not allowed to reach maturity, but are gathered in large button form. When fully expanded they are considered indigestible, and have no sale. The daily production of Paris, prior to the war, was about 25,000 kilos (about 24½ tons), worth about one franc the kilo., giving a value of 750,000 francs per month, or nine million francs per annum. Thus, not only could the needs of Paris herself be supplied, but enormous quantities were exported all over Europe.

It is to be regretted that this great industry has suffered considerably since the war. From recent information we gather that the chief causes for this would appear to be :

(1) Shortage of manure, owing to the increased use of automobiles and reduced employment of horses.

(2) Insect pests appear to be on the increase.

(3) Increased cost of labour.

(4) Mushrooms, which before the war were a common article of diet of the Parisians, have now reached such a price, 15–30 francs per kilo. (about 2¼ lb.), that they are now quite outside the reach of the middle classes, and the supply has automatically fallen off with the decreased demand.

Cultivation in England. By comparison with the scale on which the great French industry has been developed, our own efforts, and those of most other countries in this direction, are less important, this being due partly to a lack of those cultural and distributive advantages enjoyed by Paris. The French method of raising mushrooms underground has, however, been successfully introduced into this country, where in several places, disused quarry tunnels, railway tunnels, and the like, have been pressed into service. Of these, the most extensive are at Corsham, Wilts., where hundreds of pounds of mushrooms are produced daily in underground quarries, from which were formerly extracted large quantities of Bath-stone.

The Pockeridge quarries, now used by Messrs. Agaric, Ltd., for this purpose, are entered by an inclined shaft (Figs. 66 and 68), down the middle of which runs a tramway for drawing and lowering prepared manure, spent manure, mushrooms, sand, etc., a distance of about one hundred feet to and from the surface, for which purpose a steam engine is employed. From the bottom of the shaft to the actual beds (Fig. 67) is over three-quarters of a mile, the trucks being horse-drawn over this distance, and also on the surface. The area available for culture is about twenty-nine acres, capable, when fully developed, of yielding some 250,000 pounds of mushrooms per annum. Of this area, some thirteen acres are in cultivation, and from 3 to 4 cwt. is a quite usual day's picking.

Over forty tons of manure are used weekly in the making of fresh beds, and the total length of beds in various stages of cultivation is, roughly, five miles. A bed will remain in bearing for from one to four months, and by suitable rotation a more or less regular crop can be obtained throughout the year ; the spent manure being sent weekly to the fruit-growing districts of Evesham, Stratford-on-Avon, and elsewhere.

An extensive system of water-pipes has been laid down

Courtesy of The Bristol Times and Mirror

Fig. 66.—The Corsham Mushroom Industry: view of entrance to quarries, from about half-way down the shaft.

Courtesy of The Bristol Times and Mirror

Fig. 67.—The Corsham Mushroom Industry: some of the underground beds, showing pickers at work.

Courtesy of The Bristol Times and Mirror

Fig. 68.—The Corsham Mushroom Industry : part of the day's crop being hauled to the surface.

Courtesy of Lévy & Neurdein, Paris

Fig. 69.—Truffle hunting in Périgord.

to supply all the beds, while telephones communicate from the office on the surface to the various tables and packing stations below ground. Lighting is obtained by means of portable acetylene and other lamps. For the crushing of the Bath-stone for covering the beds, there is an installation consisting of oil engines, a stone crusher and a disintegrator. The mushrooms are picked every morning and sent off by passenger train almost immediately, so that they generally reach their destination the same day, being sent in the usual fruit baskets containing from four to seven pounds. A large part of the crop is sent to Covent Garden, but supplies are sent also to Southampton, Liverpool, Manchester, Scotland and elsewhere, several large shipping companies taking considerable quantities. A few miles away, at Bradford-on-Avon, the same company has similar underground beds, of about half the extent of those at Corsham. The disused underground quarries at Godstone, Surrey, are employed by another company in a similar manner; as also is a disused railway tunnel at Edinburgh.

The English method, while being somewhat similar as regards cultural details, differs in the fact that the beds are prepared either under glass or in the open, although sheds, etc., are often employed. One of the largest plants, where this system is in vogue, is that of Messrs. John F. Barter, Ltd., at Alperton, near Sudbury, Middlesex, to whom we are indebted for the subjoined account.

Site for Ridges. The ground on which ridges are to be made should have some shelter (e.g. hedgerows, buildings, etc.) from the north and east winds. On level ground the ridges should run north and south; if the ground is sloping, they should run with the slope, so that they do not interfere with the drainage. The materials used comprise horse manure, spawn of good quality, and good mould for covering the beds.

Preparation of Manure. The best manure is that from stables where plenty of straw is used, the longest litter being shaken out and dried, if possible, or thrown into a stack to dry off naturally, being then used for covering the beds. All litter less than about nine inches long should remain in the manure, which should contain about two-thirds of such litter. The manure is first made into a compact heap, in which it is allowed to remain for about four days, in order that it may heat up. It is then turned, and the outside material thrown towards the middle. This is done every other day, until it is " sweet," usually four turnings being necessary. It is then ready for making into beds.

Preparation of Beds. These consist of ridges of conical section, and are formed by a process of treading and beating the manure. The sizes of these beds vary according to the season, and are approximately of the following dimensions :

Ridges built.	Width.	Height.
In July, August, and up to the middle of September	2 ft. 6 in.	2 ft. 6 in.
From the middle of September to the end of January	3 ft.	3 ft.
In February and March ...	2 ft. 6 in.	2 ft. 6 in.
From the end of March to the beginning of July	None should be made outdoors during this interval.	

As soon as the ridge has been made, it is lightly covered with litter to prevent it from becoming sodden in wet or becoming dry in hot weather. Three days after the ridge has been built, the litter is removed, and holes nine inches apart are bored, with a one-inch iron bar, from the top of the ridge to within about nine inches of the bottom, in order to facilitate the cooling of the bed to the necessary temperature. After this operation, the litter is replaced, when, after a further period of some ten to twenty days, according to the outside temperature, the material will have become cool enough for spawning, a suitable heat being not more than 75 deg. F. at a depth of three inches below the surface, this being ascertained by the use of a plunger thermometer. The bricks of spawn are moistened, and then broken into from eight to twelve pieces, being inserted in the sides of the ridge about nine inches apart.

Casing. After the spawning, an interval of three or four days is allowed to elapse, even up to a fortnight being not too long in mild weather, to make sure that the heat of the ridge is not rising again ; after which the ridges are cased with a good loamy soil containing plenty of root and fibre, broken up fine with a fork, but not sifted. A spadeful of mould should cover about nine or ten inches square, but the thickness of the case is reduced towards the top of the ridge, to about 1½ inches *near* the top, and from half to one inch over the top. The mould is fixed in place by being lightly beaten with the spade as each spadeful is applied. The casing being finished, the litter is again put on, to a depth varying from six inches in mild weather to about fifteen when the weather is severe or very windy. Sticks are inserted down the centre of the ridge about ten yards apart, and these, if felt occasionally, will indicate the temperature of the bed. No notice is taken of a falling temperature, however low it may become, but any rise above 75 deg. Fahr. is controlled by the removal of a portion of the litter. The ridge is, however, not otherwise disturbed or examined for a month from the time of casing. At the end of that time, and on a fine day, the litter is removed and well shaken up, and froth or any other matter found on the surface of the bed, is rubbed off with a brush or a handful of straw, after which the bed is re-covered. This process will cause the spawn to " start," and it will show through most probably within a week or two. Crops are sometimes obtained in one month from the time of spawning. On the other hand, beds made up in November have been found to produce no mushrooms until the following April, when heavy crops were obtained. During the winter, when fallen snow might interfere with the gathering, mats or tarpaulins, which can be readily removed, are used to cover the beds.

Gathering. After the removal of a cluster of mushrooms, any uncovered mycelium is cut out with a knife and the hole is filled with fresh mould. All waste material, and all mushrooms which have withered away are removed, the paths and surroundings being kept clear of all mushroom débris. Gatherings should be made frequently, as mushrooms which are allowed to grow to a large size weaken the spawn and exhaust the bed. The produce is separated into two grades, one consisting of " buttons " and " cups " (i.e., closed mushrooms) ; the other of " broilers " or " flats," of which the former are worth about one-third more than the others. Unless the stalks are cut off at the time of gathering, the mush-rooms are placed in the baskets with the stems downwards, so that grit shall not enter the gills. Any dirt on the caps is removed with a piece of flannel. Care is taken to avoid touching the tender gills, on which the least pressure causes discoloration.

Growing under Glass, or in Cellars or Sheds. In these cases, much smaller beds are used than in the open. The sizes are approximately as follows :—

Beds made.	In sheds.	In vineries and cellars.
In July and August ... ... Later in the year	6 in. deep 15 in. deep	6 in. deep 9 in. deep (or with a cold cellar 15 in. deep).

The winter temperature in a shed being much lower than that of a vinery or the usual cellar, a greater depth is necessary. The beds require a covering of two or three inches of litter in a mild temperature, and of one foot to one foot three inches in a cold one. No water need be given during the first month. After that, if the soil be getting dry, water is given in very small quantities by means of a fine " rose." The temperature of houses heated artificially should be from 55 to 60 deg. Fahr.

The Cultivation of Morels. Morels (Figs. 64 and 85) are cultivated to some small extent in France on similar lines to those obtaining with the Common Mushroom, a bed being prepared in a cellar, precisely as for the latter, under the usual conditions of darkness and dampness, and with the requisite drainage. This is sown with morels cut up into small pieces, by which it is said that production can be obtained through the spring and early summer, thus ensuring a rich harvest for the grower possessed of the necessary skill. It would appear, however, that the morel presents greater difficulties than does the Common Mushroom.

Italian Cultivated Fungi.   Various fungi have been cultivated on a small scale, and the Neapolitans raise the small and delicate *Clitocybe catinus* from old coffee-grounds, which are simply kept undisturbed for a period of several months in a warm place, and watered from time to time, when the fungus makes its appearance.   In the same country is found the *Pietra fungaja*, or Fungus stone, which is simply the sclerotium of a fungus, *Polyporus tuberaster*, permeating lumps of volcanic tufa, which it has the power of compacting into a hard and almost stony form.   These " stones " are put in a warm place and kept well-watered, when in due course a crop is obtained. On occasions, the Fungus stone has been exported to this country and propagated in the same manner, with quite successful results.   This, perhaps, can hardly be described as " cultivation."

Cultivation of *Boletus edulis*.   Among other fungi, the cultivation of which has been attempted, is *Boletus edulis* (Fig. 82), where the method adopted has been to select a situation resembling its natural surroundings, and to water this freely with an infusion of the fungus. Results, however, have not been very successful.   Hay suggests that " the fecundity of spores depends on the presence also of the mycelium," [1] which is rather begging the question.

The Shii-take Industry of Japan.   No chapter on the cultivation of fungi would be complete without some account of the Japanese " Shii-take " industry, not only because of its magnitude, but also because of the remarkable cultural methods employed.   Of the large number of Japanese fungi of economic importance, most of which have previously been dealt with, the " shii-take " is that

---

[1] 1887, W. D. Hay, *Text Book of British Fungi*, p. 193.

cultivated on much the largest scale, although the total
crop of this is less than in the case of another species,
" matsu-take," which, however, is not cultivated, but
only gathered wild. The "shii-take" (*Armillaria Shii-
take*) is readily dried and preserved, in which process
there is developed and retained a very fine aroma, this
rendering it a delicate ingredient in the making of
savoury soups. In the dried state it has the advantage
of keeping for a long time, and large quantities are
annually exported in this condition, chiefly to Hong-
Kong, China and Hawaii, but also to the Straits Settlements, India, Indo-China, the Philippines, and even to
Canada and the United States. The following figures
refer to the Japanese production and export of " shii-take"
only :—

Year.	Total Crop.			
	Weight.		Value.	
	Kin.	Tons.	Yen.	£
1907	1,855,700	1094½	1,033,500	106,000
1912	—	—	—	—

Year.	Quantity Exported.			
	Weight.		Value.	
	Kin.	Tons.	Yen.	£
1907	1,626,700	960½	1,067,000	109,436
1912	1,683,834	994	1,236,237	126,794

It will be noted that the value of the exported product for the year 1907 is nominally greater than that of the total crop for the same year. It is obvious that the latter figures are more or less nominal, the value of the total production being probably obtained by multiplying the weight by the local price per kin. Naturally, if a large proportion of this is dried and exported, its value may be considerably enhanced, with the result in question. It must further be remembered that in the case of such a crop, part of which is of natural occurrence, large quantities must be gathered and consumed without appearing in such official figures as we have quoted.

This mushroom derives its name from the "Shii" tree (*Quercus cuspidata*), an evergreen oak of Central and Southern Japan on which it most frequently occurs; but in the artificial production, not only the "shii," but various oaks, and other trees, are employed. Among these are the "kunugi" (*Q. serrata*), the "konara" (*Q. glandulifera*), the "kashi" (*Q. acuta*) and the "kashiwa" (*Q. dentata*); while the "soro" (*Carpinus yedoensis*) is also very largely used.

In cultivation, logs of any of these trees are cut and soaked in water for some days, being afterwards pounded to soften the bark. Holes a few inches deep are then made, at short distances apart, in the outside; and "spawn," prepared by breaking up pieces of trees infected by the mycelium of the fungus, is placed therein, the logs being then left in a shaded part of the forest. The first mushrooms are produced in about two years, being usually very large and of an "umbrella" shape. According to Porter, they are "greatly superior in flavour to those of any other country." [1] They can be grown in rotation during most of the year, and are named differently, according to the season, " haruko," " natsuko " and " akiko," being respectively spring, summer and autumn mushroom. This method of cultivation is centuries old, and large tracts of forest are thus prepared. The profits are very large, and part of the revenue of the state forests is obtained in this manner. The districts where the industry is chiefly carried on are those of Hyuga and Bungo in Kyushu ; and of Kii, Ise and Suruga in Honshu. It is obvious that such destructive methods of cultivation must be accompanied by corresponding reafforestation, and this is obtained naturally, by permitting the growth of sprouts from the stumps of the trees already felled. These sprouts reach a size suitable for " shii-take " culture in from 18 to 25 years, and by an annual rotation of felling, a new tract of forest arrives at maturity every year.

The Japanese Pine Mushroom. The " matsu-take " or pine mushroom (*Armillaria edodes*) is a much-esteemed delicacy which is consumed in large quantities. It is found throughout Japan, that of Kyoto being considered the best. The following quaint account of it is contained in the official pamphlet already referred to : [2]

"This mushroom springs up in the forests of *Pinus densiflora* grown in the granite soil of the tertiary formation. The place best suited for the purpose is the shallow soil where weeds do not grow much. In such places it naturally grows in abundance. The output of the mushroom during the year 1907 was over

---

[1] 1915, Porter, *Japan, The New World Power*, p. 285.

[2] 1910, *Forestry of Japan*, Bureau of Forestry ; Dept. of Agriculture and Commerce, Tokyo, Japan, pp. 70–72.

3,079,700 kin [about 1819 tons] valued at 503,600 yen [£51,651]. This mushroom has the highest flavour of all kinds, and people of all classes have it at dinner.   The quality, however, is very fragile, and is impossible to keep it dried for a long time, without losing its flavour, as ' Shii-take.'   Therefore, we can taste its nice flavour for only one month in the Autumn which is the season of its growth.   In recent years, people have begun to preserve it in tin cans, and export it to foreign countries.   The most famous ' Matsu-take ' producing places are the forests belonging to Osaka Major Forest Office and Hiroshima Major Forest Office, and in certain Minor Forest Offices a greater income is obtained from the proceeds of this mushroom.   The gathering of this mushroom is very simple and done by women and children, and increasing demand of labour for gathering of mushrooms naturally causes the raising of the wages of poorer classes in those districts conferring on them no small benefits." [1]

This mushroom is eaten either roasted or boiled, and is also preserved by being salted or simply dried, when, however, as we have already seen, it tends to lose flavour and become insipid.   Whether the same thing occurs when it is exported in " tin cans," we are unable to say.

The Chinese Cultivation of the Jew's Ear.   A somewhat similar method to that of Shii-take culture is employed by the Chinese for the production of a fungus generally described as " The Jew's Ear," although, as already mentioned, it is not *Hirneola Auricula Judae* (Fig. 8), but *H. polytricha* (Fig. 52).   This fungus, the Chinese name for which is *Mu Erh*, is an export of Manchuria, and since it is also largely cultivated in provinces as distant from Manchuria as are Shen-si and Kwang-si, it is probably fairly widely spread through China.   From Shen-si, where it is grown extensively in copses of small oaks (*Quercus variabilis*), on the southern slopes of the Tsinling Mountains, it is shipped by river to Hankow for distribution.   It grows naturally on

---

[1] *Loc. cit.*

decaying oak-stumps and requires a damp atmosphere, with sufficient heat in summer, a long period of rain being particularly favourable for its development. In appearance it resembles an ear, is of a gelatinous nature, and is greatly esteemed as a delicacy, being indeed indispensable at all Chinese feasts. It is well known that the Chinese taste differs markedly from that of the Western nations, and it is therefore not surprising to read that an English traveller " did not find them very palatable, and the experiment resulted in a bad stomach-ache." [1]

In the artificial production, oak copses growing on granite hills are employed, and small sapling oaks, about 6 in. in diameter, are cut down, and the branches removed, leaving the bark entire ; after which the trunks are cut into poles 8 to 10 feet long. These are allowed to lie on the ground for several months, when they become infected by the mycelium of the fungus, and are finally stacked slantingly in scores or so. In the following year, the brown fungus appears on the dead poles, being collected as it grows.

Truffles. We may next consider the truffles, which act as a sort of link between the cultivated and the wild fungus foods, for they served the Greeks and Romans in the second capacity ; while their production has created an enormous industry of to-day. They are certainly " cultivated " to some extent nowadays, but most of their interest concerns, not their cultivation, but their " hunting," which naturally presupposes that they are wild. They were, indeed, among the most famous of the fungus foods of commerce, long before attempts to cultivate them had met with any success, and they are

---

[1] 1913, E. H. Wilson, *A Naturalist in Western China*, vol. i, p. 38.

still very largely collected in a wild state.   This industry
is chiefly carried on in Southern France, over which
truffles are very widely spread, some notable centres of
this trade being the towns of Périgueux, Apt and
Toulouse, in the Departments of the Dordogne, Vaucluse
and Haute Garonne respectively, while the most
celebrated French truffle is that of Périgord, *Tuber
melanospermum*.   These are generally found on a light
and porous soil of clay-marl, resting on limestone, and
at the edges and open spots in woods, while the ground
must be free from undergrowth.   The trees with which
they are generally associated are oaks (*Quercus coccifera,
Q. ilex, Q. robur* and *Q. sessiliflora*), but they are often
found under beech and hazel-nut trees, occurring as
curious clusters, at a depth of generally from two to eight
inches, by the roots of these trees ; this having given rise
to the conjecture that there is some connection between
the two, and that in their early stages the tubers obtain
some nourishment from the roots.

Truffle-hunting.   Owing to the subterranean habits
of these delicacies, the ordinary methods of search are
useless, but their characteristic scent enables them to be
discovered by either dogs, or pigs (Fig. 69), which have
been trained for the work.   In regard to this, Krombholz
says : " You must have a sow of five months old, a good
walker ! with her mouth shut up by a leathern strap ;
recompense her for the Truffles with acorns ; but as
they (pigs) are not easily led, are stubborn and go astray
and dig after a thousand other things, there is little to
be done with them . . . dogs are better, of them,
select a small poodle."   The pig is considered to have
the keener scent of the two, for the truffle, but is less
easy to convince, at the psychological moment, that the

find is not really for him (or rather her). Ramsbottom [1] says that pigs, or, more generally, sows, which are more docile and also better " hunters," are employed where truffles are common, and dogs where they are more scarce, presumably because, when the crop is plentiful, it is not quite such a serious matter if the sow succeeds occasionally in maintaining her rights. Also, a sow tires far more readily, for which reason it is always taken to the hunting-grounds in a cart. At any rate, both animals are commonly used. While the taste of the pig for truffles is a natural one, that of the dog is acquired, to which end its whole training is devoted. Thus, while still a puppy, finely-chopped truffle is mixed with its food, so that it always associates truffles with dinner. Later on, having been kept short of food for a day or so, it is taken out into the woods to endeavour to locate the spot where its master has previously hidden a plateful of chopped truffle and earth, first under some dried leaves ; then beneath a light sprinkling of soil ; and finally buried two or three inches deep ; the reward for finding it being a small piece of meat, or of bread and cheese. When it has become sufficiently skilled at the artificial quarry, it is used to seek out the natural one, which, having been located by the eager scratching of the dog, is dug up by means of a small fork by the *rabassier* (from *rabasso*, the Provençal word for " truffle ") ; while the dog is similarly rewarded for each find.

The Truffle Fly. In another method also used, the aid of the diminutive truffle-fly is invoked. This is *Anisotoma cinnamomea*, the larvæ of which live in the

---

[1] 1923, Ramsbottom, *Handbook of the Larger British Fungi*, p. 200.

truffle ; while the mature flies seem to regale themselves with the scent of their erstwhile home, above which they hover in clouds. By looking horizontally along the surface of the ground, usually in the evening, these clouds of minute flies are observed by the peasants, who then seek the confirmatory evidence of the fissured ground and the truffle scent, thus finding the delicacy.

Truffle Cultivation. The French truffle industry has attained large proportions and, according to Hay,[1] the annual yield of the Department of Vaucluse alone exceeds 60,000 lb. The economic importance of the truffle has naturally led to attempts at cultivation, which at first seem to have had but indifferent success. These methods perhaps can scarcely be considered as a true cultivation, but rather the stimulating to a more intensive production of the natural grounds. In a method used in Poitou, a situation on the chalk downs is selected and enclosed, being then sown with acorns. After some years' growth of the sapling oaks, truffles appear among their roots, and may be gathered for many years. It is believed by some, however, that this plan is not successful except on soil where truffles have occurred before. A second method, which has a little more claim to the title of " cultivation," is also employed. Here again a situation resembling that of the natural habitat is chosen, and " the ground is cleared, the trees are thinned, and trenches are dug. Truffles are now brought from their native site, inclosed in the earth in which they grew, and are planted in the trenches. In time they propagate, and it is said that grounds have been successfully fertilised in this way." [2] At the present day, oak plantations are

---

[1] 1887, W. D. Hay, *Text Book of British Fungi*, p. 191.
[2] Hay, *loc. cit.*

planted on a large scale in Southern France, expressly for the production of truffles.

In addition to *Tuber melanospermum*, the cultivation of which we have described above, and which does not occur in Britain, the French use also *T. aestivum*, but on a smaller scale, as it is not esteemed so highly. Ramsbottom says that this truffle probably " came into use in the courts of France and Italy some time prior to the fourteenth century. *T. melanospermum* seems to have made its appearance into Parisian cookery towards the close of the fifteenth century." [1]

We have lately received from Bergerac in Périgord, a price-list, for 1923–24, of various delicacies ("conserves de luxe exclusivement "), of which truffles are the basis, and from this we venture to extract some evidence bearing upon the present export trade in French truffles, and their products.   It had already been translated into " English," and we give it " as wrote."

> " On account of the high price of life now, The fashion is spreading more and more in France of sending at Christmas an New Year, usefull as well as agréeable presents especially foies-gras truffés pies, I offer this year to my foreigner customers the parcel ' Gift ' composed of all series of my Pâtés de foies gras truffés.
>
> " Those pies are offered in dainty pasteboard contained itself in a most artistical box.
>
> " Parcel ' Gift ' free of expense and packing.   Frs : 140.
>
> " To persons ignoring my firm, I send as the preceding years two parcels of samples by choice free of expense and packing against international money order or check of :
>
> " Frs. 36 for parcel   ...   .   No. 1.
> " Frs. 100 for parcel   ...   .   No. 2."

From detailed lists of the contents of each parcel, we note that No. 2 includes also a box of *cèpes extra au naturel*, being *Boletus edulis* (Fig. 82).   In Italy, a country

---

[1] 1923, Ramsbottom, *A Handbook of the Larger British Fungi*, p. 199.

with climatic advantages similar to those of France, the truffle industry has also attained large proportions.

The Summer Truffle. The best of the British species is *Tuber aestivum*, our Summer Truffle, which resembles a small dark-brown or almost black apple, one to three inches in diameter, having a warty surface, at times veined with white. It is found chiefly in beechwoods from June to October. In former days a considerable trade existed with this truffle " in Sussex and Wiltshire, the dogs employed being mongrel terriers. *T. aestivum* was sold usually at two and three shillings a pound. There is still a small amount of hunting done, but the trade is said to have been ruined by the taxation of dogs. It is more likely, however, that the preference for the Périgord truffle, and its greater abundance have ousted the summer truffle from the markets." [1] In this connection, it is stated in *The Times* for Feb. 14, 1859, referring to poor labourers in Wiltshire, that " many of these people . . . live by truffling and poaching, in the absence of farmer's employment," [2] and it is interesting to note that a few of the old truffle hunters are still to be found in Sussex. Besides the true truffles, other fungi, which somewhat resemble them, are known by the same popular name, and are also edible. Thus *Melanogaster variegatus*, the " Red Truffle," was formerly sold in the markets of Bath. There is also the " False Truffle " or Earth Ball, (*Scleroderma vulgare*) shown in Fig. 39, and in which a large trade is done. It is used as a substitute for the real article in various dishes, being collected in Epping Forest by gentlemen

---

[1] Ramsbottom, *loc. cit.*, p. 200.
[2] 1859, *The Times*, Feb. 14, p. 5, col. 5.

from Soho ; but, as with the Red Truffle, is of very
inferior flavour in comparison with the true truffles.

The Food Value of Fungi. In any consideration
of the fungi as foods, it is desirable to include some
account of their real food value. This has unquestionably
been somewhat overrated by certain writers, who,
probably because the flavours of many fungi resemble
those of meat, have suggested that they may rank as
substitutes for flesh foods. This is hardly correct.
Langworthy [1] lays stress on the fact that mushrooms
and other edible fungi contain " a very high percentage
of water—over 90 per cent. on an average. The 10
per cent. or so of nutritive material they contain, is
largely carbohydrates, though a little nitrogenous
material is also present. Fat is almost utterly lacking.
So it is obvious that the mushroom more nearly resembles
in composition such vegetables as a carrot or turnip
than it does meat. Mushrooms and some other edible
fungi have flavours which to many palates suggest meat,
oysters and some other animal foods. From the standpoint of flavour and palatability they are worth including
in the diet if they are relished, and alone or combined
with other materials they can be served in dishes which
suggest meat dishes in flavour and which satisfy the
palate, while the nutritive value of the meal or day's
ration can be made up to the desired standard by the
other dishes served at the meal with the mushrooms." [2]
The same view is expressed by Setchell, who remarks

---

[1] Expert in Charge of Nutrition Investigations Office of Experiment
Stations of U.S. Dept. of Agriculture.

[2] 1910, *Yearbook of the U.S. Dept. of Agriculture*, " Cheese and other
substitutes for meat in the diet," pp. 359–370 : " Mushrooms and other
edible fungi," p. 365.

" As regards nutritive value, it may be said that even
the most nutritious toadstools are of little value [as foods],
but are valuable as accessories or condiments with, not
in any wise as substitutes for, the meat or vegetables
ordinarily consumed." [1]

In any comparison, however, it is necessary to
remember that different meats also contain from about
40 to 72 per cent. of water, the latter figure applying in
the case of lean beef or mutton ; while, if one neglects
the water content in each case, and calculates only on
the dry residue, the nitrogen contained in many fungi
does not compare very unfavourably with that of meat,
which again varies in different kinds. Thus lean beef
(dry) would contain about 10·6 per cent. of nitrogen,
carrots (dry) about 1·2 per cent., and turnips (dry) about
2·1 per cent., as compared with the following figures,
quoted by Schlossberger and Döpping, for various
mushrooms (dried) :

	Nitrogen per cent.
Cantharellus cibarius	3·22
Lactarius deliciosus	4·68
Psalliota arvensis	7·26

As regards the nitrogenous portion of one's dietary,
there is thus a fairly good case for the fungi, which are
at any rate decidedly superior to either carrots or turnips.
A complicating factor is, naturally, how much of this
nitrogen is assimilable ; but this point, in view of the
scarcity of data, cannot be discussed with advantage.
Again, mushrooms are not consumed in a dry state, but
usually by cooking them directly after gathering. In
this process, however, particularly if they are fried, a

---

[1] 1913, W. A. Setchell, *California State Circular No.* 84, p. 4.

large quantity of the water is expelled, as is evidenced by by the great contraction in bulk.

The question of the fat content of fungi cannot be dismissed quite as briefly as it is by Langworthy. Thus an analysis [1] of the dried form of "shii-take," as exported, shows that it contains about 12 per cent. of albumen, 1½ per cent. of fat, nearly 70 per cent. of cellulose and other nitrogenous constituents, 4 per cent. of ash and about 12 per cent. of water. It may therefore be considered that fungi have some food value, and serve in some measure to make up the necessary amount of varied food required by the individual, but they should not be regarded either as a substitute for meat, or as a staple food, but chiefly as an agreeable addition to the dietary on the ground of flavour and palatability.

Cultivation of Fungi by Ants. It may possibly be a matter of surprise that fungus culture is not confined to man alone ; but it is deliberately practised for food purposes by the termites and leaf-cutting ants of Ceylon, Madagascar, Brazil, and other tropical and sub-tropical countries. Although this method of obtaining food has been adopted by a number of different species in widely-separated regions, the general mode of cultivation followed by them appears in all cases to be substantially the same.

In their nests, the ants allocate special chambers for this work, and in these they build up spongy masses of masticated and pounded leaf-fragments and other plant remains, which quickly become permeated with mycelial threads. This mycelium, under the methodical culti-

---

[1] Given in the catalogue of the Japanese section of the International Health Exhibition, held in London, in 1884.

vation which ensues, produces small tufts of hyphae, which have been termed " kohl-rabi clumps," and these are cut and eaten by the ants, being apparently their chief, if not their only food. These fungus gardens are systematically tended by the workers, and not only are foreign organisms weeded out, but the fungus plants are pruned to keep them both in bearing and within reasonable proportions. If the ants are removed, the fungus ceases to produce the " kohl-rabi clumps," and throws up reproductive structures, which usually burst through the top of the nest.

That the whole proceeding is as well-ordered and intensive as our own mushroom culture, is shown by the fact that each species of ant always cultivates the same variety of fungus, which, moreover, is the only species found in the nest, and which is never found growing away from it. Most of the fungi so cultivated are agarics.

CHAPTER XI

The Poisonous Fungi

" Galen affirmes, that they are all very cold and moist, and therefore to approach unto a venomous and murthering facultie, and ingender a clammy, pituitous, and cold nutriment if they be eaten. To conclude, few of them are good to be eaten, and most of them do suffocate and strangle the eater."
—1597, GERARD, *Herbal*, 2nd ed. (reprinted 1636), III., ch. 167, p. 1584.

" De nombreux décès causés par l'absorbtion de champignons vénéneux nous ont déjà été annoncés des départements du Midi, de l'Est, et même des environs de Paris. Chaque année, en octobre et novembre, une centaine d'habitants des campagnes meurent ainsi intoxiqués par les poisons extraordinairement violents et subtils que renferment surtout certains agarics du genre amanite . . . Que faire pour prévenir ces tristes accidents qui, chaque année, se renouvellent avec la régularité d'un tribut payé par nos populations à quelque moderne Locuste ? "
Le Petit Journal.

IT is common knowledge that many of the fungi are extremely poisonous, and this aspect, more than any other, has firmly impressed itself upon the public mind. Indeed, so strong is popular prejudice on the point, that it has invested with the most deadly attributes, a great number of perfectly innocuous species. Yet, on the other hand, many folk, while pronouncing anathema upon unmistakeable species of great esculence, are often only too willing to risk their lives by experimenting with anything that " looks like " a mushroom. When, therefore, the layman proposes to indulge in a pleasant repast which includes fungi, the question, whether it is quite safe, or whether it may be followed with undesirable, or even fatal, consequences, depends frequently upon the insecure foundations of the ludicrously ineffective " rules " already detailed ; and as these are usually only sketchily applied, it is not surprising that the historians of all times, and in all countries, have had to record numbers of distressing fatalities from this cause. Among the great ones of the earth, whose lives have been so sacrificed, are Pope Clement VII, the Emperor Jovian, Charles VI of France, Berronill of Naples, and the widow of Tsar Alexis; while those of less exalted rank who have paid the same dread penalty are legion. It therefore behoves us to examine a little more closely these unconscious assassins, and the lethal weapons which they unwittingly employ.

Early Classical Cases of Fungus Poisoning. The earliest records of poisoning by fungi are those of the Greeks, and date back some centuries before the Christian Era. Thus, according to Eparchides,[1] when Euripides (480–406 B.C.) was on a visit to Icarus, a woman with her daughter and two full-grown sons perished in one day through eating poisonous fungi ; while, about the same time, Hippocrates,[2] the father of medicine, who was born about 460 B.C., instances the poisoning of the daughter of Pausanias by a raw fungus, a case which, fortunately, did not terminate fatally. In the second century B.C., experience of these accidents had become more extensive, and definite if somewhat empiric remedies came into vogue.

---

[1] One of the earlier writers quoted by Athenaeus in his *Deipnosophistæ*, II., 57.

[2] Hippocrates, *Epidemicorum*, lib. VII., § 102.

Primitive Remedies. It was about this time that Nicander of Colophon, the celebrated Greek poet, physician and grammarian, described his universal prescription for fungus poisoning in the following terms :

"Let not the evil ferment of the earth which often causes swellings in the belly or strictures in the throat distress a man ; for when it has grown up under the viper's deep hollow track, it gives forth the poison and hard breathing of its mouth ; an evil ferment is that ; men generally call the ferment by the name of *fungus*, but different kinds are distinguished by different names ; but do thou take the many-coated heads of the cabbage, or cut round the twisting stems of the rue, or take the efflorescence which has accumulated on old corroded copper, or steep the ashes of clematis in vinegar, then bruise the roots of pyrethrum, adding a sprinkling of lye or soda, and the leaf of cress which grows in gardens, with the medic plant and pungent mustard, and burn wine-lees or the dung of the domestic fowl into ashes ; then, putting your right finger in your throat to make you sick, vomit forth the baneful pest." [1]

It is not recorded what success usually attended this treatment, but the remedy would appear to be almost as bad as the complaint.

Supposed Origins of the Poisons in Fungi. Later classical writers attempted to explain how the poisonous principles of fungi originated. Pliny (23–79 A.D.), whose opinions are obviously influenced by those of Nicander, says " noxious kinds must be entirely condemned ; for if there be near them a hob-nail (*caligaris clavus*) or a bit of rusty iron, or a piece of rotten cloth, forthwith the plant, as it grows, elaborates the foreign juice and flavour into poison ; who could discern the different kinds, except country-folk and those who gather them ? Moreover they imbibe other noxious qualities besides ; if, for instance, the hole of a venomous serpent be near,

---

[1] Nicander, *Alexipharmaca*, 521–536.

and the serpent breathe upon them as they open, from their natural affinity with poisonous substances, they are readily disposed to imbibe such poison. Therefore," he naïvely counsels, " it will be well to exercise care in gathering them until the serpents retire into their holes." [1] A little later, Dioscorides, the renowned Greek physician, records that " fungi have a two-fold difference, for they are either good for food or poisonous ; their poisonous nature depends on various causes, for such fungi grow either amongst rusty nails or rotten rags, or near serpents' holes, or on trees producing noxious fruits." [2] According to the same writer, even the good kinds " if partaken of too freely, are injurious, being indigestible, causing stricture and cholera," and he recommended the taking of an emetic after every meal in which fungi figured. [3] Dioscorides thus appears to have had grave doubts as to the wholesomeness of the fungi, and he cites as a common remedy, when poisonous fungi had been eaten, a dose of nitre exhibited in vinegar and water. [4]

Distrust of the Fungi. Other writers, as well they might from the numerous fatalities that occurred, shared the doubts of Dioscorides. In this connection, the opinions of Seneca, Galen and others, have already been cited in the previous section, dealing with the fungi as foods, from which aspect the consideration of the poisonous fungi is, of course, inseparable. We may also refer to an Epigram written by Martial (43–104 A.D.) upon the death of Macrinus, who died from eating

---

[1] Pliny, *Nat. Hist.*, XXII., 47.
[2] Dioscorides, *Mat. Med.*, IV., 83.
[3] Dioscorides, *Mat. Med.*, IV., 83.
[4] *Loc. cit.*, V., 130.

poisonous fungi, in which Epigram, to point the moral, the poet makes two punning allusions to the fungi : " *Defungi fungis* homines, Macrine, negabas ; *Boleti leti* causa fueri tui." [1]

> "You used to deny, Macrinus, that men could be killed by fungi ; yet Boleti destroyed yourself."

Survival of Classical Beliefs. The ingenious hypotheses advanced by the classical writers as to the origins of the fungus poisons, as with those involved in their general practice of medicine, appear to have held ground for centuries, and even at so late a period as the year 1560, Matthiolus [2] includes two serpents in his general illustration of fungi, which we reproduce in Fig. 70.

Real Origin of the Fungus Poisons. Modern research has, however, revealed the fact that the poisonous substances contained in certain fungi are, as in the case of other poisonous plants, not absorbed from without, but manufactured and liberated in the tissues of the fungus, during the normal process of metabolism. They consist of various alkaloids, glucosides, toxalbumins, etc., and are probably waste products somewhat akin to those produced in, and excreted from, the human body. It *has* been suggested that they serve in some measure as a protection against marauders, but this would appear to be fortuitous ; since they are harmless to the slug, one of the chief ravagers of fungi. Moreover, this hypothesis does not explain why certain fungi should require this protection, while other closely-allied species do not.

The Toxicology of the Fungi has not been

---

[1] Martial, ed. Delphin : Vol. II., p. 1074.
[2] Matthiolus, *Commentarii in libros sex Pedacii Dioscoridis Anazarbei de medica materia.*

230 ROMANCE OF THE FUNGUS WORLD

investigated, either from the chemical or the medical
standpoints, to the extent which the importance of the
subject warrants; but from the work which has been
done, it is evident that not only do the compositions of
these toxins often vary in the different genera, but
even in allied species of the same genus. Again, most
genera containing poisonous species include also harmless
ones. The matter is further complicated by the fact
that individual fungi sometimes contain two separate
poisons : some even more. Thus, in the present state
of our knowledge, the whole subject is exceedingly
baffling.

Classification of Fungus Poisons. This seeming
chaos has been reduced to some state of order by Roch,
a leading Swiss toxicologist, who has classified those fungi
containing specific poisons, according to the effect which
they have upon the human system, and since this aspect
is the most vital one, we have used his scheme in tabulating
our remarks on the individual species. The main groups
into which poisonous fungi, according to their toxic
effects, may be divided, are as follows :

(1) *Fungi containing poisons which, after a long period
of incubation, cause the degeneration of the cells of
the organism, particularly those of the nervous
system and the glandular parenchymatous tissues
(the liver, etc.).*

The three most poisonous fungi known are of this
type. They are characterized by toxins of a very
virulent description, rendered more deadly by their
delayed action on the human system. This delay allows
them to become completely absorbed into the blood
before the obnoxious qualities of the fungus are realized,
and remedial measures can be taken.

Fig. 70.—An early woodcut from Matthiolus (1560), illustrating the association of poisonous fungi with serpents.

Photo by A. E. Peck, Scarborough

Fig. 71.—*Entoloma lividum.* This species grows in pastures and has often been gathered with, or mistaken for, " mushrooms,"—with unfortunate results.

Photo by A. E. Peck, Scarborough

Fig. 73.—*Stropharia aeruginosa*, a suspicious species, with verdigris-coloured cap.

Photo by A. E. Peck, Scarborough

Fig. 72.—*Amanita phalloides*, the most deadly fungus known. It has been responsible for most of the fatalities from fungus poisoning.

The most lethal of these three species is *Amanita phalloides* (Figs. 25 and 72), a fungus whose harmless appearance and not unpleasant taste and smell have, in spite of the fact that the two have little in common, repeatedly led careless collectors to mistake it for the Common Mushroom. Such unhappy folk have cause, if only for a short time, to regret the error, for this fungus is capable of causing an enormous amount of suffering. After a meal in which it plays a prominent part, the unwary eater experiences little or no discomfort for some ten hours. Then he is seized with sudden abdominal cramp-like pains, accompanied by nausea, vomiting, extreme thirst and cholera-like diarrhœa, which includes the passing of blood and mucus. These and other more distressing symptoms may abate and recur for many hours, during which there is a gradual but serious loss of weight, and considerable exhaustion. The symptoms may then slowly pass away and a tardy recovery is followed by a very protracted period of convalescence. In most cases, however, the symptoms continue with greater or less intensity, and on the third to the eighth day the unhappy sufferer is released from his agony by coma and death.

The actual poison (*Amanita-toxin*) which is responsible for the calamity is an alcohol-soluble substance whose exact composition has not been ascertained, and to which no antidote is known. Another poison (*Amanita-haemolysin*), a glucoside present in the raw plant, is capable, when injected hypodermically, of destroying the red corpuscules of the blood; but, since it is decomposed by a heat less than that necessary for cooking, and also, usually, by the gastric juices, it apparently plays no part in the actual poisoning.

The two other species in this group are *Amanita*

virosa and *A. verna.* These closely resemble *A. phalloides* in appearance and probably are equally deadly in effect. This inglorious trio is responsible for *fully* ninety per cent. of the deaths from fungus poisoning.

(2) *Fungi containing poisons which, while often capable of causing serious gastric disturbances, act chiefly by exciting and then paralysing the central nervous system.*

The poisonous principles of these fungi belong to that class of toxins known as *deliriants,* which, acting on the nerve centres, produce dilation of the pupils of the eyes, spectral illusions, incoordination and delirium, and occasionally, though rarely, tetanoid spasms and paralysis. These symptoms are frequently accompanied by such gastric symptoms as vomiting, excessive thirst, etc. The most notorious member of this group, and one which almost advertises its baneful properties, is the beautiful Fly Agaric (*Amanita muscaria*), shown in Fig. 15. The bright scarlet or orange-red cap of this species, studded with white warts, should prevent anyone, however careless, from mistaking it for a mushroom ; but if this were not sufficient, its bitter acrid taste ought to discourage the most venturesome. Nevertheless, it has frequently been eaten, more especially in those countries where the allied *Amanita Caesarea* occurs, and for which species it has often been mistaken. Although its after-effects are neither so painful nor so dangerous as those of the preceding group, *yet* many deaths have resulted from it.

The poisonous principles of this species, and, therefore, their effect on the human system, appear, however, to vary in different countries, for among many of the native tribes of north-eastern Siberia and Kamchatka, it has long been employed as a stimulant, the effect being similar to that of hashish. This use has been observed by a number of travellers in these regions, notably Krasheninnikoff (1733–1744), Langsdorf (1803–1806), and Kennan (1865–67) ; and in more recent times by Lansdell (1882) and Vanderlip (1903). The effects of the fungus are so remarkable that, rather than appear to exaggerate, we will leave these writers to tell their own tales, in the course of which the reader may trace the inspiration of " The Purple Pileus " of H. G. Wells. According to Langsdorf, as translated by Greville,

"this variety of *Amanita muscaria* is used by the inhabitants of the north-eastern parts of Asia in the same manner as wine, brandy, arrack, opium, etc. is [*sic*] by other nations. Such fungi are found most plentifully about Wischna, Kamchatka, and Wilkowa Derecona, and are very abundant in some seasons, and scarce in others. They are collected in the hottest months, and hung up by a string in the air to dry ; some dry of themselves on the ground, and are said to be far more narcotic than those artificially preserved. Small deep-coloured specimens, thickly covered with warts, are also said to be more powerful than those of a larger size and paler colour. The usual mode of taking the Fungus is, to roll it up like a bolus, and swallow it without chewing, which, the Kamchatkadales say, would disorder the stomach. It is sometimes eaten fresh in soups and sauces, and then loses much of its intoxicating property ; when steeped in the juice of the berries of *Vaccinium uliginosum*, its effects are those of strong wine. One large, or two small Fungi, are a common dose to produce a pleasant intoxication for a whole day, particularly if water be drunk after it, which augments the narcotic principle. The desired effect comes on from one to two hours after taking the fungus. Giddiness and drunkenness result in the same manner as from wine or spirits ; cheerful emotions of the mind are first produced ; the countenance becomes flushed ; involuntary words and actions follow, and sometimes at last an entire loss of consciousness. It renders some remarkably active, and proves highly stimulant to muscular exertion : by too large a dose, violent spasmodic effects are produced. So very exciting to the

nervous system in many individuals is this Fungus, that the effects
are often very ludicrous. If a person under its influence wishes
to step over a straw or small stick, he takes a stride or a jump
sufficient to clear the trunk of a tree ; a talkative person cannot
keep silence or secrets ; and one fond of music is perpetually
singing." [1]

Vanderlip, who observed the customary use of this
fungus among the Koraks of Kamchatka, confirms
Langdorf's remarks on its effects, and adds :

"Curiously enough, after recovering from one of these
debauches, they claim that all the antics performed were by
command of the mushroom. The use of it is not unattended
with danger, for unless a man is well looked after he is likely to
destroy himself. The Koraks sometimes take this drug in order
to work themselves up to the point of murdering an enemy.
Three or four of the mushrooms is a moderate dose, but when
one wants to get the full effect, one takes ten or twelve." [2]

Kennan, who also visited the Koraks, and who
describes them as " a quiet inoffensive hospitable tribe
of semi-barbarians, notable only for honesty, general
amiability and comical reverence for legally-constituted
authority " [3] remarks of the fungus :

" Its habitual use, however, completely shatters the nervous
system, and its sale by Russian traders to the natives has
consequently been made a penal offence by Russian law.   In spite
of all prohibitions, the trade is still secretly carried on, and I have
seen twenty dollars worth of furs bought with a single fungus. [4]
The Koraks would gather it for themselves but it requires the
shelter of timber for its growth and is not to be found on the
barren steppes over which they wander ; so that they are obliged
for the most part to buy it, at enormous prices, from the Russian
traders. . . . As the supply of these toadstools is by no means

---

[1] Langsdorf, *Annalen der Wetterauschen Gesellschaft für die gesammte
Naturkunde*, vol. i., p. 249.
[2] 1903 Vanderlip, *In Search of a Siberian Klondike*, p. 212.
[3] 1870, Kennan, *Tent Life in Siberia*, pp. 155, 203–4.
[4] Lansdell (1882, *Through Siberia*, p. 645) says " a mushroom of
this kind sells for three or four reindeer."

equal to the demand, Korak ingenuity has been greatly exercised in the endeavour to economise the precious stimulant, and make it go as far as possible. Sometimes in the course of human events, it becomes imperatively necessary that a whole band should get drunk together and they have only one toadstool to do it with. For a description of the manner in which this band gets drunk collectively and individually upon one fungus, and keeps drunk for a week, the curious reader is referred to Goldsmith's ' Citizen of the World,' Letter 32. It is but just to say, that this horrible practice is almost confined to the settled Koraks of Penzhinsk Gulf—the lowest, most degraded portion of the whole tribe. It may prevail to a limited extent among the wandering natives but I have never heard of more than one such instance outside of the Penzhinsk Gulf settlements.''

Whether the consumption of such large, yet non-fatal, doses of an admittedly poisonous fungus is due to a less virulent form, or to a hardier people inured through generations to its use, is difficult to say. Certainly, the species is sufficiently poisonous in more temperate countries. The active principles of this species are a number of toxins, of which the best known is the alkaloid, *muscarine*. Among other poisonous fungi which belong to this class are *Amanita pantherina, Stropharia coronaria*, etc.

(3) *Fungi containing irritant principles which cause gastro-enteritis, by direct action on the mucous membrane of the digestive system.*

It is this group to which the vast bulk of poisonous fungi would appear to belong. Their active principles are probably of varying constitution, but their action on the human system is materially the same. Owing to the solubility of these acrid principles, the fungi produce symptoms soon after they are eaten, and these usually appear as griping pains in the stomach, a quickening and weakening of the pulse, depression, lethargy and vertigo, accompanied by vomiting and diarrhœa. These symptoms usually abate soon after the fungus is removed from the system, and recovery is in most cases rapid. Only in rare instances, where the patient is of weak constitution, or where a large quantity of the fungus has been eaten, does death occur. To this group belong the acrid species of *Russula*, *Lactarius* and *Boletus*, some species of *Amanita*, *Entoloma lividum* (Fig. 71), and several others.

(4) *Fungi containing haemolytic or blood-destroying principles.*

Curiously enough, this group is composed almost wholly of fungi which are generally considered to be edible, namely, the morels (*Morchella sp.*) ; the helvells (*Helvella sp.*) ; *Gyromitra esculenta* (Fig. 59), *Amanita rubescens*, etc. The explanation of this seeming paradox is found in the unstable nature of these *haemolysins*, which, while present in the raw fungus, are partially removed by the preliminary preparation of washing, while the remainder are destroyed in cooking. It follows, therefore, that the rare cases of poisoning which have been caused by eating these fungi, are probably always due to insufficient cooking. In such cases, the poisonous substances act by attacking and partially destroying the red corpuscles of the blood, the process being accompanied by symptoms of uneasiness, vertigo, vomiting and the passing of blood, and sometimes by convulsions and profound sleep.

(5) *Fungi containing substances which excite the muscular system, especially the smooth muscle fibres (the uterus, vessels, etc.).*

These poisonous fungi (ergot of rye, etc.) are mostly very minute, and are only eaten inadvertently as contaminants of the more usual foods. In this connection reference has already been made to them (p. 94). In some cases, the toxins are employed in medicine, and this aspect is dealt with elsewhere.

DOUBTFUL FUNGI. In addition to these five classes of fungi, in which the presence of specific poisons has already been proved, there is also a certain number of species whose wholesomeness is open to grave doubt. True, many of them have been eaten by some persons without the slightest ill-effects ; while with others the reverse has been the case. The question of digestive idiosyncracies must not be overlooked, for, as with lobsters and various other foods, certain people become ill through eating quite wholesome fungi, which do not at all affect normal individuals. This personal peculiarity has at times brought harmless species under unjust suspicion. Again, the eating of fungi normally quite innocuous may have harmful effects in certain diseases, e.g., parenchymatous nephritis. Kakowski cites *Boletus edulis* (Fig. 82) in this connection. There are also the questions of the freshness of the specimens, their mode of preparation and of cooking, and the quantity eaten. The variable effects of these fungi do not indicate whether they should be regarded as definitely edible or equally definitely poisonous. Therefore, until further information is available, it is best to regard them all with suspicion. These species are too numerous to tabulate, and lest this be considered a serious omission, it may be pointed out that it is better for the reader to learn what he *may* eat, rather than what he *may not*.

Treatment. No account of the poisonous fungi could be considered complete without some remarks on the treatment to be adopted in cases of fungus poisoning. Yet, so obviously is this a matter for the medical man, that we hesitate in making any suggestions which might be construed as an attempt to usurp his powers. On the other hand, the severity of an attack, and its after effects, can be considerably lessened by prompt treatment, and since so many of these cases occur in country districts, where a certain delay in obtaining a doctor is often inevitable, it is desirable that everyone who is in the habit of collecting and eating fungi, should be capable of applying first-aid remedies. Therefore, in giving the following facts, we are animated rather with the desire to lighten the physician's labour than to trespass on his preserves.

When any one, after eating fungi of any description, is seized with symptoms akin to those described, no time should be lost in summoning a doctor, who should be informed of the nature of the case which he is required to attend, so that he may bring with him appropriate appliances. In the interval, preliminary treatment may be commenced. The general aims of the treatment are :—

(i) To remove from the system the remains of the fungi eaten.
(ii) To bring about the elimination or exhaustion of the toxins already absorbed by the blood.
(iii) To counteract pain and all other distressing symptoms.
(iv) To guard against collapse, and generally to keep a watch on the action of the heart.

Of these items, the attendant will probably only be required to act on the first. Indeed, so long as valuable time is not lost in so doing, as much as possible should be left to the doctor.

(i) EXPULSION OF THE FUNGUS. In cases of poisoning, the usual procedure is to resort immediately to emetics. With fungus poisoning, these may not only be useless, but actually harmful, for the first symptoms are usually violent sickness, during which practically the whole of the fungus in the stomach is rejected. Therefore, there is no point in increasing the irritation to this organ, by deliberately causing further retching. In some cases, however, the patient is unable to vomit, when a table-spoonful of mustard in half a tumblerful of warm water should be given. Apomorphine, tartar emetic or zinc sulphate may alternatively be used. Since, however, each is, in itself, a powerful poison, any of these should only be employed under medical direction. *On no account should salt and water be administered, as unless this acts at once, it merely accentuates the solubility of the poisons.*

If possible, the stomach should afterwards be washed out by means of a stomach tube, or, failing this, copious draughts of warm water should be given.

After this treatment, any of the fungus not accounted for has naturally passed into the intestines, and therefore the next step should be to administer a purgative, preferably of an alkaline nature, such as :—

Sulphate of soda (Glauber's salt) : $\frac{1}{4} - \frac{1}{2}$ oz. dose.[1]
Sulphate of magnesium (Epsom salts) : $\frac{1}{4} - \frac{1}{2}$ oz. dose.[1]

either in a tumblerful of warm water. Should there be severe abdominal griping, it is better to substitute for the above, one tablespoonful of castor oil in a little milk, while a further soothing drink is two tablespoonfuls of

---

[1] From one to two *level* dessert-spoonfuls.

olive oil, beaten up with the yolk of an egg, and four or five tablespoonfuls of milk or warm water, to which, *under the doctor's instructions*, may be added 20 drops of laudanum.

(ii) THE ELIMINATION OF THE TOXIN. The natural elimination or exhaustion of the poison which has already been absorbed into the blood, can only be assisted or expedited by subcutaneous injections of atropine, and other medical means only possible to a doctor.

(iii) THE COUNTERACTION OF THE VARIOUS DISTRESSING SYMPTOMS which almost always accompany an attack of fungus poisoning should likewise be left in the hands of the doctor. In case of delirium, sedatives such as potassium bromide are necessary ; lethargy and depression can be counteracted by strong tea or coffee, dry friction, etc. ; pain, by the use of various opium compounds ; while prolonged and excessive vomiting can be combated with soda water (aerated water) or by giving the patient small pieces of ice to suck.

(iv) EFFECT ON THE HEART. Many fungi have a very marked effect on the heart's action, and resort may have to be made to stimulants.

The Utilization of Poisonous Fungi as Foods. Having already emphasized the serious danger of eating fungi without knowing precisely what they are, any consideration of the gastronomic use of fungi which are unquestionably poisonous may at first appear not only a folly, but almost a madness. However, there's method in it, and since undoubtedly many poisonous kinds *are* so used, the practice being furthermore of very ancient standing, it is interesting to discuss it. The crux of the matter is, that these poisons are soluble, and may first in various ways be extracted, when the remainder of the fungus may be consumed without harm. At the same time, he would be a very foolish person who would recommend experimenting with any of them, when there are so many harmless edible species available, and nothing is further from our thoughts. The consideration of the matter, however, can do no harm, and for the novice it will be safer to stop at that.

The Ancient Use of Poisonous Fungi.   Dealing first with the historical side of the matter, Celsus, who lived about the beginning of the Christian era, tells us that poisonous fungi " can be rendered serviceable by a mode of cooking them ; for if they have been boiled in oil or with the young twig of a pear tree, they become free from any bad quality," [1] while Pliny (23–79 A.D.) says that fungi " are rendered more safe still if they are cooked with meat or with pear stalks ; indeed, it is good to eat pears immediately after fungi. Vinegar being of a nature contrary to them neutralizes their dangerous qualities." [2]   That the ancients were substantially correct with regard to the efficacy of vinegar has since been amply demonstrated by the experiments of Paulet and Gérard, referred to below. As to the virtue of pears, we are not so certain, but the belief evidently survived after so long an interval as to the year 1495 A.D., for Trevisa says that " yf perys ben sodde [=boiled] wyth tode stoles they take awaye fro them all greyf and malyce." [3]

The Experiments of Paulet and Gérard.   In the year 1793, Paulet stated that if poisonous fungi are cut up into small pieces, and soaked in water containing either

---

[1] Celsus, *De Medicina*, V., 27, 17.

[2] Pliny, *Nat. Hist.*, XXII., 47.

[3] Trevisa, *Barth. De. P. R.*, xvii., cxxiv. (W. de W.).

salt, vinegar or alcohol, the poisons are extracted, so that they become innocuous to animals fed on them.[1]   About half a century later, it was demonstrated by the experiments of Gérard, that even the deadly *Amanita phalloides* and *A. muscaria*, when so treated, are rendered equally harmless to man.   In 1851, Gérard communicated to the Conseil de Salubrité of Paris, an account of various experiments he had made on the preparation of poisonous fungi, so as to render them quite safe for consumption, and stated that, as a result of these, he and his family were in the habit of eating, without any ill-effects, all kinds of deadly varieties, to the extent even of 75 kilogrammes (about 1½ cwt.) within one month. To investigate these claims, a commission of three was delegated by the Conseil, and in the presence of these gentlemen, Gérard, after preparation according to his method, consumed 500 grammes (a little more than 1 lb.) of *Amanita muscaria*, and 70 grammes (about 2½ oz.) of *A. phalloides*, without harm, to the complete persuasion of the commission, two of whose members even had the temerity to taste some small pieces themselves, no doubt with some inward trepidation, with which one can entirely sympathize.   The commission reported, however, that there was no doubt as to the success of the demonstration.

Similar Uses among Peasants, etc.   The practice of eating poisonous fungi, after the poisons had been extracted, was current in parts of France long before Gérard, in this notable manner, brought it to public notice, and it was similarly practised in other countries ; while, from the evidence of Pliny, it no doubt dates back

---

[1] Paulet, *Traité des Champignons*, Paris, Tom. 2, p. 25.

to remote antiquity. Buller suggests that "the secret may have been known only to groups of peasants in various localities. That it was not known universally appears to be shown by the numerous references in classical literature to cases of fungus poisoning." [1]

In Russia and Germany, many different species, edible and poisonous alike, have long been largely gathered for winter consumption, being preserved in vinegar, which extracts the toxic alkaloids contained in many of those used, thus preventing the ill-effects that would otherwise result. Some interesting details of a similar practice among the French peasants round Sérignan are given by Fabre, who says:

"Often, when rambling in the neighbouring woods, I inspect the baskets of the mushroom-pickers, who are delighted for me to look. I see things fit to make mycological experts stand aghast. I often find the purple boletus [*B. purpureus*], which is classed among the dangerous varieties. I made the remark one day. The man carrying the basket stared at me in astonishment:

"'That a poison! The wolf's bread' [2] he said, patting the plump boletus with his hand. 'What an idea! Its beef-marrow, sir, regular beef-marrow!'

"He smiled at my apprehensions and went away with a poor opinion of my knowledge in the matter of mushrooms.

In the baskets aforesaid, I find the ringed agaric (*Armillaria mellea*), which is stigmatized as *valde venenatus* by Persoon,[3] an expert on the subject. It is even the mushroom most frequently made use of, because of its being so plentiful, especially at the foot of the mulberry-trees. I find the Satanic boletus [*B. Satanas*], that dangerous tempter; the belted milk-mushroom (*Lactarius zonarius*), whose burning flavour rivals the pepper of its woolly kinsman; the smooth-headed amanita (*Amanita leiocephala*),

---

[1] Buller, "The Fungus Lore of the Greeks and Romans," *Trans. Brit. Myc. Soc.*, 1914, vol. v., Part I.

[2] The boleti are known hereabouts by the generic name of *pan de loup*, or "wolf's bread."

[3] Christiaan Hendrik Persoon (1770–1836), a naturalist of Dutch descent, and author of various mycological works.

a magnificent white dome rising out of an ample volva and fringed at the edges with flowery relics resembling flakes of casein. Its poisonous smell and soapy after-taste should lead to suspicion of this ivory dome ; but nobody seems to mind them.

" How, with such careless picking, are accidents avoided ? In my village and for a long way round, the rule is to blanch the mushrooms, that is to say, to bring them to the boil in water with a little salt in it. A few rinsings in cold water conclude the treatment. They are then prepared in whatever manner one pleases. In this way, what might at first be dangerous becomes harmless, because the preliminary boiling and rinsing have removed the noxious elements." [1]

Fabre says further that during the thirty years that he lived at Sérignan, he never heard of one case of mushroom poisoning, even the mildest, in the village. This may well have been the case, if the villagers confined their attentions to the species indicated, for, as we now know, not one of them is poisonous.

In the light of this evidence, it is not surprising to find it quite a usual practice with certain of the negro women of the United States to eat *Amanita muscaria* with impunity, after a suitable preparation involving extraction by both salt and vinegar, thus carrying out very thoroughly the recommendations of Gérard, although the worthy ladies have probably never even heard of him. Some interesting details of this custom are given by Coville.[2] It appears that most of the coloured women of the Washington markets wisely regard the species in question with dread, and its use as a food is confined to a few, one of whom " recited in detail how she was in the habit of cooking it. She

---

[1] Fabre, *The Life of the Fly*, English translation by A. T. de Mattos (1913), ch. xviii., p. 420.

[2] 1898, Circular No. 13 (Revised edition) of the U.S. Dept. of Agriculture, Division of Botany : " Observations on recent cases of mushroom poisoning in the District of Columbia," p. 19.

prepared the stem by scraping, the cap by removing the gills and peeling the upper surface. Thus dressed, the mushrooms were first boiled in salt and water, and afterwards steeped in vinegar. They were then washed in clear water, cooked in gravy like ordinary mushrooms, and served with beef steak. This is an exceedingly interesting operation from the fact that although its author was wholly ignorant of the chemistry of mushroom poisons, she had, nevertheless, been employing a process for the removal of these poisons which was scientifically correct. The gills, according to various pharmacological researches, are the chief seat of the poisonous principles, and their removal at once takes away a large part of the poison. The salt and water would remove phallin or any other toxalbumin the mushroom contained, and although the presence of phallin or any of this class of poisons has not been demonstrated in *Amanita muscaria*, there is a strong suspicion that it may occur in slight amount. The vinegar, secondly, removes the alkaloid poison, muscarine, and the mushroom after the two treatments is free from poisons. This process is cited, not to recommend its wider use, but as a matter of general interest. The writer's recommendation is that a mushroom containing such a deadly poison should not be used for food in any form, particularly at a season when excellent non-poisonous species may be had in abundance," [1] with which opinion we entirely agree, and there we may leave the matter.

---

[1] *Loc. cit.*

CHAPTER XII

The Curious Phenomena Exhibited by Fungi

"The giant puffball [*Lycoperdon Bovista*] . . . increases from the size of a pea to that of a melon in a single night."
—1861, H. MacMillan, *Footnotes from the Page of Nature*, 199.

"Matthiolus mentions mushrooms which weighed thirty pounds each, and were as yellow as gold; Fer. Imperatus tells us, he saw some which weighed above a hundred pounds a-piece; and to add no more, the Journal des Sçavans furnishes us with an account of some growing on the frontiers of Hungary, which made a full cart-load."
—1819, Rees, *Cyclopaedia*, Vol. 24, under "Mushroom."

ALTHOUGH popular antipathy to the fungi is certainly due in no small measure to the poisonous qualities which many possess, there are other characters which, to the layman, appear strange and inexplicable, and these have doubtless assisted in maintaining these plants in the invidious position which they hold in popular estimation. The uncanny mode of appearance; the rapidity of growth of some species, often inordinately magnified in general belief; the huge sizes frequently attained; the power, enormous for such frail bodies, which many are capable of exerting; the chameleon-like tendency, which certain species show, to change colour when broken; their phosphorescence; and the often unpleasant mode of dissolution—such characters are enough in themselves to make the casual wayfarer a little chary of closer investigation. Yet, when any of these seemingly magical properties is examined more closely, one can see how truly it is governed by natural causes, and, incidentally, how erroneous are many popular conceptions concerning fungi.

Rapidity of Growth. Among the phenomena which are usually considered to be characteristic of fungi, that which has most firmly impressed itself upon the public mind is that they grow at an enormously rapid rate. One is continually encountering the statement that mushrooms grow up in a night, while puffballs of stupendous size are said to appear suddenly in places where there was nothing before ; and so on. We need adduce no further examples—this belief is proverbial— and although for reasons which we shall shortly enumerate. there is a good deal of truth in the statement, yet in another sense, it must to some extent be discounted.

In the first place, it should be remembered that the fruiting bodies of fungi are produced for a specific purpose—that of generating spores—a process which, in most cases, must be accomplished rapidly at a time when climatic conditions are suitable. It is therefore only natural that these plants should prepare for this eventuality by constructing organs, which can be gorged with water, and rapidly distended and erected at this appropriate time. From this point of view, it is not surprising that their growth should be comparatively rapid.

Further, it should be pointed out that in what is usually regarded as the " growth " of fungi, at least two different factors are operating. There is in the first place the *true* growth, which we may regard as the formation of new tissue ; and, secondly, there is an *apparent* growth, which consists of the rapid distension of tissue already formed, but previously unexpanded. The two senses are not quite the same. The apparent growth of unexpanded tissue may be likened to the regular expansion of a deflated tube on pumping in air, or of a dry sponge which has become full of water.

Leaving for a moment the question of the rapidity of " true " growth and the reasons for it, we may consider briefly one effect of the " apparent " growth, which is undoubtedly that responsible for the popular belief that mushrooms grow in a night. In the egg stage, and as an example we may take that of the Dog Stinkhorn (*Mutinus caninus*), shown in Fig. 77, the substance of the stalk is much compressed ; and when the spores are formed, the hymenial part of the fungus perforates and bursts through the peridium, and is carried upwards by a very rapid elongation of the stalk. The rate of elongation in the case of an ally, the Common Stinkhorn (*Phallus impudicus*), has been recorded by Lees as about six or eight inches in two or three hours. With both fungi the egg itself is often an inconspicuous object, partly buried in the ground and sometimes partly or almost entirely covered by grass or fallen leaves ; while on the other hand, the expanded fungus is very prominent, and some idea of the relative noticeability of the two may be gained from Fig. 14, in which the egg is shown with the fungus emerging therefrom. There is thus a very good reason for thinking that it has " grown " in a night, and the same remarks apply in much the same degree to the Common Mushroom. Extended preparation has, of course, been made on the part of the plant *for* such growth ; but without a knowledge, on the part of the observer, of the causes which have led up to it, the result is naturally somewhat startling.

It must, at the same time, be realized that the true growth of fungi is much more rapid than in the case of most other plants. On consideration, the reasons for this are quite clear. Fungi occur usually in places where unlimited supplies of food material are found; this material is already in a state fit for immediate utilization; the vast majority of fungi contain very little solid matter, but are composed very largely of water, which can be absorbed very quickly; while finally, fungi have in general a large number of growing points, instead of the very limited and localized growing layers found in most other plants.

These factors, as a whole, combine to produce in many of the fungi that " rapidity of growth " which has always been a source of amazement to the casual observer, and even when all considerations are appreciated, one can still marvel at the enormous size of many of the fruiting bodies, and the relative speed at which they are constructed, when compared with the total quantity of mycelium from which they arise.

We have quoted, at the head of this chapter, a statement by MacMillan, concerning the rate of development of the Giant Puffball (Fig. 78), which well illustrates popular belief in the matter, but which can scarcely be correct. Sowerby cites the instance of a specimen of *Polyporus squamosus* (Frontispiece), as having attained a weight of 34 lb. in three weeks from the time of its first appearance, which is at the rate of over 1½ lb. per day, and this is probably by no means unusual for this and allied species in our own country.

As something of a counterblast, we may refer the

reader to the illustrations of *Lepiota procera* shown in Figs. 74 and 75, from which he can obtain some idea of the amount of development which takes place in this species in the course of twenty-four hours.

Sizes attained.   Very closely related to the question of rapidity of growth is that of the size which, under favourable conditions, may be attained, and some possibly exaggerated examples of this have been quoted in the heading to this chapter.   In the case of the larger polypores, a weight of thirty pounds is quite possible, and under exceptional conditions, those, for example, of the tropics, there would appear no reason why a much greater development should not occur.   When, however, we read of some " on the frontier of Hungary, which made a full cart-load," we are moved to enquire as to the size of the cart.   Bulliard certainly mentions puffballs of nine feet in circumference, and some of the tropical fungi are said to have been mistaken for sleeping lions, but it would not be a very large cart for which either would constitute a " load " within the meaning of the term.

To consider some examples which have been recorded with a little more exactitude, we note a field mushroom from Bewdley, weighing 13½ oz. and 30 inches in circumference ; [1] while of the same year and county, a Mr. Cuthbert Bede records that " field mushrooms would seem to have been very large this year.   In my own meadow I gathered several of great size, two of which measured respectively 33¼ and 36½ inches in circumference." [2]   In this present year of 1924, large examples

---

[1] 1886, G. Shaw, Letter to *The Standard*, Aug. 26th.
[2] 1886, C. Bede, *Notes and Queries*, 7th Ser., II, Sept. 25, p. 245.

Photo by A. E. Peck, Scarborough

Fig. 75.—The same, twenty-four hours later.

Photo by A. E. Peck, Scarborough

Fig. 74.—*Lepiota procera*, in young state.

Photo by A. E. Peck, Scarborough

Fig. 77.—The Dog Stinkhorn (*Mutinus caninus*), showing the relative prominence of the "egg" and the mature plant.

Photo by Authors

Fig. 76.—A "Shaggy Cap" (*Coprinus comatus*) in old state, showing deliquesced and reflexed cap. Compare with fig. 60.

have also been found. From Ingoldisthorpe, Norfolk, is recorded one measuring 15½ in. across and 47½ in. round, and weighing 3 lb. 2 oz.[1] This is, however, by no means a record for this species, and an example four feet in circumference and weighing five pounds was found by a farmer in the woods near Château Roux, in France.[2] It is, however, extremely doubtful if most of the large mushrooms recorded are really Field Mushrooms (*Psalliota arvensis*). More probably are they *P. villaticus*, a much larger fungus. The record for abnormal size appears to be held by a specimen of the Common Mushroom grown in 1846 in the quarries at Vitry, near Paris, and presented by the growers to King Louis Philippe. The cap of this mushroom had a circumference of a little over 43 inches, and the stalk one of 18½ inches, while the weight was over 5½ pounds.

We have shown in Fig. 78, a good-sized puffball (*Lycoperdon Bovista*), which was found in a meadow at Goldington, near Bedford, about the end of July, 1894. When found, it was 34½ inches in circumference and weighed over 9 lb. When, three days later, it came into the possession of our friend, Mr. E. M. Langley, M.A., it was 33½ inches round and weighed just over 6 lb. ; while to-day, thirty years later, it is very small and shrivelled, and weighs 10 oz. This of course is by no means unusual, and is indeed insignificant, when compared with an American example of the same species which has been described. This measured 5 ft. 4 in. in its greatest diameter, by 4 ft. 6 in. in its

---

[1] 1924, *Daily Express*, June 26th.
[2] 1924, *Ibid.*, July 21st.

least, and was 9½ in. high.   A simple calculation will show that this specimen was approximately 15½ feet in circumference, which is certainly phenomenal.

The Forces Exerted by Growing Fungi.   There have, from time to time, been recorded instances of paving stones and similar heavy bodies being forced upward from their positions by the levitational action of fungi growing under them, and great astonishment is often expressed that such fragile organisms should be capable of exerting such tremendous forces.   Some cases may, with advantage, be referred to.   In the town of Basingstoke, in the year 1830, a large paving-stone measuring 22 by 21 in., and weighing 83 lb., which had been cemented down, was dislodged and elevated an inch and a half out of its bed by the growth of two mushrooms beneath it, and other stones becoming deranged for a similar reason and in varying degrees, much perturbation was naturally occasioned to the paving contractor, who had but recently completed the work, " for it seemed doubtful whether the whole town of Basingstoke might not want re-paving during the term of his contract,"[1] but whether, as Cooke asserts,[2] the whole town *was* re-paved, we are not able to say, and are certainly doubtful whether such a heroic expedient could have been really necessary.   Cooke records a similar incident, which came under his own notice, " of a large kitchen hearth-stone, which was forced up from its bed by an under-growing fungus, and had to be relaid two or three times, until at last it reposed in peace, the old bed having been removed to a depth of six inches, and a new

---

[1] Burnett, *Botany*, p. 239.
[2] 1862, Cooke, *British Fungi*, p. 7.

foundation laid." [1]   Many similar cases, most of which have been due to *Coprinus atramentarius*, have occurred, for example, at Cheltenham in 1840, at Ely in 1901, and elsewhere. Another remarkable instance of a fungus growth is related by Sir Joseph Banks. A cask of wine, which had been left undisturbed for three years in a cellar, was at the end of that time found firmly fixed against the roof of the same, having been carried thereto in the embrace of an enormous growth of fungus, evidently developed from the leakage of the wine from the cask, which was empty.

From the superficial evidence, such occurrences are certainly puzzling. If, however, the matter be carefully considered, it becomes fairly obvious that the water absorbed by the thousands, possibly millions, of mycelial threads, during the simultaneous fruiting, enables the vessels to act as minute hydraulic rams, the combined effort resulting in a slow but inexorable movement. It is clear, also, that no greater pressure can be generated than the individual vessels are able to stand. Even so, the results are sufficiently astonishing.

The Colour Changes Exhibited by Fungi.   Among the many queer characteristics of the fungi, this is not the least curious. That fungi, which change colour when broken, are unwholesome, has already been cited, as one of the empirical and quite valueless " rules " by which poisonous species may be detected. Such a colour change is well shown in many species of Boletus and in representatives of various other groups, the flesh of which, when broken and exposed to the air, changes from white

---

[1] *Loc. cit.*

or yellow to a deep indigo blue. According to Bourquelot and Bertrand,[1] the change is due to the presence in the fungus of an oxidizing ferment, which they call tyrinosase, and such fungi apparently also contain chromogenous substances which when thus oxidized are converted into coloured products.[2] An analogous change of colour is seen when the flesh of an apple is exposed to the air for a short time.

The Luminosity of Fungi. Another somewhat eerie manifestation occurring in some fungi is their luminosity, of which many examples have been recorded. In a description of a forest in Sumatra, Forbes says : " The stem of every tree blinked with a pale greenish-white light which undulated also across the surface of the ground like moonlight coming and going behind the clouds, from a minute thread-like fungus invisible in the day time to the unassisted eye ; and here and there thick dumpy mushrooms displayed a sharp, clear dome of light, whose intensity never varied or changed till the break of day ; long phosphorescent caterpillars and centipedes crawled out of every corner, leaving a trail of light behind them, while fire-flies darted about above like a lower firmament." [3] A remarkable account is given by Berkeley,[4] which shows how striking this phenomenon

---

[1] 1896, Bourquelot and Bertrand, *Bull. Soc. Myc.*, p. 17.

[2] It may be remarked that the colour shown by such species as *Lactarius deliciosus* (Fig. 84), *Russula lepida*, and *Clitocybe inversa* is considered to be due to colour changes brought about by the oxidation of such materials giving rise to coloured pigments in the hyphae of the cuticle of the fungus. This conjecture is supported by the fact that in many species where the cap is normally coloured, such portions of it as are accidentally protected from oxidation by the adherence of a leaf, or in some other manner, remain colourless.

[3] H. O. Forbes, *A Naturalist's Wanderings in the Eastern Archipelago.*

[4] 1872, Berkeley, *Gardener's Chronicle*, p. 1258.

may be. A quantity of wood, having been bought in an adjoining parish, had to be dragged up a very steep hill to its destination. Part of the consignment consisted of a log of larch or spruce, it is not quite certain which, about twenty-four feet long and a foot in diameter. The same night, some young people, having occasion to go up this hill, were astonished to find the roadway strewn with luminous particles, which, on investigation, were found to consist of small pieces of bark and wood. Following the trail, they came to a very strong blaze of white light, proceeding from the log in question. On closer investigation, it was found that the whole of the inside of the bark was covered by a white byssoid mycelium, having an extremely strong smell, but unfortunately so damaged that its true form could not be determined. It was from the mycelium that the light was proceeding, and the brightness was most intense in places where the spawn had penetrated more deeply, where, indeed, the roughest treatment, if, for example, one attempted to rub off the luminous matter, only caused it to glow more brightly. If wrapped up in five folds of paper, the light shone as strongly through the paper as if the specimen had been fully exposed, and if placed in the pocket, the latter on opening again was a perfect blaze of light. When these tests were made, the luminosity had been going on for three days. Fabre considers the mechanism of the luminosity to be an expression of the respiration of the cells of the fungus, and says :—

" Let us begin by questioning the olive-tree agaric or luminous mushroom (*Pleurotus phosphoreus*), a magnificent mushroom coloured jujube-red. . . . A more remarkable feature distinguishes it from all the other European mushrooms ; it is phosphorescent. On the lower surface and there only, it sheds a soft, white gleam, similar to that of the Glow-worm. It lights up to celebrate its

nuptials and the emission of its spores. There is no question of
chemists' phosphorus here. This is a slow combustion, a sort of
more active respiration than usual. The luminous emission is
extinguished in the unbreathable gases, nitrogen and carbonic
acid ; it continues in aerated water, it ceases in water deprived
of its air by boiling. It is exceedingly faint, however, so much
so that it is not perceptible except in the deepest darkness. At
night and even by day, if the eyes have been prepared for it by a
preliminary wait in the darkness of a cellar, this agaric is a wonderful
sight, looking indeed like a piece of the full moon." [1]

The most interesting aspect of this luminosity is its
reason, for Nature does not work blindly, although to
mankind its object may sometimes be obscure. To seek
such a parallel from the animal world as is afforded by the
glow-worm, it would appear not unreasonable to suppose
that luminosity is sometimes a device to attract insects
and so ensure spore dissemination, and it must obviously
be the night-flying insects which are so attracted, in much
the same manner as the brilliant tints of flowers serve to
allure those which fly by day. That any luminous object
possesses an irresistible attraction for night-flying insects
is proverbial, and since flies and beetles use certain
luminous fungi in which to lay their eggs, the conjecture
is a not unlikely one. This explanation, however,
cannot always hold good, for in certain cases, e.g., that
of *Armillaria mellea*, it is only the young mycelium that
is luminous, and not the fruiting bodies. Why some
fungi should possess this property, and others not, is as
inscrutable as is the erratic manner in which poisons
occur in fungi. It should be noted that fungi are only
luminous while growing, and the emission ceases when
the plant is dead.

---

[1] 1913, J. H. Fabre, *The Life of the Fly*, English ed., by A. T. de
Mattos, ch. xviii, p. 418.

Fungi Responsible for the Rain of Blood, and Allied Phenomena. There have been recorded, from time to time, instances of the falling of coloured rain, sometimes blood-red, which the superstitious have naturally regarded as a warning of the direst calamities ; sometimes of other colours, giving rains of ink, or of sulphur, according to the prevailing hue ; each alike being probably vastly disquieting to the uninitiated. It would appear that various causes may at different times be responsible for these effects, which were closely studied by Ehrenberg, and may be sometimes due to soot, sometimes to pollen of different trees, and in other cases to the presence of fungi. The red rain is generally considered to be caused by a fungus of the lowest order, and in the opinion of Berkeley " it is a state of some mould analogous to the gelatinous spots of various colours which appear on meat or paste when in a state of incipient decomposition. It increases with immense rapidity, and is easily propagated, a very singular circumstance being that from particular spots multitudes of lesser spots extend in a straight line, as if blood had been spurted out from a wounded artery."[1] The appearance of blood-coloured spots on various articles of food was very common in the hot days of July, 1853, particularly in France, and when at Rouen at this time, Montagne investigated many such cases, on both animal and vegetable food, which became so spotted in a few hours. Food cooked in the evening was found the next day to be covered with this growth. Montagne found the red substance to be the same as that previously investigated by Ehrenberg, in Berlin, and he was able to propagate it with ease on rice paste. It is by this means

---

[1] 1857, Berkeley, *Introduction to Cryptogamic Botany*, p. 264.

that the supposed appearance, in mediaeval times, of stains of blood upon the Host, which was then naturally regarded as miraculous, has been explained.

Curious Growths of Fungi.   It is a not uncommon thing to find two mushrooms growing with their caps joined together at the edge in a Siamese-twin manner.   An even more curious example of the blewitt (*Tricholoma personatum*), shown to the authors, had three individuals growing one above, and out of, the other, in the form of a pagoda.   In another interesting case which was brought to our notice, the growth of a large Parasol (*Lepiota procera*) had carried upwards on its cap a small quantity of humus and mycelium, out of which was growing a complete but smaller specimen of the same species.   A large number of monstrosities have no doubt been observed.

The Rapidity of Decay of Fungi.   This is naturally intimately related to that of rapidity of growth. When compared with that of most of the flowering plants, the reproductive portion of most fungi not only grows to maturity, but, its purpose accomplished, decays also so rapidly that it would appear to have been given a dose of that new accelerator, the effects of which one of our authors has so humorously described.   Thus, in the space of some forty-eight hours, many species of *Coprinus* will erect their caps, fructify, and deliquesce into a collapsed, black and semi-liquid mass, popularly regarded as " a horrible putrescence." When this process is considered by an enquiring mind, however, one loses such a viewpoint and, instead, can have nothing but admiration for another of Nature's devices by which spore dissemination is facilitated.   In the first place, these fungi are auto-digestive, and contain a ferment or

Courtesy of E. M. Langley, Bedford

Fig. 78.—A Giant Puffball (*Lycoperdon Bovista*).

Photo by Authors

Fig. 79.—The Candle-Snuff Fungus (*Xylaria hypoxylon*), in which the young mycelium is luminous.

Photo by A. E. Peck, Scarborough

Fig. 80.—The Oyster Fungus (*Pleurotus ostreatus*), at home.

Photo by Authors

Fig. 81.—The Common Parasol (*Lepiota procera*), at home.

oxidizing enzyme which gives the dark colour to the liquid produced. The fact that fungi are composed very largely of water naturally simplifies such a process, which, by the removal of those portions of the gills which have already discharged their spores, provides the necessary space for the shedding of others in their turn, this being further facilitated by the gradual opening and reflexion of the cap as the process continues. It must be pre-supposed that fructification only takes place when external conditions are favourable, and thus, by the speeding-up of the whole process of fructification, it is sought to ensure that the spores will be liberated while such conditions continue. The change in the appearance of the fungus during this process is often phenomenal ; indeed, the neophyte might be forgiven for refusing to credit the identity of the old, with the young form of the same species. This is exemplified on comparing Fig. 60, of *Coprinus comatus* in the young stage, with Fig. 76, of the same when old.

Many other curious phenomena are exhibited by fungi, but it has here been our object, in the first place, to illustrate some of those characteristics of the fungi which have often excited popular speculation, and, secondly, to give some explanation as to the causes for the results observed. In spite of the view which holds *omne ignotum pro magnifico*, we think that the reasons often afford as much additional cause for wonder as the original phenomena, in which belief we hope for the support of the reader.

CHAPTER XIII

The Study of the Fungi as a Hobby

"Let me assure the student that all times, seasons, and localities will afford him some species for examination; and whether he has felt interested in them before, or now, for the first time, adopts these interesting plants as objects worthy of his special regard, I would commend them to his patient and persevering attention, in the assurance that this pursuit will 'lead from joy to joy.'"

1862, M. C. COOKE, *British Fungi*, p. vi.

IT has long been recognized that the investigation, if in but desultory fashion, of some group of the natural objects which surround us, provides an excellent relaxation from the more serious pursuits of life ; and thus, wild flowers, trees, birds and their eggs, butterflies, etc., have in turn received their modicum of attention at the hands of the enthusiastic nature-lover, who has incidentally in this way been responsible for a number of important discoveries. Of the various branches of nature study so covered, none has received less attention than the fungi. The reason for this is to be found primarily in the prejudice, already described, with which this group of plants has been hedged around in the past, and which we trust we have already done something to dissipate. But to this may be added the fact that the time of year at which there is the greatest abundance of specimens, is also the season when our fields and woods are wearing their most depressing garb ; when all is sodden and muddy underfoot, and when, therefore, to many, a book and a chair in front of a cheerful fire offer superior attractions. There is a further disadvantage for those who would make the study of these queer plants their hobby, that, with the fungi, one of the principal joys of the devotee—that of arranging and rearranging his spoils—must, to a large extent, be lacking ; for the evanescent nature of most kinds, their bulk, together with the fact that no altogether satisfactory method has yet been devised for preserving the vast proportion, render a reference collection somewhat impracticable. This disadvantage, incidentally, is more apparent than real, for no method, however perfect, could hope to preserve the more delicate shades of colour and the finer details of structure, so fleeting and yet so necessary for the identification of many species. Still, in spite of these drawbacks, we feel confident in asserting that, once the natural and hereditary distaste for these plants is overcome, the fungi possess an interest equal to that of any other group of natural objects, and one which deepens as acquaintance with them grows. Thus their study will not only supply the newcomer with those hours of unalloyed pleasure which always accompany the investigation of some new phase of the workings of Nature's world, but will bring him an additional reward, if any be needed, in the form of many a succulent dish, some fit to grace a gourmet's table. This, albeit a somewhat base and immoral method of raising enthusiasm for the fungi, certainly cannot be said of some of the other branches of natural history we have mentioned.

The Haunts of the Fungi. As with other plants, fungi have their respective seasons and localities. The time of year when there is the greatest abundance is the autumn, from the middle of September until the setting-in of winter; but spring and summer have also their representatives, while the woody perennial kinds are naturally to be found even in winter.

An autumn walk abroad in the woods and fields will generally enable the fungus hunter to find many of the larger fleshy kinds of toadstools and puffballs, but particular kinds may not be found quite so readily. In searching for a particular species, it is necessary to know its haunts, and since fungi are dependent on organic matter for their sustenance, the localities in which they are found vary with the type of food available. Most of the fungi are terrestrial and are found in fields, woods and waste places; a number confine their attention to dead tree-trunks and decaying wood generally; others attack the living trees in our woods and forests, while a few are even parasitic upon other fungi. In short, fungi occur almost anywhere, and most damp, shady and undisturbed spots will yield their quota of specimens. Many terrestrial fungi are found among fallen leaves, where their brown and buff colours cause them to be sometimes overlooked.

The Field Study of the Fungi. For any serious study of the fungi, it is necessary to note certain habits and features, which can only be observed when they are growing; and study in the field must, therefore, always precede such botanical investigations as one can pursue later. It is thus important to note the situation in which a specimen is found, whether on the ground or on wood, in the former case whether in the open or under trees, whether the species is solitary, gregarious or crowded; when growing in a wood, whether this is composed principally of beeches, of oaks, etc.; if on a tree, the kind of tree on which it is growing, on what part of the host, whether the latter is living or dead, and so on. It may be remarked that even in the case of species found in woods, there are variations in habitat, some preferring the more open parts at the edges, and others the denser and more shaded portions.

If a species with stalk and cap, the appearance of the cap should be noted, whether smooth and silky, or scaly, etc.; whether the scales are large or small, and the colour. The same remarks apply to the stem. The under surface of the cap may show the gills of the Agaricini, the pores of the Polyporei, or other features; and the colour of the gills or pores is a useful aid to ready recognition of a specimen encountered in the field. There is also the question, whether the substance of the specimen is more or less persistent, or rapidly deliquescent. It is surprising to find how soon one is able, from its more salient characteristics, if not to identify precisely the particular genus to which a species belongs, at least to say in which two or three closely-allied genera it will most probably be found.

One should note also the smell of the fungus, which in some cases is most characteristic. Thus one usually becomes aware of the presence of a Stinkhorn, on being assailed by its powerful and fetid odour, before actually seeing it. Quite a large number of species possess well-marked odours, such as those " of tarragon, of new-mown hay, of violets, of anise, of walnuts, of new meal, etc.; while there are others, which, we must confess, have the odour of onions, of garlic, of tainted meat, of fish, and equally unpleasant substances ; and others, again, which are devoid of any perceptible odour." [1]

Another distinguishing feature is the taste, whether acrid, pungent or mild ; and for this test, one naturally rejects the morsel after the necessary impression has been produced on the tongue, taking possibly such other measures, to avoid any unpleasant after-effects, as the discretion of the individual may commend.

The importance of field study is emphasized, when it is realized that many species vary enormously in passing from the young to the old state, so greatly indeed, that the novice might be forgiven for refusing to credit the identity ; and these relations are naturally best noted when specimens in all stages are found growing together.

Besides the general appearance, some of the other characteristics which are an aid to identification, also change as the specimen becomes old. Thus the surface of the pileus may be dry or viscid, but a species viscid when young may be quite dry in age, and this factor must be allowed for, when observing an old specimen. In such a case, the finding of leaves, twigs, etc., firmly fixed to the cap, or the perceptible adherence to the same of a moistened finger, is a fairly clear indication that the species possesses this property. Any such distinguishing feature as the presence of a volva should be carefully looked for, and for the enthusiast it is the surest method to dig up the entire specimen and so avoid missing anything.

Methods of Delineation. For purposes of study, in view of the difficulty of preserving the individual, it is perhaps advisable to fall back on its representation,

---

[1] 1862, Cooke, *British Fungi*, p. 11.

and here such means suggest themselves as the camera, the pencil and the brush. The first is within the reach of everyone, and, if properly employed, supplies the most faithful method of recording the various details of structure, but, unless colour photography be practised, must obviously fail to record the tints. The other means are only for those equipped with the necessary powers. It must be presumed that the reader has a general knowledge of photography and, therefore, it need only be added that the photographing of fungi does not differ materially from that of other natural objects, and any camera suitable for the latter is equally so for fungi, with perhaps an additional contrivance. Thus, in photographing fungi on the ground, in order to get sufficiently near, it is often necessary, with an ordinary field camera and tripod, to straddle the legs of the latter until there is difficulty in making them stick properly into the ground, and the camera is so insecurely supported that there is a great risk of movement during exposure. This can be avoided either by having a special short-reach tripod, or by the use of a hinged tilting-table, one part of which screws on to the tripod table, and the other supports the camera itself, while the two parts can be clamped at any convenient angle ; if necessary, at 90°, so that the camera points straight downwards. Hand-cameras are almost useless for the photographing of fungi.

It must be remembered that objects near the ground in woods, which are not so well lighted as they would appear, require a generous exposure, and the period of this should be ascertained by means of an exposure meter ; while to obtain a correct rendering of the colour values, panchromatic plates should preferably be employed. Many fungi, for example the Shaggy-cap (*Coprinus comatus*) or the Oyster (*Pleurotus ostreatus*) in their young states, are a most intense white ; and with ordinary or process plates, the latter being those which we generally employ, there is very great halation, unless the plates are backed with dead black. The result is quite hopeless. Even those plates which are backed with a red colour-wash are very little better. Halation is a most serious cause of trouble, unless the precaution in question is taken.

In selecting toadstools for one's operations, it should be borne in mind that, in order to illustrate all the characters of the species, a certain amount of manipulation of the subject may be necessary, and this is certainly permissible, so long as it does not change any of the fundamental characters of growth. Fungi which grow in solitary state should not be crowded together in order to obtain " a nice group " ; nor should those which seek sanctuary in long grass be removed to a lawn ; but short of these and other such character-destroying upheavals, it is desirable from the view-point of " study " to arrange for the inclusion in a photograph of immature as well as mature specimens, together with one (or more) which has been uprooted, or even sectioned, to display structures which might otherwise be hidden. To those purists who would deprecate any readjustment of Nature's scheme, it may be remarked that the result desired is, primarily, a record of the species for future comparison, and not merely a picture. It should here be stated that most of the photographs included in the present volume were not taken chiefly for the purpose of study and, therefore, do not follow the lines we have just laid down.

For those who possess the necessary skill, the finished

print may be coloured, preferably with transparent washes. Alternatively, sketches may be made and coloured. In either case the colours should be matched from an actual specimen, and not from memory, or from notes made in the field. If the sketch is not coloured or if a photograph only is taken, the colours of the cap, the stem and the gills of an agaric should be noted as accurately as possible, and if a standard colour chart is systematically employed, so that the complication of personal colour idiosyncracy can be ruled out, one's records become more exact and therefore much more valuable for comparative purposes.

The prints or sketches should be mounted on stiff sheets of standard size, on which should be recorded the name, the date when found, and the habitat of the species, together with any other notes which may seem desirable, and some of which we have already indicated. The sheets may then be fixed in a loose-leaf album, or arranged, card-index fashion, in a cabinet, either method permitting of easy reference, and the interpolation of other records as they come to hand.

Collecting. In collecting a fungus to take away for further examination, one uses either a vasculum or basket, the latter being probably better, and the larger specimens should be put in separate paper bags, this being almost essential in the case of different species, so as to avoid any confusion in the case of loose parts. Smaller and more delicate kinds require special precautions in packing, and should be put in small boxes or tins, with packing of moss, paper, or similar material. If transported in paper bags, the colour of the spores is often immediately obvious on inspection of the inside of the bag ; but if a spore print is desired, it can be readily obtained by placing the cap, top uppermost, on a sheet of white paper and allowing it to remain for a few hours. Although not really necessary for field study, a microscope is most useful, revealing many beauties previously unsuspected, while its employment is naturally essential for any systematic study of the fungi.

Identification. It is beyond our present scope to discuss the classification and the means of identification of the various fungi one encounters, but the former matter has already to some extent been dealt with.[1] When one desires to find out the name of an unknown species, it is necessary to compare its characteristics with those detailed in a " key," or tabular method of classification, by means of which one is enabled by a process of elimination to run it to ground. The reader who desires to pursue this branch of the subject further will be safe in the capable hands of those who have already written books to this end. Among those works, which can be heartily recommended, are the following :—

British Fungi, by George Massee, with 40 coloured plates, George Routledge & Sons, 1911, 10/6 net.

A Handbook of the Larger British Fungi, by John Ramsbottom, with 141 figures in the text, British Museum (N.H.), 1923, 7/6 net.

Fungi and how to know them, an introduction to Field Mycology, by E. W. Swanton, with 16 coloured plates and 32 black and white plates, Methuen & Co., 1909, 10/6 net.

In conjunction with any of these, one may use the cheap and handy little books of photographs by Somerville

---

[1] See ch. IV : The Fungi in Reality : their structure and characteristics.

Hastings, *Toadstools at Home*, Gowans & Gray, Ltd., Series 1 and 2, 1906 and 1911, at 1/- each.

The Preservation of Fungi. We have already referred to the difficulty of making a permanent collection of fungi. The enthusiast can, however, do something in the matter. A certain number of fungi, such as the polypores, are of a woody or leathery consistency, and can be dried fairly well in the air, being afterwards treated with a 0·1 per cent. solution of corrosive sublimate in alcohol, as a preservative against attack by insects. Corrosive sublimate being a dangerous poison, care must be used in this process. Instead of alcohol, turpentine may be used, in which the sublimate does not dissolve, but merely remains suspended. It must, therefore, be finely powdered, and the bottle requires shaking before applying the liquid. It should be noted that even specimens which have been treated with the sublimate wash must be kept in a dry room, and frequently inspected, and if necessary treated anew, for they are liable to fresh attack. One reason for this is that the first application of the sublimate, although destroying the perfect insects and the larvae, will not destroy the eggs, from which another batch of insects may hatch out later. In time, however, by further treatment, all may be destroyed. The possibility of an entirely fresh attack must also be guarded against.

The same method is also applicable with such smaller species as *Marasmius*, *Panus*, etc., which are originally soft, and which dry without becoming rotten ; and also to some of the larger kinds which are less watery and, therefore, amenable to the same process. Many puffballs, Geasters, etc., dry quite well, and will keep indefinitely, of course, in a somewhat shrivelled condition, while morels become almost stone-like in consistency and keeping qualities. In some species of the Gasteromycetes, which are covered with spines or warts, these fall away during drying, but may then be kept loose. The value of an accurate sketch, or a photograph, in addition to the dried specimen, becomes, however, obvious.

The chief difficulty arises in the case of the very great number of species which are largely composed of water, and which, instead of drying, so as to retain a good deal of their original character, become rotten. To attempt the preservation of the whole of such a species in spirit is a somewhat expensive and troublesome expedient, and the difficulties of the storage and display of a large number of such specimens in glass bottles will act as an effective deterrent to most people. A 2 per cent. solution of boric acid or a 0·1 per cent. solution of corrosive sublimate in alcohol may be used for this purpose. Withering recommends a preliminary treatment of the specimen in a solution of two oz. of copper sulphate (blue vitriol) in a pint of water, to which has then been added half a pint of spirits of wine. After soaking in this for three or four hours, the specimen is placed permanently in a solution of three fluid ounces of spirits of wine to a pint of water. This mode of preservation should really be only employed as supplementary to other methods, for the specimens lose not only their colours but some other characteristics.

There are less cumbrous ways of preservation, all, however, involving a certain amount of trouble. A method used extensively by Klotsch [1] is to divide the fungus in half, from the top of the pileus to the base of the stem, and then to take a thin slice from each half ;

---

[1] *Linn.*, vol. v., p. 478 and 626, tab. 9, Klotsch in Hook. *Bot. Misc.*, vol. 2, p. 159.

these slices being carefully dried, first in the air, and then under slight pressure between dry blotting paper, changing the papers from time to time, exactly as in drying other plants. These sections show the vertical outline of the whole fungus, the structure and details of the stem, whether hollow, spongy or solid, and the details of the gills, pores, etc. In the case of the two remaining portions, the nearly halves of the original fungus, each portion of the cap is carefully separated from the stem, and the gills, if an agaric ; or tubes, if a Boletus, are removed ; after which the four pieces are thoroughly dried as before. When the process is complete, the portions are mounted on white paper, the respective halves of the pileus upon those of the stem, in their original position, so as to give three aspects of the fungus, of which one is the section. In the case of a specimen having a volva or ring, these must also be carefully dried and mounted. The same remarks apply with regard to the need for inspection, and further treatment with the wash, as have already been made in reference to the keeping of the dried specimens of polypores, etc. Owing to the great changes which occur in the different stages of growth, it is obvious that specimens of various ages should be preserved.

Another satisfactory method of preserving a thin section of one of the larger fleshy fungi is described by Constantin and Dufour. A solution, still hot, of 100 grammes (roughly 4 oz.) of gelatine in 500 grammes (about 0·9 pint) of water is applied with a brush to the surface of strong white paper, which is then allowed to dry. At the moment of use, the paper is moistened again and roughly dried with blotting paper, when the section is placed on it in the desired position, and dried under moderate pressure, changing the top paper from time to time as necessary. An analogous method is recommended for fixing a spore print, a solution of four parts of essence of terebenthene to one part of Canada balsam being applied to the under surface or back of the sheet of paper on which the spores have been deposited, so that they are not disturbed.

This then gives the reader some idea of the possibilities of the fungi as a hobby. Whether these plants are sufficiently attractive, we must leave him to judge. But if we have imbued him with sufficient enthusiasm to arrive at an affirmative decision, we shall have achieved our object, and in leaving the embryo " fungus-hunter," we would wish him " good hunting " in that new and fascinating world, on the threshold of which he stands.

CHAPTER XIV

Some further Historical Aspects of the Fungi

FOR those to whom the field study of the fungi presents no attractions, but who may, nevertheless, feel loath to leave the subject at this stage, it should be of interest to consider it historically.

The origins of the fungi lie hid in the remote past, long anteceding all records, and are possibly coeval with, or comparatively little later than, the beginnings of plant life on this planet. Their conjectured botanical origin from the protists has already been discussed,[1] and need not be dealt with any further here, for we are now not so much concerned with that extremely vexed question, but rather with their association with mankind.

Geological Records of the Fungi. It may, however, be remarked in passing that the earliest records are naturally the geological ones, but, owing to the perishable nature of the fungi, it is not to be expected that these plants will have left geological traces commensurate in number with their probable abundance. It is, however, clear, from the work of Kidston and Lang,[2] that the fungi are at least as old as the Devonian rocks, which are thought

---

[1] See ch. IV.: The Fungi in Reality: their structure and characteristics.

[2] 1921, Kidston and Lang, On Old Red Sandstone Plants showing structure, etc. Part V. *Trans. Roy. Soc. Edin.*, LII., p. 855.

by various geological authorities to have been laid down some fifty million years ago ; and in Carboniferous times they certainly constituted an important section of the plant world, for fungi are quite commonly found permeating the tissues of many of the fossil cryptogamic stems of the Coal Measures, thus demonstrating that their relation to the so-called " higher " plants, as saprophytes and parasites upon them, was precisely the same in that period as it is at the present day.

Early References to Fungi. Some consideration has already been given to the Biblical references to the diseases of crops, and such other phenomena as were probably also due to the activities of these plants [1]. There is no mention in the Bible of such larger fungi as the mushrooms and truffles. The first classical allusions to these plants occur in the writings of Euripides [2] and Hippocrates [3] in the fifth century B.C. As we have already seen, both mention cases of fungus poisoning. Hippocrates also describes the use of a fungus for cauterization in certain complaints, to which previous reference has been made. [4]

First Botanical Consideration of the Fungi. The first philosophical or botanical observations upon the structure and characteristics of fungi are found a little later, in the writings of Theophrastus, who describes to some extent the differences between the fungi, which in general he refers to as *muketes*, and the flowering plants ;

---

[1] See ch. VII. : The Damage caused by Fungi, and its Effect on Mankind.

[2] According to Eparchides, quoted by Athenaeus, *Deipnosophistae*, II., 57.

[3] Hippocrates, *Epidemicorum*, lib. vii., § 102.

[4] See ch. VIII. : The Uses of Fungi : in Medicine.

pointing out that the latter are differentiated into a large number of members, such as root, stem, branches, leaves, buds, fruit, etc., while the former are not.[1] Fungi, he says, grow out of, and near the roots of oaks and other trees,[2] while their stems have a certain uniform structure or evenness.[3] Again, in his book on odours, he says that the fungi which grow on dung have no bad smell.[4] Theophrastus describes also what are evidently particular fungi under various names, such as the *udnon, pezis* and *keraunion.* As with the *muketes,* these have no root ; the *udnon,* he remarks, has neither root, stem, branch, bud, leaf, flower, nor fruit ; again neither bark, pith, fibres nor veins.[1]

Identity of Fungi mentioned in Classics. If we had to rely on Theophrastus, the problem as to what particular species is represented by each of these names would present great difficulty. The matter is considerably simplified, however, on comparing with the somewhat scanty descriptions of Theophrastus, the matter contained in the writings of later writers, such as Pliny, Athenaeus, Dioscorides and others, who borrowed from Theophrastus, sometimes using the sense, or even his precise wording, and who give additional data, by means of which conjecture can be converted into reasonable certainty. As will be seen later, this is particularly well exemplified in the case of the *udnon,* which undoubtedly represented the truffle, while the *keraunion* was a particular variety of truffle and the *pezis* a puffball, possibly *Lycoperdon Bovista* (Fig. 78).

---

[1] Theophrastus, *Hist. Plant,* I., 1, § 11, ed. Teubner.
[2] *Ibid.,* III., 7, § 6.
[3] *Ibid.,* I., 5, § 3.
[4] Theophrastus, *De Odoribus,* Frag. IV., 1, § 3, ed. Teubner.

Classical Beliefs as to their Origins. It is not surprising that the nature of the truffles was a mystery to the ancients, and a common belief among the early Greeks was that they were produced by thunder, this, however, not being a general one. Theophrastus says : " With regard to these things [truffles], peculiar beliefs are held, for they say that they are produced during autumn rains, and thunderstorms especially, which are the main reason of their growing, and that they do not last more than a year, and are best for food in the spring. Some think they are produced from seed, because those which grow on the shore of the Mityleneans only appear after floods, which bring down the seed from Tiarae, where many *udna* are found. They grow on the shore where there is much sand. They are found around Lampsacus of Abarnis, and in Alopeconnesus (Asia), and in Elis." [1] Theophrastus adds that the truffles from Cyrene (on the African coast, opposite to the Peloponnesus, and where there were Greek settlements with which trade was carried on) surpassed all the other kinds in flavour. He also says that neither truffles nor wild onions were found near the Hellespont ; but since Lampsacus (the modern Lapsaki) was at the northern end of the Hellespont, this seems rather contradictory.

To Pliny, who obviously borrowed some of his information concerning truffles from Theophrastus, these plants appear to have given much food for cogitation, for he says : " Among the most wonderful of all things is the fact that anything can spring up and live without a root. These are called Truffles (*tubera*) ; they are surrounded on all sides by earth, and are supported by

---

[1] Theophrastus, *Hist. Plant.*, I, 6, § 13 (ed. Schneider).

no fibres or only by hair-like root threads (*capillamentis*) ; nor does the place in which they are produced swell out into any protuberance or present any fissure ; they do not adhere to the earth ; they are surrounded by a bark, so that one cannot say they are altogether composed of earth, but are a kind of earthy concretion ; they generally grow in dry sandy places which are overgrown with shrubs ; in size they are often as large as quinces and weigh as much as a pound.   There are two kinds : one is sandy and injures the teeth, the other is without any foreign matter (*sincera*) ; they are distinguished by their colours being red, or black, or white within ; those of Africa are most esteemed.   Now whether this imperfection of the earth (*vitium terrae*)—for it cannot be said to be anything else—grows, or whether it has at once assumed its full globular size, whether it lives or not, are matters which I think cannot be easily understood. In their being liable to become rotten, these things resemble wood," [1] while he closes his account of the truffles in the following manner : " The thing which they call *misy*, in the province of Cyrene, is of this kind, but it is more fleshy, and of a finer taste and smell." [2]   It is clear that Pliny, from his reference to the *capillamentis*, or hair-like threads, had observed the fine filaments from which the truffle proper is developed, and which are now called the *mycelium ;* but he had obviously no conception of its true function, which has been discussed. [3]

Survival of Classical Beliefs.   The early belief held by some of the Greeks, and cited by Theophrastus,

---

[1] Pliny, *Nat. Hist.*, XIX., ii.

[2] *Ibid.*, XIX., iii.

[3] See ch. IV. : The Fungi in Reality : their structure and characteristics.

as to the origin of truffles, was still current nearly four centuries later, there being still, however, contrary opinions, and supporters of the various theories often engaged in hot debate on the matter. Plutarch, who was of middle age when Pliny died, indulges in a long discourse upon the subject : "Why Truffles are thought to be produced by thunder," [1] and he records that at a banquet in Elis, which was noted for its truffles at the time of Theophrastus, some very large truffles appeared on the table. These having been duly admired, a guest who was not a believer in the Jovian theory of their origin, observed in jest " These are worthy of the late thunder," whereupon Agemachus, the host, begged his guests not to think a thing was incredible, simply because it was strange " for this ridiculous bulb, which has become quite a proverb for absurdity, does not escape the lightning on account of its small size, but because it has a property the exact opposite to it," and he finished by saying : " It is absurd to wonder at these things, when we see the most incredible things imaginable in thunder, as flame arising out of moist vapour, and from soft clouds such deafening noises." The conclusion finally reached by a majority of the company was that truffles were produced by a certain generating fluid contained in the thunder, which, on being mixed with heat, penetrates into the earth, turning and rolling it round, and thus, by a local alteration of the earth, producing the tubers.

The Roman, Juvenal, who flourished about the same time as Plutarch, also believed that truffles were so produced, for in a description of another banquet, he relates : " Before him there smokes the liver of a

---

[1] Plutarch, *Symposiaca* (Table Talk), Book IV., Question 2.

large goose, fit to be eaten by geese, and a boar's head, worthy of the sword of the yellow-hair'd Meleager. After this, Truffles will be handed round if it is spring, and if the longed-for thunders have produced the precious dainties." [1]   It is curious that the same belief was held in comparatively recent times—in fact, when the nineteenth century had almost dawned, as to the origin of fairy-rings.

The Truffles used by The Ancients.   Two later Greek writers, Dioscorides, who lived during the second century of the Christian era, and Athenaeus, towards the end of the same century, also dealt with truffles, and quoted from the earlier works of Theophrastus. Dioscorides says that " among the other exports of Thrace and Macedonia were . . . truffles " ; [2] while Athenaeus speaks of the *udnon* as found in the lofty downs of Thrace, and, like the Cyrenean *misy*, possessing an agreeable odour resembling that of animal food. [3] Dioscorides says, of the Cyrenean truffles, that some of them were of a reddish hue, [4] which suggests that they were a different species, and that more than one kind of truffle was exported from Cyrene.

The general Latin name for the truffle, including the *misy*, and *keraunion*, of Pliny, was " Tuber " ; and Pliny's three differently-coloured varieties have been identified as follows :—

> *Tuber colore nigro* = *Tuber brumale* and *T. melanospermum.*
> *Tuber colore intus candido* = *T. magnatum.*
> *Tuber colore rufo* = *T. rufum.*

---

[1] Juvenal, *Sat.*, V., 116-119.
[2] Dioscorides, *De Medicina*, iii., 26.
[3] Athenaeus, *Deipnosophistae*, ii., 62.
[4] Dioscorides, *loc. cit.*, i, 25.

T. rufum is common in Italy to-day, being their well-known wild truffle, having a reddish and smooth coat ; and it is considered a poor article of food, being little used. *T. melanospermum* is the so-called French truffle, a black rough-coated form, and if it was undoubtedly Pliny's *tuber colore nigro*, it should not have suffered in comparison with the African species. It may, however, have been inferior in flavour to the present Périgord variety. *T. magnatum* is also well known in Italy at the present time, its garlic flavour being much appreciated by the poorer Italians, who roast it in ashes.

The Terfez. The African or Libyan truffle, much prized by the Romans, was identical with the Cyrenean *misy* of Pliny, and of the earlier Greek writers from whom Pliny quoted, and is undoubtedly the delicate terfez (*Terfezia Leonis*) of Leo Africanus and the moderns, sometimes described as *kema* by the Africans, and referred to by the Arabian writers as *cantha* and *camaha*. This has a white coat and a very fine flavour. The terfez is collected by the Arabs at the present day, and differs from the " Tubera " in being found only in sandy soils, while the latter prefer a calcareous one. Where the ancients refer specifically to a sandy habitat, the terfez must have been in question, and it is still quite common in various Mediterranean regions. Martial speaks of the Libyan sand truffles, which he describes as breaking the surface of the earth into cracks, which show where they are to be found ; and Leo Africanus mentions the same effect, which, it will be observed, is quite contrary to the opinion of Theophrastus, previously quoted. This method of finding them appears to have been the one generally followed, and it is still employed by the Arabs, who note the " slight bulging and breaking of the soil

around the roots of the plants under which they grow." [1]
The same effect is seen in the case of the Périgord
truffle, where, however, as has been described, a more
positive method of locating them is employed, by means
of their scent.   There is no reference in classical literature
to the use of pigs or dogs for this purpose.   According to
Walpole,[2] in Greece, in more recent times, the divining
rod has been employed in the search.

Plautus and the Fungi.   Leaving the truffles and
their supposed origin, we may go back to a time a little
later than that of Theophrastus, to consider the aspect
in which the fungi were then regarded by the Romans.
Some fifty years after Theophrastus was first considering
the nature and structure of the fungi, they figured largely
in the plays of the celebrated Roman comic dramatist,
Plautus (254–184 B.C.), being employed in a humorous
sense, which can best be illustrated by some examples.

Thus in his *Trinummus*, when old Charmides, himself
unobserved, sees the sycophant come in, wearing a hat
with a very wide brim, he says " By Pollux, he's just like
a mushroom : he's completely covered by his head." [3]
The slave Sangarimus, in the *Stichus*, says that it is just
as impossible for him to have too much dancing, as it is
for a mushroom to have too much rain.[4]   In the second
act of the *Bacchides*, old Nicobulus complains to the
slave Chrysalus of the perfidy of Archidemides, saying
" Wasn't I a fungus to trust him ? " [5]   In the fourth

---

[1] 1920, Duggar, *Mushroom Growing*, p. 215.

[2] Walpole, *Mem.*, i, 284.

[3] Plautus, Scriptorum Classicorum Bibliotheca Oxoniensis, Oxonii,
Comoediae, *Trinummus*, IV., 2, 9.

[4] Plautus, *loc. cit.*, *Stichus*, V., 7, 5–6.

[5] Plautus, *loc. cit.*, *Bacchides*, II., 3, 49.

act of the same play, Chrysalus says derisively of his master that " he has been travelling up and down this earth, a perfect nuisance ; he has neither sense nor feeling ; he's no more good than a rotten fungus ! " [1] while in the fifth act, Nicobulus himself appears to be by way of sharing the opinion of Chrysalus, for he thus denounces himself : " Of all people here in the world or already dead or yet to be born, who are fools, blockheads, idiots, *fungi*, dullards, drivellers and babblers, I, quite unaided, surpass them all in my folly." [2]   The word " fungus " was obviously used at this time by the Romans as a term of derision, much as is the word " ass " by ourselves to-day.

It is curious to find that the word " mushroom " was comparatively recently being employed in exactly the same sense in this country.   As an example may be quoted the following : " I will make a filthy bustle before I dye among the Clergy of the nation, as contemptible a mushrump and silly ignoramus as some do make me." [3] Other instances of the same usage have already been given in another connection. [4]

Gap in Greek Records of Fungi.   Nicander of Colophon, from whose *Alexipharmaca* we have already quoted, anent the poisonous fungi, was born some time towards the end of Plautus' life, and died before the middle of the second century B.C.   If one refers to Greek literature, there is found a gap from the date of Nicander to that of Plutarch, who lived towards the end of the first century of the Christian era, and for more than two

---

[1] Plautus, *loc. cit., Ibid.*, IV., 7, 23–24.
[2] Plautus, *loc. cit., Bacchides*, V., 1, 1–2.
[3] 1680, D. Granville, in *Life* (1902), 224.
[4] See ch. III. : The Fungi in Fiction.

centuries the word "fungus" (*mukes*) is not to be found either in the works of the Greek poets, tragic or comic, or of the historians. An exception to this statement may perhaps be made, since Athenaeus, who wrote about the end of the second century A.D., quotes from earlier Greek writers who dealt with fungi (*muketes*), but whose original writings have been lost. There is no doubt, however, that during this period their use as foods continued. In the case of the Romans, there is no such hiatus, and some account has already been given of the many references that are to be found in their literature about the beginning of the Christian era.[1]

The Identity of some other Classical Fungi. At about the same time, descriptions of certain fungi are given by different writers, from which accounts they may be identified with some degree of sureness. For example, the genus *Amanita*, of which an example is figured on p. 58, was well known to the Romans, and the modern *A. Caesarea* is unquestionably the species which Pliny had in mind when he refers to " certain kinds which are dry and like nitre, and which bear on their heads, as it were, spots formed from their own coating; for the earth first produces a wrapper (" volva ") and afterwards itself (i.e., the boletus) within the volva, like the yolk in the egg; the young boletus with its volva is very good for food. As the boletus grows, the volva is burst; by and by its substance is borne on the stem; there are seldom two heads on one stem. Their origin is from mud and the acrid juices of moist earth, or frequently from those of acorn-bearing trees; at first it appears as a kind of tenacious foam (*spuma lentior*), then as a

---

[1] See ch. IX. : The Uses of Fungi : as Foods.

membranous body; afterwards the young boletus appears, as we have said." [1] *Amanita Caesarea* is common in Italian markets in September and October at the present day, and Lenz records as modern Italian names for this fungus, *uovolo*, *uovolo ordinario*, *uovolo commune*, *uovolo rancio* (orange-coloured); at Verona *fongo ovo*, *fongo bolado*, and *bolè*. The term *uovolo* recalls Pliny's description of it as being "like the yolk in the egg"; while in *bolado* and *bolè* we have obvious survivals of *boletus*, its original Roman name. The description might serve to some extent for *A. muscaria* and *A. pantherina*, although the volva in these two species is friable, and not wrapper-like, as in *A. Caesarea* (and *A. phalloides*). Buller identifies Pliny's species with *A. pantherina*, but since Pliny was specifically referring to an edible species, which the Panther Cap certainly is not, it must be considered that *A. Caesarea* was the species in question. Houghton [2] quotes Bicknell, who travelled in North Italy in the autumn of 1884, as saying that he saw *A. Caesarea* on sale in the markets of Milan, Bergamo, Brescia, Verona, Cremona, Bologna and other Lombard cities, from the middle of September to the middle of October. He usually had it cut up, and stewed or fried in butter. At the beginning of the season, it was worth about one shilling the pound. Pliny is probably indicating another species of the same genus, *A. muscaria*, the Fly Agaric (Fig. 15), when he says that "some of the poisonous kinds are easily known by a dilute red colour (*diluto rubore*), a loathsome aspect, and internally by a livid hue; they

---

[1] Pliny, *Nat. Hist.*, XXII., 22.
[2] 1885, W. Houghton, Notices of Fungi in Greek and Latin Authors, *Annals and Magazine of Natural History*, Series 5, Vol. 15, pp. 22–49. See p. 30.

have gaping cracks (*rimosa stria*) and a pale lip round the margin." [1]   He goes on to say that "these characters are not seen in certain other kinds" [2] and then proceeds with the description of *A. Caesarea* in question.

The Earliest Illustration of a Fungus. Pliny also describes other kinds of fungi which he considers good for food. Those which he calls "fungi tutissimi, qui rubent callo, minus diluto rubore quam boleti" [3] cannot be identified with absolute certainty by colour only, and this character, conjoined with the property of being esculent, is all that Pliny tells us about this species. Comes identifies it with *Lactarius deliciosus* (Fig. 84), which species he also considers to be represented in the earliest illustration of a fungus which has up to the present been discovered. It is interesting to note that this picture also dates back to the time of Pliny and occurs in a fresco or mural decoration in Pompeii, which, together with its neighbour Herculaneum, was buried by an eruption of Vesuvius in the year 79 A.D., the first of the reign of Titus. It is a curious coincidence that Pliny himself also lost his life at the same place in this eruption, which, although stifling and destroying the inhabitants, did little real harm to many of the buildings or their contents, thus preserving for us a great number of valuable records of the past.

Plants quite commonly occur in the rural landscapes which many of these paintings depict, and one of them shows, in black and white, a number of mushrooms,

---

[1] Pliny, *Nat. Hist.*, XXII., 22.
[2] *Ibid.*
[3] *Ibid.*, XXII, 47.

lying together after being picked.[1]   Comes made a study
of the plants represented in these paintings, and arrived
at the conclusion that it was *Lactarius deliciosus* which
is there shown, and that this is the same species of which
Pliny writes that " the safest fungi are those whose skin
becomes red, but a deeper red than that of the boleti." [2]
Lenz, however, considered the species referred to by
Pliny to be probably *Russula alutacea,* which he says is
still known in Verona as *fungo rosetto,* and in Italy generally
as *rossola buona di gambo lungo,* " the good long-stemmed
red fungus."   In default of further evidence, either of
these two determinations may be correct.

Coprinus comatus.   Another edible species is
described by Pliny as " fungi candidi, velut apice Flaminis
insignibus pediculis," [3] " the white fungi whose head
stems are similar in form to the caps of the Flamens."
These caps are always shown on coins and bas-reliefs of
the Roman emperors as of a conical and cylindrical form,
which, according to Houghton, " reminds one of the
cylindrical pileus of the very excellent *Coprinus comatus*
before it expands and deliquesces, at least I know of no
other edible fungus which so much resembles the figures
of these priestly caps." [4]   Badham, writing in 1847,
states that *Coprinus comatus* is still " largely eaten "
about Lucca at the present day, but it is not given
in Vittadini's list of Italian edible fungi, nor was it seen
by Bicknell in the Italian markets.

---

[1] O. Comes, *Illustratione delle piante nei dipinti pompeiani,* Napoli,
1879, p. 9.   The illustration referred to is No. 102 of the Museo Nazionale,
and is reproduced in the *Pitture di Ercolano e contorni,* Napoli, 1757,
Vol. II., t. 56.

[2] Pliny, *Nat. Hist.,* XXII., 47.

[3] Pliny, *Nat. Hist.,* XXII, 23.

[4] *Loc. cit.,* p. 32.

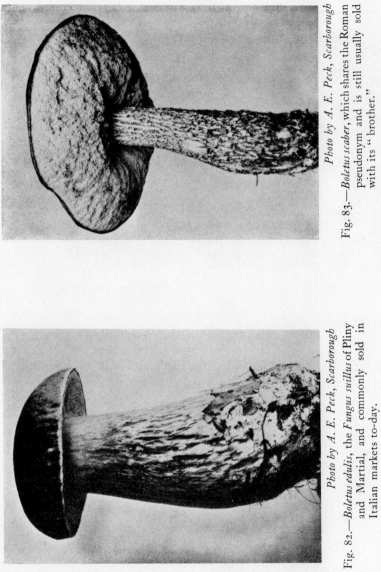

Photo by A. E. Peck, Scarborough

Fig. 82.—*Boletus edulis*, the *Fungus suillus* of Pliny and Martial, and commonly sold in Italian markets to-day.

Photo by A. E. Peck, Scarborough

Fig. 83.—*Boletus scaber*, which shares the Roman pseudonym and is still usually sold with its " brother."

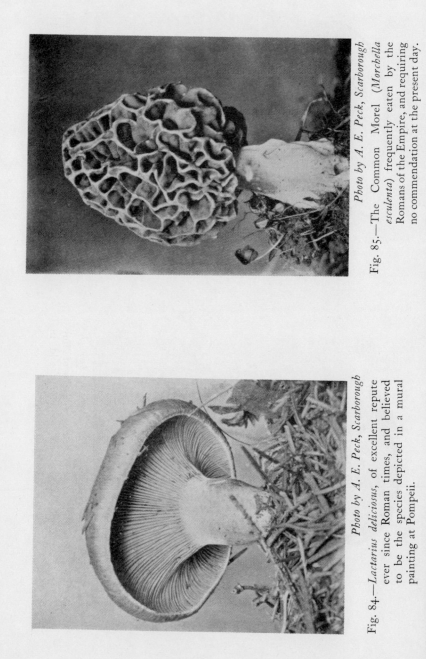

Photo by A. E. Peck, Scarborough

Fig. 84.—*Lactarius deliciosus*, of excellent repute ever since Roman times, and believed to be the species depicted in a mural painting at Pompeii.

Photo by A. E. Peck, Scarborough

Fig. 85.—The Common Morel (*Morchella esculenta*) frequently eaten by the Romans of the Empire, and requiring no commendation at the present day.

Fungi Suilli. The *fungi suilli* of Pliny and Martial, so called because pigs were very fond of them, are usually identified with *Boletus edulis* (Fig. 82), which is known in Italy to-day as *porcino* and *bolè porcin*, evidently the modern forms of the name under which this species was known to the Romans. Bicknell says this fungus was the one most commonly sold in Italy at the time he made his visit. In the market of Bergamo it was being sold at 40c. per pound; at Brescia it was 10c. dearer. In Florence and Parma, there was no other fungus on sale. He adds that when cooked they are usually filled with bread-crumbs, and that they may be bought in almost any grocer's shop. It is probable that the ancient *suillus* included, besides *B. edulis*, *B. scaber* (Fig. 83), which is also very common in the Italian markets, and is known by the name of *porcinello*, or " the little-pig fungus." [1]

A number of other fungi known to the ancients have been identified with a greater or less degree of certainty, and are included in the table given below, which has been compiled largely from the sources previously mentioned.

Modern botanical name.	Name under which the species was known	
	To the Greeks.	To the Romans.
Amanita Caesarea	*Bolitus* of Galen	*Boletus* of Pliny and of all the Latin authors.
A. muscaria ...	—	*Boleti veneni, diluto rubore, rancido aspectu, livido intus colore, rimosa stria, pallido per ambitum labro* of Pliny.
Boletus edulis ... *B. scaber*	—	*Fungi suilli* of Pliny and Martial: *Fungi farnei* of Apicius (?)

[1] Houghton, *loc. cit.*, p. 33.

Modern botanical name.	Name under which the species was known	
	To the Greeks.	To the Romans.
Coprinus comatus	—	*Fungi candidi, velut apice Flaminis insignibus pediculis* of Pliny.
Fomes fomentarius	*Mukes* of Hippocrates	*Aridus fomes fungorum* of Pliny.
Lactarius deliciosus (Comes)	—	*Fungi tutissimi, qui rubent callo, minus diluto rubore quam boleti* of Pliny.
Russula alutacea (Lenz)		
Lycoperdon Bovista	*Pezis* of Theophrastus	*Pezicae* of Pliny.
Morchella esculenta	—	*Spongiae in humore pratorum nascentes* of Pliny. *Sfonduli, Funguli* or *Spongioli* of Apicius.
Pholiota aegerita	*Muketes aigeiritai* of the *Geoponica*	*Fungi populi* of Pliny and Dioscorides.
Pleurotus nebrodensis	—	*Fungus ferulae* of Pliny.
Pl. olearius ...	—	Fungi of the Olive of Athenaeus.
Polyporus, sp. ...	*Muketes apo ton pizas kai para tas pizas phomenoi* of Theophrastus.	—
P. officinalis ...	*Agarikon* of Dioscorides.	*Agaricum* of Pliny.
Psalliota campestris	*Amanitai* of Galen.	*Fungi pratenses* of Horace. *Fungi albi* of Ovid.
Puccinia graminis	—	*Robigo veris* of Pliny, Ovid, &c.
Terfezia Leonis ...	—	*Misy* of Pliny and Athenaeus : *Tuber veris* of Juvenal.
Tuber	*Udnon* of Theophrastus and the Greek writers	The general Latin name for the truffle, including the *misy* and *keraunion* of Pliny.
T. brumale ... *T. melanospermum*	—	*Tuber colore nigro* of Pliny.
T. magnatum ...	—	*Tuber colore intus candido* of Pliny.
T. rufum ...	—	*Tuber colore rufo* of Pliny.

Lightning and the Fairy Rings. Long after classical times, the origins of the fungi were still a matter for contentious debate, and in the sixteenth century, when the belief in fairies was losing strength, earnest seekers after scientific truth evolved what they considered a more probable explanation of the causes of the rings, than that they were made by the fairies' dancing. Their hypothesis was, unfortunately, an equally erroneous one. It was that the rings were caused by thunderbolts. It was conjectured that the diameter of the ring represented that of the bolt, or "lightning-effect," and that only where it came into contact with the air, or along its surface, did combustion occur, burning in the grass a ring of the same diameter. The dead vegetable matter so produced was considered to give rise later on to a more vigorous growth, turning the grass to the dark green colour which is characteristic of that growing on the boundary of the ring.

Among others, Fulke, that stormy prelate and virulent opponent of Romanism, representing what was then no doubt considered as "the modern school of scientific thought," was scornful of the popular conception, and was convinced that lightning was the true cause of "those round circles that ignorant people affirme to be the rings of the Fairies dances." [1] This recalls the similar belief, that we have already discussed, held by many of the Greeks and Romans as to the origin of truffles. The thunderbolt belief is also expressed in the following reference :

---

[1] 1563, Fulke, *A Goodly Gallerye, with a most pleasant prospect into the garden of naturall contemplation, to behold the naturall causes of all kynde of meteors* (1640), 68 b.

"So from dark clouds the playful lightning springs,
Rives the firm Oak, or prints the Fairy rings." [1]

The fact that the rings increased in size from year to
year might have been supposed to present some difficulties
to the advocates of this theory, but it was readily
accounted for by these ingenious fellows, and Dr. Plot
suggested that the lightning might give a kind of herpetic
quality to the ground, "a sort of shingles, qui in unâ
parte sanescens, in proximâ serpit." [2]   It is curious that
Erasmus Darwin, who was a grandfather of the author
of *The Origin of Species*, should still, at so late a period
as the year 1791, be a disciple of the same false doctrine.
It was a few years later, in 1796, that Withering put
forward the correct explanation, which has been already
dealt with.

Another Erroneous Hypothesis.   Later still, with
reference to the fungi in general, Smith says that "Ellis's
beautiful discoveries, relative to corals and their inhabiting
polypes, led to the strange analogical hypothesis that
these insects formed the fungus, which Munchausen and
others have asserted.   Some have thought fungi were
composed of the sap of corrupted wood, transmuted into
a new sort of being, an idea as unphilosophical as the
former, and unsupported by any semblance of truth." [3]
But in view of their strange habits, it is not surprising
that queer conjectures should have been made concerning
the fungi, and the march of scientific knowledge, in
refuting many ancient beliefs, has given us as much to
marvel at as it has destroyed.

---

[1] 1791, E. Darwin, *Bot. Garden*, I., 36.
[2] 1686, Plot, *History of Staffordshire*, p. 9.
[3] 1807, Sir J. E. Smith, *Introduction to Physiological and Systematical Botany* (1836), p. 279.

A Curious Myth.   We may close this chapter with a fitting historical reference to the fungi, relating to a curious myth, connecting them with our reputed ancestors, Adam and Eve.   This is seen in a fresco in a ruined chapel at Plaincourault, in France, dating back to 1291, and purporting to depict the fall of man.   A reproduction of this is shown,[1] and the Tree of Life is represented as a branching *Amanita muscaria,* with the Serpent twining himself in its " branches," while Eve, having eaten of the forbidden fruit, appears from her attitude to be in some doubt as to its after effects, which it is gratifying to know caused her no serious harm.   It is impossible to say whether this picture is merely a quaint conception on the part of the artist, or whether it has any better traditional foundation.

---

[1] (1911) *Bull. Soc. Mycologique de France,* xxvii., p. 31.

CHAPTER XV

The Derivation of Fungus Names

" Salmasius thinks they are so called—a *musco*, because they grow—ubi brevissima est herba, et plerumque non-nisi *muscus*, where the herbage is very short, and scarcely aught except moss."

1627, Bacon, *Naturall Historie*, § 546.

NOT the least interesting matter relating to the fungi is the derivation of their names, many of which, notably in the case of the terms "mushroom" and "toadstool," are very much in dispute. The derivations of the various popular terms that have been applied to them are dealt with alphabetically as follows :—

Agaric is from the Latin *agaricum* and the Greek *agarikon*, which denoted *Polyporus officinalis*, the fungus used as tinder, said by Dioscorides[1] to be called after Agaria, a town in Sarmatia, where it grew very abundantly. According to the same author, it was found " also in Asia, namely in Galatia and Cilicia, on cedar trees." [1] On this point, Badham, however, says : " What Dioscorides meant by agarikon is another uncertainty, to resolve which we have not sufficient data ; one thing seems plain, that it could not have been our officinal *Agaric*, for that grows on the *larch*, whereas his *Agarikon* grew upon the cedar. Julius Scaliger amuses himself at the expense of Athenaeus for saying that *Agaricus* is so

---

[1] Dioscorides, *De Medicina*, III., i.

called, from the country of Agaria, whence he would make out that it originally came ; whereas there never was such a country, his Agaria being like our Poiatia, only another synonyme for Fancy's fairy land." [1] The bulk of modern opinion, however, regards Dioscorides' *agarikon* as certainly referring to *Polyporus officinalis*,[2] while Julius Scaliger (1484–1558), who was frequently in error, appears to have been quite wrong in his statement as to the mythical character of Agaria. It is not only Athenaeus, but Pliny,[3] Dioscorides [4] and Galen [5] who lend support to the belief that this was a real country. The Agari (Gr. *Agaroi*) were, in fact, a Scythian people of Sarmatia Europaea, on the north shore of Palus Maeotis (or Sea of Azov), about a promontory Agarum and a river Agarus, probably not far east of the Isthmus. Diodorus [6] speaks also of Agarus, a king of the Scythians, near the Cimmerian Bosphorus, in B.C. 240. The original derivation appears thus to have been perfectly correct.

Fungus is from the Latin *fungus*, commonly believed to be cognate with or derived from the Greek *sphoggos*, *spoggos*=sponge.[7] The Romans applied the term, however, to certain particular kinds, including representatives of several of our modern genera, and not to the fungi as

---

[1] 1847, Badham, *Esculent Funguses of England*, pp. 4 and 5.
[2] See Buller, "The Fungus Lore of the Greeks and Romans," *Proc. Brit. Myc. Soc.*, 1914, Vol. v, part I.
[3] Pliny, *Nat. Hist.*, XXV., 9, S. 57.
[4] Dioscorides, *loc. cit.*
[5] Galen, *De fac. simp. med.*, p. 150.
[6] Diodorus, XX., 24.
[7] It should be remembered that the Greek " g " was pronounced " ng."

a whole as we now consider them. This aspect of the matter is dealt with elsewhere.[1]

Morel, of which old writers give several different spellings, is said by Murray to be certainly from some form of Teutonic word represented by the Old High German *morhila* (a diminutive of *morha*), from which the Modern German *morchel* is derived. " In Old High German, the diminutive, like the primary word, occurs only for ' carrot ' or ' parsnip ' ; in Middle High German, both were applied also to the fungus ; in Modern German, *morchel* means only the fungus." [2]   The French form is *morille* (16th century in Hatz.-Darm.).

Mushroom has been variously derived from several different roots.   The term has been spelt in many ways, and the list on p. 295, although not complete, serves as a guide in the difficult task of deciding which derivation is the most probable one.

The respective derivations are as follows :

(*a*) From the French *mousseron* (Old French *moisseron*, 1389 in Hatz.-Darm.) generally considered to be from *mousse*=moss, which Diez in his " Romance Dictionary " cites as coming originally from Old High German *mos*, our moss.   The idea is elaborated in the quotation from Bacon at the beginning of this chapter.   Diez follows the same lines, and suggests that it is because the plant grows in moss, or where the grass is short and mossy. This explanation does not seem altogether convincing. An alternative suggestion is that *mousse* bears the sense of softness or nap, referring to the texture of the mushroom.   This, again, is not quite conclusive.   However,

---

[1] See ch. IX : The Uses of Fungi : as Foods.
[2] Murray's *New English Dictionary*.

in spite of the doubt as to the exact shade of meaning that is conveyed by the term *mousse*, the weight of opinion is strongly in favour of this derivation.

Date.	Spelling.	Authority.	Reference.
a.1440	Muscheron	—	*Promptorium Parvulorum*, 349/1.
14...	Mussetum, musserouns	—	Wr.-Wülcker, 597/13.
1527	Muscheroms	Andrew	*Brunswyke's Distyll. Waters*, E vj b.
1533	Musherons	Elyot	*Cast. Helthe* (1539), 89.
1562	Moushrimpes	Bulleyn	*Bk. Simples*, 3 b.
1563	Mushrooms	Hyll	*Art Garden* (1593), 30.
1567	Mushrom	Maplet	*Gr. Forest*, 52.
1578	Mousheroms	Lyte	*Dodoens*, 261.
a.1593	Mushrump	Marlowe	*Edw. II.* (1598), C I b.
1594	Mushroms	Greene	*Selimus*, Wks. (Grosart) XIV., 282.
1595	Mushrumpes	Southwell	*Spirituall Poems* (Grosart), 69.
1601	Mushrome	Holland	*Pliny* (1634), II., 133.
1612	Mesrumes	Parkes	*Curtaine-Dr.*, 20.
1622	Mushrumpes	—	*Interpreter*, A 3 b.
1648	Mushromes	Prynne	*Plea for Lords*, 2.
1651	Mushrumps	Howell	*Venice*, 204.
1655	Mucerons	Mayerne	*Archimag. Anglo-Gall.*, XX. (1658), 19.
1656	Muscherons	Marnette	*Perf. Cook.*, I., 312.
1670	Mushrooms	Gataker	*Antid.Errour*, Ep. Ded., A ij b.
1676	Musrumes	D'Urfey	*Mad. Fickle*, II., i.
1680	Mushrump	Granville	*Life* (1902), 224.
1732	Mushrooms	Arbuthnot	*Rules of Diet* in *Aliments*, etc., I., 258.

(*b*) From a combination of the Welsh or Old British *maes*, a field, and *rhum*, a thing that bulges out, i.e., knob. Hence the Welsh *maesrhin*. Hay thus accounts for the older form " mushrump " and later " mushroom," [1] and

---

[1] See *Notes and Queries*, No. 138, June 19, 1852, p. 598 ; also W. D. Hay, *Text-Book of British Fungi*, 1887, p. 2.

suggests that as this usage is older than the derivation from the French *mousseron*, it thus appears "most plausible." It will, however, be seen, from the table of the different spellings of the term, that we have not been able to confirm this theory, and the earliest references undoubtedly suggest the derivation from *mousseron*, which has much more support than the other.

(*c*) From Old French *mousche*, a fly (from the Latin *musca*). This derivation is chiefly based on the following quotation from Albertus Magnus :

"Vocatur fungus muscārum, eo quod in lacte pulverizatus interficit muscas." [1]

Dr. Prior accepts this as the real source of the word,[2] and some of the earlier spellings appear to lend support to this hypothesis.

Puffball is a corruption of *puck* or *poukball*, formerly called *puckfist*. The word *puck* is of Celtic origin, appearing in slightly varying forms as the Irish *puca*, the Welsh *pwca* or *pwci*, the Icelandic and Swedish *puke* and the Scottish *puck*, all denoting an elf, hobgoblin or demon. The form *puckfist* appears in "The Lancashire Witches." The Saxon word for the toadstool was *pulkerfist*. In view of the habit of these particular fungi, the change from *puckball* to *puffball* is not surprising, and is analogous to those seen in *crayfish*, *posthumous* and other words.

Toadstool, as with "mushroom," has been variously derived, but there is here less doubt as to the correct origin. A list of early spellings, with the reference for each, is given below :

---

[1] Albertus Magnus, I, vii., 345.
[2] 1863, Prior, *Popular Names of British Plants* (1879), 164.

Date.	Spelling.	Authority.	Reference.
1398	Tadstoles	Trevisa	*Barth. De P. R.*, xvi, xxxi (Tollem. MS.).
1398	Tode stoles	Trevisa	*Barth. De P. R.*, xvii, cxxiv (1495), 686.
1440	Toodys hatte	—	*Promptorium Parvulorum*, 349/1
1483	Tade stole	—	*Cath. Angl.*, 377/1.
1519	Todestolys	Horman	*Vulg.*, 101 b.
1527	Tode stoles	Andrew	*Brunswyke's Distyll. Waters*, E vj b.
1530	Tode stole	Palsgrave	281/2.
1562	Todestolles	Turner	*Herbal*, II., Pref.
1562	Todstole	Turner	*Herbal*, II., 29 b.
1563	Toad stooles	Hyll	*Art Garden* (1593), 30.
1567	Toadstoole	Maplet	*Gr. Forest*, 52.
1578	Tadstooles	Lyte	*Dodoens*, 261.
1579	Tode-stoole	Spenser	*Shepheard's Calender*, "December," 12, 67–70.
1594	Tad-stoole	T.B.	*La Primaud. Fr. Acad.*, II., 97.
1601	Tadstoole	Barlow	*Serm. Paules Crosse*, 50.
1601	Toadstoole	Holland	*Pliny* (1634), II., 133.
1607	Toad-stool	Topsell	*History of Four-footed Beasts* (1658), 204.
1682	Toadstool	Somers	*Tracts* (Scott), VII., 68.

There are probably other variants of the word, which has been variously derived from the following sources :

(*a*) From *toad* and *stool*.

The word " toad " is found in Middle English (1200–1500 A.D.) as *tode* or *toode*, derived from Anglo-Saxon *tádige*, of which the root is unknown, and that the first part of " toadstool " represents the animal, is clear from the *Promptorium Parvulorum* (about 1440), where the name appears as *toodys hatte*. Further, there are several other references, at about the same period, in which the first part of the word appears as *padok* or *paddok*, an old

Scottish word for the frog, and incidentally not the toad. However, the last is a small point. Some of these references are given below :

Date.	Spelling.	Reference.
14—	Padokchese	*Harl. MS.*, 1002, lf. 144, b/2.
1450	Paddocstol	*Alphita* (Anecd. Oxon.), 70/7.
1483	Paddokstole	*Cath. Angl.*, 265/2.

The word is still commonly used in Scotland and the North of England as *paddock* or *puddockstool*. In other languages, the same connection is to be found. Thus the toadstool is, in Dutch, *paddestoel*, from *pad*=toad ; in Belgian, *paddenstoel,* and in German *kröten-schwamm,* from *kröte*=toad. In local dialects in England we find " frog-seat " (Northamptonshire) and " toadsmeat " (Isle of Wight). What, however, is the connection between the toad (or frog) and the toadstool ? It has been suggested that since the toad was formerly regarded as venomous and as many toadstools are also, the name of the one was applied to the other. Minsheu in his Dictionary says it is so called, " because the toades doe greatly loue it." Spenser[1] emphasizes that toads are to be found on toadstools, while in Lyly's " Euphues " the following passage is found : " I am of this minde with Homer, that as the Snayle that crept out of hir shell was turned eftsoones into a Toad, and therby was forced to make a stoole to sit on, disdaining hir own house : so the Trauailer that stragleth from his own countrey, is in short-tyme transformed into so monstrous a shape, that

---

[1] 1579, Spenser, *Shepheard's Calender*, " December," 12, 67–70.

hee is faine to alter his mansion with his manners, and to liue where hee canne, not where hee would." [1]   The second half of the word is obviously suggested by the shape of most of the commoner fungi.

(*b*) From the Icelandic *tad*=dung, from the animal's horrid appearance, the toadstool being similarly called after the same, for the reasons already discussed.   This is Webster's derivation, but appears an improbable one.

(*c*) From the Norse *tūtna*=to swell or be blown up. Wedgwood [2] so derives it, from the toad's habit of distending itself, in relation to the rapidity of growth exhibited by the plant.   This, he suggests, accounts for its Danish name *tudse*.   As a parallel case, he cites the French *bouffer* as coming from the Latin *bufo* and the Greek *phusalos*=toad, from *phusao*=to distend.   On the whole, this derivation, although possible, seems less likely than the first.

(*d*) From the Saxon or Old English *tod*, meaning a bunch, cluster or bush, and *stool*, from its shape.   This is suggested by Hay, who quotes Coleridge's line :

" The ivy *tod* is heavy with snow,"

and goes on to say " Evidently the word was first applied to those clusters of fungi often seen on tree-roots and elsewhere.   The erroneous idea connecting toads with these plants seems to be due to Spenser, or to some poet before him, possibly.   Once received, it became converted into ' paddickstool ' in the North, paddick being the name there given to the toad." [3]   But this is obviously

---

[1] 1579, P. Lyly, *Euphues : The Anatomy of Wit*, ed. Arber, p. 239.

[2] 1867, Wedgwood, *Dictionary of English Etymology*, Vol. III., pt. ii., under " toadstool."

[3] 1887, W. D. Hay : *Text Book of British Fungi*, p. 3.

incorrect, for it has already been shown that the term "paddokstole" long antedated Spenser, and there is no evidence of any "other poet" to put against the strong testimony in favour of the relationship of the toadstool to the animal.

Truffle is of uncertain origin and has been differently derived as follows :

(*a*) From French *trufe*, *truffe* (1370 in Hatz.-Darm.), from Latin *tūber*, conjectured to have been altered at an early date to *tūfer*—whence *tūfre*, *trūfe*, *tuffe*. According to Murray, the change of gender has been accounted for by supposing the neuter plural *tūbera* to have been treated as a feminine singular ; according to Graff, *tūbera* appears as a feminine singular in some German glossaries of the ninth century. A form without *r* is found in Swiss Romand and Languedoc as *tufelle*, *tufeda*.

(*b*) As a derivative from the same, but considered to be related to Spanish *trufa*, meaning deceit, imposition or *truffles*, the name having been applied because the plant grows entirely underground and has to be located by scent, the term being thus connected with the Italian *traffare*, to deceive.

(*c*) As an alternative to (*a*), Murray suggests that it is related to the "Italian *tartuffo*, Milanese *tartuffel*, Venetian *tartuf*, *tartufola*, Piedmont *tartifla*, Rheto-Rumansch *tartufe*, Languedoc *tartifle* and Berry *tartrufle*. These mean 'potato' and have been explained by Miège as=*terrae tuber ;* whence the German *kartoffel*, dial. *tartoffel*, Icelandic *tartuflur*, plural, potatoes."

It will thus be seen that the same doubt and mystery which has generally enshrouded the fungi has extended even to their names, regarding the derivation of most of which it is inadvisable to be dogmatic.

"And thus, having through God's assistance discoursed somewhat at large of . . . certaine excrescences of the earth, with other things moe, incident to the historie thereof, we conclude and end our present Volume." [1]

---

[1] 1597, Gerard, *Herbal*, 2nd ed. (reprinted 1636), lib. 3, p. 1589.

Index

*A*CHORION
    SCHONLEINII, 96, 97
Adam and Eve, 291
Agaricaceae, 57
" Agarick," 128, 130, 132, 135,
    146, 163, 292.
Albertus Magnus, 296.
Amadou, 128, 158, 159
Amanita Caesarea, 168, 283
    ,,   *muscaria*, 33, 140, 164,
        232, 284, 291
    ,,   *phalloides*, 37, 58, 231
Anaesthetics, use of fungi as,
    137.
Armillaria edodes, 213
    ,,   *Shiitake*, 211
Asci, 51
Ascomycetes, 72
Aspergillosis, 98

*B*ACON, Francis, 16, 177, 292
    Badham, 17, 292
Barber's Itch, 96
Basidia, 51
Basidiomycetes, 57
Bee Wine, 154
Beef-Steak Fungus, 16, 62
Beer, 153
Berkeley, 2, 139, 162, 178, 257
Black Spot of meat, 121
Blight of potato, 109
Boletus edulis, 131, 210, 287
Boletus of Romans, 168

Boletus scaber, 287
Bordeaux Mixture, 108, 113
Botrytis Bassiana, 98
Brand, 12, 13
Bread making, 150
Brooks, F. T., 22
Brooks and Hansford, 121
Brown Rot of fruit, 123
Buller, 158, 243
Butter of Witches, 13

*C*ATHARTICS, Use of fungi
    as, 135
Chlorosplenium aeruginosum, 161
Cider, 153
Cladosporium herbarum, 122
Classical Writings, Fungi in :
    Apicius, 173
    Athenaeus, 193, 226, 279, 283
    Celsus, 241
    Cicero, 168, 170
    Dioscorides, 130, 192, 198,
        228, 279, 292
    Galen, 171
    Geoponica, 198
    Hippocrates, 128, 226
    Horace, 192
    Juvenal, 168, 169, 278
    Martial, 169, 172, 229, 280
    Nicander, 227
    Ovid, 103
    Plautus, 281

Pliny, 101, 102, 131, 157, 168, 192, 227, 241, 276, 283, 284, 285, 286
Plutarch, 173, 278
Seneca, 170
Suetonius, 169
Theophrastus, 101, 274, 276
Clavariaceae, 66
Claviceps purpurea, 94, 142
Comes, 286
Coniophora cerebella, 117
Connold, 14
Cooke, 160, 161, 164, 252, 260, 264
Coprinus atramentarius, 164, 253
  ,,   *comatus*, 25, 59, 163, 259, 286
Cordyceps sinensis, 141
Counter-irritants, use of fungi as, 128
Coville, 244
" Cramp-balls," 139
Cultivation of fungi, 197
    Boletus edulis, 210
    by ants, 223
    Common Mushroom, 199
        English method, 205
        French method, 200
        French method in England, 203
    Early Attempts at, 197
    in Italy, 210
    Jew's Ear of China, 214
    Methods involving burning, 198
    Morels, 209
    Poplar Fungi, 198
    Shii-take Industry of Japan, 210
    Truffles, 218

Curry-combs, 162

D*AEDALEA QUERCINA*, 162
Darwin, Erasmus, 290
Derivation of Fungus Names, 292
Dermycoses, 96
Devil, The, 15
Discomycetes, 73
Doran, Dr., 134
Doyle, Conan, 11
" Dry-rot," 63, 117
    counter measures, 119
Duggar, 183
Dyeing, use of fungi in, 162

E*DIBLE* Fungi : See under *Foods*
Edible Fungi discriminated from poisonous do., 191
Empusa muscae, 54, 98
Ergot of Maize, 145
    ,,   Rye, 94, 142
Ergotism, 94
Exidia glandulosa, 12, 13
Exoascus, 14.

F*ABRE*, J. H., 168, 194, 243, 255
Fairy Butter, 12
   ,,   rings, 7, 27, 47, 289
    Superstitions concerning, 9
Favus, 96, 97
Fermentation, 145, 148
Fiction and Poetry, Fungi in :
    Ainsworth, Harrison, 29
    Barrie, J. M., 22
    Black, Andrew, 26.
    Bramah, Ernest, 36

Browne, 8
Carroll, Lewis, 29
Clemens, S. L. (" Mark Twain "), 160
Dickens, 19, 22, 32
Doyle, Conan, 2
Drayton, 7
Gay, 30
Glyn, Elinor, 32
Hardy, Thomas, 26
Kipling, Rudyard, 27
Longfellow, 24
Mant, Bishop, 1
Oppenheim, E. P., 24, 25
Phillpotts, Eden, 23
Poe, 23
Pope, 8, 30
Raspe, R. E. (" Baron Munchausen "), 20, 26
Shakespeare, 8, 9, 10
Shelley, 18, 25
Spenser, 1
Stevenson, 24
Tennyson, 9, 26
Thackeray, 30
Verne, 21
Wells, H. G., 19, 20, 32, 33
Winchelsea, Countess, 30
Fistulina hepatica, 16, 62
Flower and Fruit parasites, 85
Flowering Plants, compared with Flowerless do., 41
  mode of nutrition, 40
  reproduction, 39
Flowerless Plants, compared with Flowering do., 41
  mode of nutrition, 41
  reproduction, 40
Fomes fomentarius, 128, 158, 164
Food Value of Fungi, 221

Foods, Use of fungi as :
  among civilised races, 179
  by Greeks, 166, 173, 198, 215, 275
  by Romans, 167, 215, 241, 275
  by savage races, 178
  in Australasia, 189
  in China, 189, 214
  in France, 180, 195, 200, 209, 216, 218
  in Germany, 183
  in Great Britain, 190, 203, 205, 220
  in India, 185
  in Italy, 183, 199, 210
  in Japan, 187, 210, 213
  in Switzerland, 182
  in Tibet, 187
  in United States, 190
  Mediaeval, 174
  Need of greater encouragement of, 191
Forbes, H. O., 254
Forsyth, 107
Friend, 12, 15, 16
Fruit moulds, 123
Fruiting Bodies, 44, 50
Fulke, 289
Fungi : as intoxicants, 33, 233
  as poisons, 36, 225
  associated with Desolation and Ruin, 22
  Beauty of, 4
  Classification of, 55
  Cultivated, 197
  Damage caused by, 93
  Depredations of Saprophytic, 115
  Distrust of, 228

Doubtful, 237
Evil Smell of, 25
Evolution of, 42
Extent of, 43
Figurative Uses of, 37, 281
Food of, 76, 93
Food Value of, 221
Geological Records of, 273
Historical Aspects of, 273
in Fiction and Poetry, 18
in Mythology and Folk-lore,
    7, 27
Reality, their modes of
    existence, 76
in Reality, their structure and
    characteristics, 39
in the Bible, 101, 116, 274
in the Classics, 166, 198, 215,
    241, 275
intermediate between
    parasites and saprophytes,
    89
More pleasing Aspects of, 26
Parasitic, 81, 93
Phenomena, Curious,
    exhibited by, 246
Place in Nature's Scheme, 5
Poisonous, 225
Rapidity of growth of, 20, 247
Saprophytic, 78, 115
Strangeness of, 19
Study of, 260
Use as Foods, 30, 166, 197
Use in Industry, 148
Use in Medicine, 16, 127
Fungi and Witches, 13
" Fungus," Derivation of, 293
Fungus Diseases of Man and
    other Animals, 94
    of Plants, 99

Foods of Commerce, 197
Galls, 14, 86
Names, Derivation of, 292
Fungus suillus, 131, 172, 287

GAUTIER, 140, 162
    Gerard, 132, 139, 175,
    225, 301
Gérard, 241
German Tinder, 128, 158, 159
" Green Oak," 161
Glomerella rufomaculans, 123

" HARD TONGUE," 97
    Hay, W. D., 3, 299
Helvelleae, 74
Hemi-parasites, 89
Hemi-saprophytes, 89
Hesse, Heinrich, 106
Heteroecism, 88
Hirneola Auricula-Judae, 15,
    139
    polytricha, 189, 214
Hooker, J. D., 129
Hosts, effects of parasitic fungi
    on, 85
    effects on fungus, 87
Houghton, W., 173, 284, 286
Hydnaceae, 63
Hygrometers, 164
Hymenium, 45
Hymenogastraceae, 72
Hyphae, 47

IBN-AL-AWAM, 104
    Illustration of a Fungus,
    Earliest, 285
Ink, 163

" JEW'S EAR," 15, 139,
    189, 214

Johnson, Samuel, 163
Judas Iscariot, 15

KAMCHATKADALES, 233
Kennan, 234
Koraks : See *Kamchatkadales*
Krombholz, 216

LACHAUME, 200
Lactarius deliciosus, 285
Langsdorf, 233
Langworthy, 221
Lansdell, 234
Leaf Parasites, 84
Lenz, 284, 286
Lichens, 90
" Lumpy Jaw," 97
Lycoperdaceae, 70
Lycoperdon Bovista, 251
Lyly, 298

" MADURA FOOT," 96
Mandeville, Sir John, 15, 176
Massee, G., 112
Matthiolus, 229
Meat-moulds, 120
Medicine, Use of fungi in, 127
Medicines, Universal, 130
Merulius lacrymans, 63, 117
Mildew, Downy, of potato, 109
    ,,   ,,   tomato, 124
    ,,   ,,   vine, 108
Millardet, 108
" Mithridate," 133
Monilia fructigena, 123
Morel, 30, 173, 177, 199, 209, 294
Mucor, 121, 155

Muscardine Disease of Silk-worms, 98
Mushroom, Common, 43, 199, 251
  Field, 250
  Japanese Pine, 213
" Mushroom," Derivation of, 294
Mutinus caninus, 248
Mycelium, Function of, 49
  Mode of development of, 46
Mycoderma aceti, 156
Mycorrhiza, 91

NIDULARIACEAE, 72

OIDIUM ALBICANS, 96, 97

PARASITIC FUNGI, 81, 93
  Effect on Hosts, 85
  Effect of Hosts on, 87
  on Animals, 82
  on Plants, 83
Paulet, 241
Penicillium, 123, 125
  expansum, 122
Pezizae, 73
Phalloidaceae, 68
Phallus impudicus, 26, 69, 248
Phenomena, Curious, exhibited by Fungi, 246
  Colour Changes when broken, 253
  Curious Growths, 258
  Forces exerted in growing, 252
  Luminosity, 254

" Rain of Blood," etc., 257
Rapidity of Decay, 258
Rapidity of Growth, 247
Sizes attained, 250
Pholiota aegerita, 198
Phosphorescent Fungi, 160
Phytophthora infestans, 109, 124
Plant Diseases, 99
    Classical References to, 101
    Control of, 112
    Early References to, 100
    Effects on Mankind, 109
    Legal Enactments against,
        105, 107
    Mediaeval References to, 104
    Modern Developments in
        Study of, 107
    Monetary Losses occasioned
        by, 111
    Study of, in Eighteenth
        Century, 106
Plasmopara viticolor, 108
Pleurotus phosphoreus, 255
Plot, Dr., 290
Poisoning by Fungi, 195, 225
    Early Classical Cases, 226
    Extent of, 195, 225, 226
    Primitive Remedies, 227
    Treatment for, 237
Poisonous Fungi, 225
    discriminated from Edible
        Kinds, 191
    Toxicology of, 229
    Use as Foods, 240
        Ancient, 241
        Experiments of Paulet and
            Gérard, 241
        by Peasants, 242
Poisons of Fungi :
    Classification of, 230

Real Origins of, 229
Supposed Origins of, 227, 229
Polyporaceae, 61
Polyporus betulinus, 159, 161
    corylinus, 199
    cryptarum, 116
    Mylittae, 178
    officinalis, 128, 130, 146, 158,
        163, 292
    squamosus, 161, 249
    vaporarius, 118
Power Alcohol, 155
Prior, 13
Protists, 42
Psalliota arvensis, 251
    campestris, 43, 199, 251
Puccinia graminis, 88, 104, 111
Puffball, 20, 251, 296
Puffballs and Fairies, 11
Pyrenomycetes, 74

QUICK VINEGAR
    PROCESS, 156

RAMSBOTTOM, J., 10, 193,
    219, 220
Ray, 197
Razor Strops, 161
Rees, 129, 246
Rein, 187
Rhizomorphs, 49, 117
Ringworm, 96, 97
Robigo veris, 103
Roch, 230
Root Parasites, 85
Rubigalia, 103
Russula alutacea, 286
Rust, 88, 102, 103, 105, 106,
    111

SACCHAROMYCES
   CEREVISIAE, 145, 150
  pyriformis, 155
Saprolegnia ferax, 98
Saprolegniae, 98
Saprophytic Fungi, 78, 115
Scleroderma vulgare, 71, 220
Sclerodermaceae, 71
Sclerotia, 49
Setchell, W. A., 221
Smith, Sir J. E., 290
Snuff, 162
Soft Rot of Fruit, 123
" Spawn," 46
Spirits, 155
Spore Colours, 58
  Dispersal, 52
  Germination, 46
Sporophores, 50
Sporotrichum carnis, 121
Spraying, 113, 114
Stanley, H. M., 179
Stem Parasites, 84
Stinkhorn, Common, 26, 53, 96, 248
  Dog, 248
Storage Bodies, 49
Styptics, use of fungi as, 135
Swanton, E. W., 137, 139, 159, 161
Symbiotic Unions, 90

TERFEZ, 280

Terfezia Leonis, 280
Thamnidium, 121
Thelephoraceae, 64
" Thrush," 96, 97
Tinder, 157

" Toadstool," Derivation of, 296
" Tong-chong-ha-cho," 141
Topsell, 176
Torula botryoides, 122
Tremellinaceae, 67
" Trench feet," 96
Trevisa, 241
Trichophyton tonsurans, 96, 97
Truffle, 30, 173, 177, 215, 276, 278, 300
  False, 220
  Hunting, 216
  Summer, 220
Truffle Fly, 217
Tuber aestivum, 220
  magnatum, 279
  melanospermum, 216, 279
  rufum, 279
Tuberaceae, 74
Tunbridge Ware, 161
Turner, 158

USTILAGO MAYDIS, 145

VANDERLIP, 234

Vinegar, 156

WINE, 151

Witches' Brooms, etc., 14, 86
Wood Rots, 116
Writing Materials, 163

YEAST, 145, 148

A CATALOGUE OF SELECTED DOVER BOOKS
IN ALL FIELDS OF INTEREST

A CATALOGUE OF SELECTED DOVER BOOKS
IN ALL FIELDS OF INTEREST

AMERICA'S OLD MASTERS, James T. Flexner. Four men emerged unexpectedly from provincial 18th century America to leadership in European art: Benjamin West, J. S. Copley, C. R. Peale, Gilbert Stuart. Brilliant coverage of lives and contributions. Revised, 1967 edition. 69 plates. 365pp. of text.
21806-6 Paperbound $3.00

FIRST FLOWERS OF OUR WILDERNESS: AMERICAN PAINTING, THE COLONIAL PERIOD, James T. Flexner. Painters, and regional painting traditions from earliest Colonial times up to the emergence of Copley, West and Peale Sr., Foster, Gustavus Hesselius, Feke, John Smibert and many anonymous painters in the primitive manner. Engaging presentation, with 162 illustrations. xxii + 368pp.
22180-6 Paperbound $3.50

THE LIGHT OF DISTANT SKIES: AMERICAN PAINTING, 1760-1835, James T. Flexner. The great generation of early American painters goes to Europe to learn and to teach: West, Copley, Gilbert Stuart and others. Allston, Trumbull, Morse; also contemporary American painters—primitives, derivatives, academics—who remained in America. 102 illustrations. xiii + 306pp. 22179-2 Paperbound $3.50

A HISTORY OF THE RISE AND PROGRESS OF THE ARTS OF DESIGN IN THE UNITED STATES, William Dunlap. Much the richest mine of information on early American painters, sculptors, architects, engravers, miniaturists, etc. The only source of information for scores of artists, the major primary source for many others. Unabridged reprint of rare original 1834 edition, with new introduction by James T. Flexner, and 394 new illustrations. Edited by Rita Weiss. 6⅝ x 9⅝.
21695-0, 21696-9, 21697-7 Three volumes, Paperbound $15.00

EPOCHS OF CHINESE AND JAPANESE ART, Ernest F. Fenollosa. From primitive Chinese art to the 20th century, thorough history, explanation of every important art period and form, including Japanese woodcuts; main stress on China and Japan, but Tibet, Korea also included. Still unexcelled for its detailed, rich coverage of cultural background, aesthetic elements, diffusion studies, particularly of the historical period. 2nd, 1913 edition. 242 illustrations. lii + 439pp. of text.
20364-6, 20365-4 Two volumes, Paperbound $6.00

THE GENTLE ART OF MAKING ENEMIES, James A. M. Whistler. Greatest wit of his day deflates Oscar Wilde, Ruskin, Swinburne; strikes back at inane critics, exhibitions, art journalism; aesthetics of impressionist revolution in most striking form. Highly readable classic by great painter. Reproduction of edition designed by Whistler. Introduction by Alfred Werner. xxxvi + 334pp.
21875-9 Paperbound $3.00

VISUAL ILLUSIONS: THEIR CAUSES, CHARACTERISTICS, AND APPLICATIONS, Matthew Luckiesh. Thorough description and discussion of optical illusion, geometric and perspective, particularly; size and shape distortions, illusions of color, of motion; natural illusions; use of illusion in art and magic, industry, etc. Most useful today with op art, also for classical art. Scores of effects illustrated. Introduction by William H. Ittleson. 100 illustrations. xxi + 252pp.
21530-X Paperbound $2.00

A HANDBOOK OF ANATOMY FOR ART STUDENTS, Arthur Thomson. Thorough, virtually exhaustive coverage of skeletal structure, musculature, etc. Full text, supplemented by anatomical diagrams and drawings and by photographs of undraped figures. Unique in its comparison of male and female forms, pointing out differences of contour, texture, form. 211 figures, 40 drawings, 86 photographs. xx + 459pp. 5⅜ x 8⅜.
21163-0 Paperbound $3.50

150 MASTERPIECES OF DRAWING, Selected by Anthony Toney. Full page reproductions of drawings from the early 16th to the end of the 18th century, all beautifully reproduced: Rembrandt, Michelangelo, Dürer, Fragonard, Urs, Graf, Wouwerman, many others. First-rate browsing book, model book for artists. xviii + 150pp. 8⅜ x 11¼.
21032-4 Paperbound $2.50

THE LATER WORK OF AUBREY BEARDSLEY, Aubrey Beardsley. Exotic, erotic, ironic masterpieces in full maturity: Comedy Ballet, Venus and Tannhauser, Pierrot, Lysistrata, Rape of the Lock, Savoy material, Ali Baba, Volpone, etc. This material revolutionized the art world, and is still powerful, fresh, brilliant. With *The Early Work*, all Beardsley's finest work. 174 plates, 2 in color. xiv + 176pp. 8⅛ x 11.
21817-1 Paperbound $3.00

DRAWINGS OF REMBRANDT, Rembrandt van Rijn. Complete reproduction of fabulously rare edition by Lippmann and Hofstede de Groot, completely reedited, updated, improved by Prof. Seymour Slive, Fogg Museum. Portraits, Biblical sketches, landscapes, Oriental types, nudes, episodes from classical mythology—All Rembrandt's fertile genius. Also selection of drawings by his pupils and followers. "Stunning volumes," *Saturday Review*. 550 illustrations. lxxviii + 552pp. 9⅛ x 12¼.
21485-0, 21486-9 Two volumes, Paperbound $10.00

THE DISASTERS OF WAR, Francisco Goya. One of the masterpieces of Western civilization—83 etchings that record Goya's shattering, bitter reaction to the Napoleonic war that swept through Spain after the insurrection of 1808 and to war in general. Reprint of the first edition, with three additional plates from Boston's Museum of Fine Arts. All plates facsimile size. Introduction by Philip Hofer, Fogg Museum. v + 97pp. 9⅜ x 8¼.
21872-4 Paperbound $2.00

GRAPHIC WORKS OF ODILON REDON. Largest collection of Redon's graphic works ever assembled: 172 lithographs, 28 etchings and engravings, 9 drawings. These include some of his most famous works. All the plates from *Odilon Redon: oeuvre graphique complet,* plus additional plates. New introduction and caption translations by Alfred Werner. 209 illustrations. xxvii + 209pp. 9⅛ x 12¼.
21966-8 Paperbound $4.50

DESIGN BY ACCIDENT; A BOOK OF "ACCIDENTAL EFFECTS" FOR ARTISTS AND DESIGNERS, James F. O'Brien. Create your own unique, striking, imaginative effects by "controlled accident" interaction of materials: paints and lacquers, oil and water based paints, splatter, crackling materials, shatter, similar items. Everything you do will be different; first book on this limitless art, so useful to both fine artist and commercial artist. Full instructions. 192 plates showing "accidents," 8 in color. viii + 215pp. 8⅜ x 11¼.   21942-9 Paperbound $3.75

THE BOOK OF SIGNS, Rudolf Koch. Famed German type designer draws 493 beautiful symbols: religious, mystical, alchemical, imperial, property marks, runes, etc. Remarkable fusion of traditional and modern. Good for suggestions of timelessness, smartness, modernity. Text. vi + 104pp. 6⅛ x 9¼.
        20162-7 Paperbound $1.25

HISTORY OF INDIAN AND INDONESIAN ART, Ananda K. Coomaraswamy. An unabridged republication of one of the finest books by a great scholar in Eastern art. Rich in descriptive material, history, social backgrounds; Sunga reliefs, Rajput paintings, Gupta temples, Burmese frescoes, textiles, jewelry, sculpture, etc. 400 photos. viii + 423pp. 6⅜ x 9¾.   21436-2 Paperbound $5.00

PRIMITIVE ART, Franz Boas. America's foremost anthropologist surveys textiles, ceramics, woodcarving, basketry, metalwork, etc.; patterns, technology, creation of symbols, style origins. All areas of world, but very full on Northwest Coast Indians. More than 350 illustrations of baskets, boxes, totem poles, weapons, etc. 378 pp.
        20025-6 Paperbound $3.00

THE GENTLEMAN AND CABINET MAKER'S DIRECTOR, Thomas Chippendale. Full reprint (third edition, 1762) of most influential furniture book of all time, by master cabinetmaker. 200 plates, illustrating chairs, sofas, mirrors, tables, cabinets, plus 24 photographs of surviving pieces. Biographical introduction by N. Bienenstock. vi + 249pp. 9⅞ x 12¾.   21601-2 Paperbound $4.00

AMERICAN ANTIQUE FURNITURE, Edgar G. Miller, Jr. The basic coverage of all American furniture before 1840. Individual chapters cover type of furniture—clocks, tables, sideboards, etc.—chronologically, with inexhaustible wealth of data. More than 2100 photographs, all identified, commented on. Essential to all early American collectors. Introduction by H. E. Keyes. vi + 1106pp. 7⅞ x 10¾.
    21599-7, 21600-4 Two volumes, Paperbound $11.00

PENNSYLVANIA DUTCH AMERICAN FOLK ART, Henry J. Kauffman. 279 photos, 28 drawings of tulipware, Fraktur script, painted tinware, toys, flowered furniture, quilts, samplers, hex signs, house interiors, etc. Full descriptive text. Excellent for tourist, rewarding for designer, collector. Map. 146pp. 7⅞ x 10¾.
        21205-X Paperbound $2.50

EARLY NEW ENGLAND GRAVESTONE RUBBINGS, Edmund V. Gillon, Jr. 43 photographs, 226 carefully reproduced rubbings show heavily symbolic, sometimes macabre early gravestones, up to early 19th century. Remarkable early American primitive art, occasionally strikingly beautiful; always powerful. Text. xxvi + 207pp. 8⅜ x 11¼.   21380-3 Paperbound $3.50

ALPHABETS AND ORNAMENTS, Ernst Lehner. Well-known pictorial source for decorative alphabets, script examples, cartouches, frames, decorative title pages, calligraphic initials, borders, similar material. 14th to 19th century, mostly European. Useful in almost any graphic arts designing, varied styles. 750 illustrations. 256pp. 7 x 10.   21905-4 Paperbound $4.00

PAINTING: A CREATIVE APPROACH, Norman Colquhoun. For the beginner simple guide provides an instructive approach to painting: major stumbling blocks for beginner; overcoming them, technical points; paints and pigments; oil painting; watercolor and other media and color. New section on "plastic" paints. Glossary. Formerly *Paint Your Own Pictures*. 221pp.   22000-1 Paperbound $1.75

THE ENJOYMENT AND USE OF COLOR, Walter Sargent. Explanation of the relations between colors themselves and between colors in nature and art, including hundreds of little-known facts about color values, intensities, effects of high and low illumination, complementary colors. Many practical hints for painters, references to great masters. 7 color plates, 29 illustrations. x + 274pp.
20944-X Paperbound $2.75

THE NOTEBOOKS OF LEONARDO DA VINCI, compiled and edited by Jean Paul Richter. 1566 extracts from original manuscripts reveal the full range of Leonardo's versatile genius: all his writings on painting, sculpture, architecture, anatomy, astronomy, geography, topography, physiology, mining, music, etc., in both Italian and English, with 186 plates of manuscript pages and more than 500 additional drawings. Includes studies for the Last Supper, the lost Sforza monument, and other works. Total of xlvii + 866pp. 7⅞ x 10¾.
22572-0, 22573-9 Two volumes, Paperbound $11.00

MONTGOMERY WARD CATALOGUE OF 1895. Tea gowns, yards of flannel and pillow-case lace, stereoscopes, books of gospel hymns, the New Improved Singer Sewing Machine, side saddles, milk skimmers, straight-edged razors, high-button shoes, spittoons, and on and on . . . listing some 25,000 items, practically all illustrated. Essential to the shoppers of the 1890's, it is our truest record of the spirit of the period. Unaltered reprint of Issue No. 57, Spring and Summer 1895. Introduction by Boris Emmet. Innumerable illustrations. xiii + 624pp. 8½ x 11⅝.
22377-9 Paperbound $6.95

THE CRYSTAL PALACE EXHIBITION ILLUSTRATED CATALOGUE (LONDON, 1851). One of the wonders of the modern world—the Crystal Palace Exhibition in which all the nations of the civilized world exhibited their achievements in the arts and sciences—presented in an equally important illustrated catalogue. More than 1700 items pictured with accompanying text—ceramics, textiles, cast-iron work, carpets, pianos, sleds, razors, wall-papers, billiard tables, beehives, silverware and hundreds of other artifacts—represent the focal point of Victorian culture in the Western World. Probably the largest collection of Victorian decorative art ever assembled— indispensable for antiquarians and designers. Unabridged republication of the Art-Journal Catalogue of the Great Exhibition of 1851, with all terminal essays. New introduction by John Gloag, F.S.A. xxxiv + 426pp. 9 x 12.
22503-8 Paperbound $5.00

A HISTORY OF COSTUME, Carl Köhler. Definitive history, based on surviving pieces of clothing primarily, and paintings, statues, etc. secondarily. Highly readable text, supplemented by 594 illustrations of costumes of the ancient Mediterranean peoples, Greece and Rome, the Teutonic prehistoric period; costumes of the Middle Ages, Renaissance, Baroque, 18th and 19th centuries. Clear, measured patterns are provided for many clothing articles. Approach is practical throughout. Enlarged by Emma von Sichart. 464pp. 21030-8 Paperbound $3.50.

ORIENTAL RUGS, ANTIQUE AND MODERN, Walter A. Hawley. A complete and authoritative treatise on the Oriental rug—where they are made, by whom and how, designs and symbols, characteristics in detail of the six major groups, how to distinguish them and how to buy them. Detailed technical data is provided on periods, weaves, warps, wefts, textures, sides, ends and knots, although no technical background is required for an understanding. 11 color plates, 80 halftones, 4 maps. vi + 320pp. 6⅛ x 9⅛. 22366-3 Paperbound $5.00

TEN BOOKS ON ARCHITECTURE, Vitruvius. By any standards the most important book on architecture ever written. Early Roman discussion of aesthetics of building, construction methods, orders, sites, and every other aspect of architecture has inspired, instructed architecture for about 2,000 years. Stands behind Palladio, Michelangelo, Bramante, Wren, countless others. Definitive Morris H. Morgan translation. 68 illustrations. xii + 331pp. 20645-9 Paperbound $3.00

THE FOUR BOOKS OF ARCHITECTURE, Andrea Palladio. Translated into every major Western European language in the two centuries following its publication in 1570, this has been one of the most influential books in the history of architecture. Complete reprint of the 1738 Isaac Ware edition. New introduction by Adolf Placzek, Columbia Univ. 216 plates. xxii + 110pp. of text. 9½ x 12¾. 21308-0 Clothbound $12.50

STICKS AND STONES: A STUDY OF AMERICAN ARCHITECTURE AND CIVILIZATION, Lewis Mumford. One of the great classics of American cultural history. American architecture from the medieval-inspired earliest forms to the early 20th century; evolution of structure and style, and reciprocal influences on environment. 21 photographic illustrations. 238pp. 20202-X Paperbound $2.00

THE AMERICAN BUILDER'S COMPANION, Asher Benjamin. The most widely used early 19th century architectural style and source book, for colonial up into Greek Revival periods. Extensive development of geometry of carpentering, construction of sashes, frames, doors, stairs; plans and elevations of domestic and other buildings. Hundreds of thousands of houses were built according to this book, now invaluable to historians, architects, restorers, etc. 1827 edition. 59 plates. 114pp. 7⅞ x 10¾. 22236-5 Paperbound $3.50

DUTCH HOUSES IN THE HUDSON VALLEY BEFORE 1776, Helen Wilkinson Reynolds. The standard survey of the Dutch colonial house and outbuildings, with constructional features, decoration, and local history associated with individual homesteads. Introduction by Franklin D. Roosevelt. Map. 150 illustrations. 469pp. 6⅝ x 9¼. 21469-9 Paperbound $5.00

THE ARCHITECTURE OF COUNTRY HOUSES, Andrew J. Downing. Together with Vaux's *Villas and Cottages* this is the basic book for Hudson River Gothic architecture of the middle Victorian period. Full, sound discussions of general aspects of housing, architecture, style, decoration, furnishing, together with scores of detailed house plans, illustrations of specific buildings, accompanied by full text. Perhaps the most influential single American architectural book. 1850 edition. Introduction by J. Stewart Johnson. 321 figures, 34 architectural designs. xvi + 560pp.

22003-6 Paperbound $4.00

LOST EXAMPLES OF COLONIAL ARCHITECTURE, John Mead Howells. Full-page photographs of buildings that have disappeared or been so altered as to be denatured, including many designed by major early American architects. 245 plates. xvii + 248pp. 7⅞ x 10¾. 21143-6 Paperbound $3.50

DOMESTIC ARCHITECTURE OF THE AMERICAN COLONIES AND OF THE EARLY REPUBLIC, Fiske Kimball. Foremost architect and restorer of Williamsburg and Monticello covers nearly 200 homes between 1620-1825. Architectural details, construction, style features, special fixtures, floor plans, etc. Generally considered finest work in its area. 219 illustrations of houses, doorways, windows, capital mantels. xx + 314pp. 7⅞ x 10¾. 21743-4 Paperbound $4.00

EARLY AMERICAN ROOMS: 1650-1858, edited by Russell Hawes Kettell. Tour of 12 rooms, each representative of a different era in American history and each furnished, decorated, designed and occupied in the style of the era. 72 plans and elevations, 8-page color section, etc., show fabrics, wall papers, arrangements, etc. Full descriptive text. xvii + 200pp. of text. 8⅜ x 11¼.

21633-0 Paperbound $5.00

THE FITZWILLIAM VIRGINAL BOOK, edited by J. Fuller Maitland and W. B. Squire. Full modern printing of famous early 17th-century ms. volume of 300 works by Morley, Byrd, Bull, Gibbons, etc. For piano or other modern keyboard instrument; easy to read format. xxxvi + 938pp. 8⅜ x 11.

21068-5, 21069-3 Two volumes, Paperbound $10.00

KEYBOARD MUSIC, Johann Sebastian Bach. Bach Gesellschaft edition. A rich selection of Bach's masterpieces for the harpsichord: the six English Suites, six French Suites, the six Partitas (Clavierübung part I), the Goldberg Variations (Clavierübung part IV), the fifteen Two-Part Inventions and the fifteen Three-Part Sinfonias. Clearly reproduced on large sheets with ample margins; eminently playable. vi + 312pp. 8⅛ x 11. 22360-4 Paperbound $5.00

THE MUSIC OF BACH: AN INTRODUCTION, Charles Sanford Terry. A fine, nontechnical introduction to Bach's music, both instrumental and vocal. Covers organ music, chamber music, passion music, other types. Analyzes themes, developments, innovations. x + 114pp. 21075-8 Paperbound $1.50

BEETHOVEN AND HIS NINE SYMPHONIES, Sir George Grove. Noted British musicologist provides best history, analysis, commentary on symphonies. Very thorough, rigorously accurate; necessary to both advanced student and amateur music lover. 436 musical passages. vii + 407 pp. 20334-4 Paperbound $2.75

JOHANN SEBASTIAN BACH, Philipp Spitta. One of the great classics of musicology, this definitive analysis of Bach's music (and life) has never been surpassed. Lucid, nontechnical analyses of hundreds of pieces (30 pages devoted to St. Matthew Passion, 26 to B Minor Mass). Also includes major analysis of 18th-century music. 450 musical examples. 40-page musical supplement. Total of xx + 1799pp.
(EUK) 22278-0, 22279-9 Two volumes, Clothbound $17.50

MOZART AND HIS PIANO CONCERTOS, Cuthbert Girdlestone. The only full-length study of an important area of Mozart's creativity. Provides detailed analyses of all 23 concertos, traces inspirational sources. 417 musical examples. Second edition. 509pp.
21271-8 Paperbound $3.50

THE PERFECT WAGNERITE: A COMMENTARY ON THE NIBLUNG'S RING, George Bernard Shaw. Brilliant and still relevant criticism in remarkable essays on Wagner's Ring cycle, Shaw's ideas on political and social ideology behind the plots, role of Leitmotifs, vocal requisites, etc. Prefaces. xxi + 136pp.
(USO) 21707-8 Paperbound $1.75

DON GIOVANNI, W. A. Mozart. Complete libretto, modern English translation; biographies of composer and librettist; accounts of early performances and critical reaction. Lavishly illustrated. All the material you need to understand and appreciate this great work. Dover Opera Guide and Libretto Series; translated and introduced by Ellen Bleiler. 92 illustrations. 209pp.
21134-7 Paperbound $2.00

BASIC ELECTRICITY, U. S. Bureau of Naval Personel. Originally a training course, best non-technical coverage of basic theory of electricity and its applications. Fundamental concepts, batteries, circuits, conductors and wiring techniques, AC and DC, inductance and capacitance, generators, motors, transformers, magnetic amplifiers, synchros, servomechanisms, etc. Also covers blue-prints, electrical diagrams, etc. Many questions, with answers. 349 illustrations. x + 448pp. 6½ x 9¼.
20973-3 Paperbound $3.50

REPRODUCTION OF SOUND, Edgar Villchur. Thorough coverage for laymen of high fidelity systems, reproducing systems in general, needles, amplifiers, preamps, loudspeakers, feedback, explaining physical background. "A rare talent for making technicalities vividly comprehensible," R. Darrell, High Fidelity. 69 figures. iv + 92pp.
21515-6 Paperbound $1.35

HEAR ME TALKIN' TO YA: THE STORY OF JAZZ AS TOLD BY THE MEN WHO MADE IT, Nat Shapiro and Nat Hentoff. Louis Armstrong, Fats Waller, Jo Jones, Clarence Williams, Billy Holiday, Duke Ellington, Jelly Roll Morton and dozens of other jazz greats tell how it was in Chicago's South Side, New Orleans, depression Harlem and the modern West Coast as jazz was born and grew. xvi + 429pp.
21726-4 Paperbound $3.00

FABLES OF AESOP, translated by Sir Roger L'Estrange. A reproduction of the very rare 1931 Paris edition; a selection of the most interesting fables, together with 50 imaginative drawings by Alexander Calder. v + 128pp. 6½x9¼.
21780-9 Paperbound $1.50

AGAINST THE GRAIN (A REBOURS), Joris K. Huysmans. Filled with weird images, evidences of a bizarre imagination, exotic experiments with hallucinatory drugs, rich tastes and smells and the diversions of its sybarite hero Duc Jean des Esseintes, this classic novel pushed 19th-century literary decadence to its limits. Full unabridged edition. Do not confuse this with abridged editions generally sold. Introduction by Havelock Ellis. xlix + 206pp. 22190-3 Paperbound $2.50

VARIORUM SHAKESPEARE: HAMLET. Edited by Horace H. Furness; a landmark of American scholarship. Exhaustive footnotes and appendices treat all doubtful words and phrases, as well as suggested critical emendations throughout the play's history. First volume contains editor's own text, collated with all Quartos and Folios. Second volume contains full first Quarto, translations of Shakespeare's sources (Belleforest, and Saxo Grammaticus), Der Bestrafte Brudermord, and many essays on critical and historical points of interest by major authorities of past and present. Includes details of staging and costuming over the years. By far the best edition available for serious students of Shakespeare. Total of xx + 905pp. 21004-9, 21005-7, 2 volumes, Paperbound $7.00

A LIFE OF WILLIAM SHAKESPEARE, Sir Sidney Lee. This is the standard life of Shakespeare, summarizing everything known about Shakespeare and his plays. Incredibly rich in material, broad in coverage, clear and judicious, it has served thousands as the best introduction to Shakespeare. 1931 edition. 9 plates. xxix + 792pp. 21967-4 Paperbound $3.75

MASTERS OF THE DRAMA, John Gassner. Most comprehensive history of the drama in print, covering every tradition from Greeks to modern Europe and America, including India, Far East, etc. Covers more than 800 dramatists, 2000 plays, with biographical material, plot summaries, theatre history, criticism, etc. "Best of its kind in English," *New Republic*. 77 illustrations. xxii + 890pp. 20100-7 Clothbound $10.00

THE EVOLUTION OF THE ENGLISH LANGUAGE, George McKnight. The growth of English, from the 14th century to the present. Unusual, non-technical account presents basic information in very interesting form: sound shifts, change in grammar and syntax, vocabulary growth, similar topics. Abundantly illustrated with quotations. Formerly *Modern English in the Making*. xii + 590pp. 21932-1 Paperbound $3.50

AN ETYMOLOGICAL DICTIONARY OF MODERN ENGLISH, Ernest Weekley. Fullest, richest work of its sort, by foremost British lexicographer. Detailed word histories, including many colloquial and archaic words; extensive quotations. Do not confuse this with the Concise Etymological Dictionary, which is much abridged. Total of xxvii + 830pp. 6½ x 9¼. 21873-2, 21874-0 Two volumes, Paperbound $7.90

FLATLAND: A ROMANCE OF MANY DIMENSIONS, E. A. Abbott. Classic of science-fiction explores ramifications of life in a two-dimensional world, and what happens when a three-dimensional being intrudes. Amusing reading, but also useful as introduction to thought about hyperspace. Introduction by Banesh Hoffmann. 16 illustrations. xx + 103pp. 20001-9 Paperbound $1.00

POEMS OF ANNE BRADSTREET, edited with an introduction by Robert Hutchinson. A new selection of poems by America's first poet and perhaps the first significant woman poet in the English language. 48 poems display her development in works of considerable variety—love poems, domestic poems, religious meditations, formal elegies, "quaternions," etc. Notes, bibliography. viii + 222pp.

22160-1 Paperbound $2.50

THREE GOTHIC NOVELS: THE CASTLE OF OTRANTO BY HORACE WALPOLE; VATHEK BY WILLIAM BECKFORD; THE VAMPYRE BY JOHN POLIDORI, WITH FRAGMENT OF A NOVEL BY LORD BYRON, edited by E. F. Bleiler. The first Gothic novel, by Walpole; the finest Oriental tale in English, by Beckford; powerful Romantic supernatural story in versions by Polidori and Byron. All extremely important in history of literature; all still exciting, packed with supernatural thrills, ghosts, haunted castles, magic, etc. xl + 291pp.

21232-7 Paperbound $2.50

THE BEST TALES OF HOFFMANN, E. T. A. Hoffmann. 10 of Hoffmann's most important stories, in modern re-editings of standard translations: Nutcracker and the King of Mice, Signor Formica, Automata, The Sandman, Rath Krespel, The Golden Flowerpot, Master Martin the Cooper, The Mines of Falun, The King's Betrothed, A New Year's Eve Adventure. 7 illustrations by Hoffmann. Edited by E. F. Bleiler. xxxix + 419pp.

21793-0 Paperbound $3.00

GHOST AND HORROR STORIES OF AMBROSE BIERCE, Ambrose Bierce. 23 strikingly modern stories of the horrors latent in the human mind: The Eyes of the Panther, The Damned Thing, An Occurrence at Owl Creek Bridge, An Inhabitant of Carcosa, etc., plus the dream-essay, Visions of the Night. Edited by E. F. Bleiler. xxii + 199pp.

20767-6 Paperbound $1.50

BEST GHOST STORIES OF J. S. LEFANU, J. Sheridan LeFanu. Finest stories by Victorian master often considered greatest supernatural writer of all. Carmilla, Green Tea, The Haunted Baronet, The Familiar, and 12 others. Most never before available in the U. S. A. Edited by E. F. Bleiler. 8 illustrations from Victorian publications. xvii + 467pp.

20415-4 Paperbound $3.00

MATHEMATICAL FOUNDATIONS OF INFORMATION THEORY, A. I. Khinchin. Comprehensive introduction to work of Shannon, McMillan, Feinstein and Khinchin, placing these investigations on a rigorous mathematical basis. Covers entropy concept in probability theory, uniqueness theorem, Shannon's inequality, ergodic sources, the E property, martingale concept, noise, Feinstein's fundamental lemma, Shanon's first and second theorems. Translated by R. A. Silverman and M. D. Friedman. iii + 120pp.

60434-9 Paperbound $2.00

SEVEN SCIENCE FICTION NOVELS, H. G. Wells. The standard collection of the great novels. Complete, unabridged. *First Men in the Moon, Island of Dr. Moreau, War of the Worlds, Food of the Gods, Invisible Man, Time Machine, In the Days of the Comet.* Not only science fiction fans, but every educated person owes it to himself to read these novels. 1015pp. (USO) 20264-X Clothbound $6.00

LAST AND FIRST MEN AND STAR MAKER, TWO SCIENCE FICTION NOVELS, Olaf Stapledon. Greatest future histories in science fiction. In the first, human intelligence is the "hero," through strange paths of evolution, interplanetary invasions, incredible technologies, near extinctions and reemergences. Star Maker describes the quest of a band of star rovers for intelligence itself, through time and space: weird inhuman civilizations, crustacean minds, symbiotic worlds, etc. Complete, unabridged. v + 438pp. (USO) 21962-3 Paperbound $2.50

THREE PROPHETIC NOVELS, H. G. WELLS. Stages of a consistently planned future for mankind. *When the Sleeper Wakes,* and *A Story of the Days to Come,* anticipate *Brave New World* and *1984,* in the 21st Century; *The Time Machine,* only complete version in print, shows farther future and the end of mankind. All show Wells's greatest gifts as storyteller and novelist. Edited by E. F. Bleiler. x + 335pp. (USO) 20605-X Paperbound $2.50

THE DEVIL'S DICTIONARY, Ambrose Bierce. America's own Oscar Wilde—Ambrose Bierce—offers his barbed iconoclastic wisdom in over 1,000 definitions hailed by H. L. Mencken as "some of the most gorgeous witticisms in the English language." 145pp. 20487-1 Paperbound $1.25

MAX AND MORITZ, Wilhelm Busch. Great children's classic, father of comic strip, of two bad boys, Max and Moritz. Also Ker and Plunk (Plisch und Plumm), Cat and Mouse, Deceitful Henry, Ice-Peter, The Boy and the Pipe, and five other pieces. Original German, with English translation. Edited by H. Arthur Klein; translations by various hands and H. Arthur Klein. vi + 216pp.
20181-3 Paperbound $2.00

PIGS IS PIGS AND OTHER FAVORITES, Ellis Parker Butler. The title story is one of the best humor short stories, as Mike Flannery obfuscates biology and English. Also included, That Pup of Murchison's, The Great American Pie Company, and Perkins of Portland. 14 illustrations. v + 109pp. 21532-6 Paperbound $1.25

THE PETERKIN PAPERS, Lucretia P. Hale. It takes genius to be as stupidly mad as the Peterkins, as they decide to become wise, celebrate the "Fourth," keep a cow, and otherwise strain the resources of the Lady from Philadelphia. Basic book of American humor. 153 illustrations. 219pp. 20794-3 Paperbound $2.00

PERRAULT'S FAIRY TALES, translated by A. E. Johnson and S. R. Littlewood, with 34 full-page illustrations by Gustave Doré. All the original Perrault stories—Cinderella, Sleeping Beauty, Bluebeard, Little Red Riding Hood, Puss in Boots, Tom Thumb, etc.—with their witty verse morals and the magnificent illustrations of Doré. One of the five or six great books of European fairy tales. viii + 117pp. 8⅛ x 11. 22311-6 Paperbound $2.00

OLD HUNGARIAN FAIRY TALES, Baroness Orczy. Favorites translated and adapted by author of the *Scarlet Pimpernel.* Eight fairy tales include "The Suitors of Princess Fire-Fly," "The Twin Hunchbacks," "Mr. Cuttlefish's Love Story," and "The Enchanted Cat." This little volume of magic and adventure will captivate children as it has for generations. 90 drawings by Montagu Barstow. 96pp.
(USO) 22293-4 Paperbound $1.95

THE RED FAIRY BOOK, Andrew Lang. Lang's color fairy books have long been children's favorites. This volume includes Rapunzel, Jack and the Bean-stalk and 35 other stories, familiar and unfamiliar. 4 plates, 93 illustrations x + 367pp.
21673-X Paperbound $2.50

THE BLUE FAIRY BOOK, Andrew Lang. Lang's tales come from all countries and all times. Here are 37 tales from Grimm, the Arabian Nights, Greek Mythology, and other fascinating sources. 8 plates, 130 illustrations. xi + 390pp.
21437-0 Paperbound $2.50

HOUSEHOLD STORIES BY THE BROTHERS GRIMM. Classic English-language edition of the well-known tales — Rumpelstiltskin, Snow White, Hansel and Gretel, The Twelve Brothers, Faithful John, Rapunzel, Tom Thumb (52 stories in all). Translated into simple, straightforward English by Lucy Crane. Ornamented with headpieces, vignettes, elaborate decorative initials and a dozen full-page illustrations by Walter Crane. x + 269pp. 21080-4 Paperbound **$2.00**

THE MERRY ADVENTURES OF ROBIN HOOD, Howard Pyle. The finest modern versions of the traditional ballads and tales about the great English outlaw. Howard Pyle's complete prose version, with every word, every illustration of the first edition. Do not confuse this facsimile of the original (1883) with modern editions that change text or illustrations. 23 plates plus many page decorations. xxii + 296pp.
22043-5 Paperbound $2.50

THE STORY OF KING ARTHUR AND HIS KNIGHTS, Howard Pyle. The finest children's version of the life of King Arthur; brilliantly retold by Pyle, with 48 of his most imaginative illustrations. xviii + 313pp. 6⅛ x 9¼.
21445-1 Paperbound $2.50

THE WONDERFUL WIZARD OF OZ, L. Frank Baum. America's finest children's book in facsimile of first edition with all Denslow illustrations in full color. The edition a child should have. Introduction by Martin Gardner. 23 color plates, scores of drawings. iv + 267pp. 20691-2 Paperbound $2.50

THE MARVELOUS LAND OF OZ, L. Frank Baum. The second Oz book, every bit as imaginative as the Wizard. The hero is a boy named Tip, but the Scarecrow and the Tin Woodman are back, as is the Oz magic. 16 color plates, 120 drawings by John R. Neill. 287pp. 20692-0 Paperbound $2.50

THE MAGICAL MONARCH OF MO, L. Frank Baum. Remarkable adventures in a land even stranger than Oz. The best of Baum's books not in the Oz series. 15 color plates and dozens of drawings by Frank Verbeck. xviii + 237pp.
21892-9 Paperbound $2.25

THE BAD CHILD'S BOOK OF BEASTS, MORE BEASTS FOR WORSE CHILDREN, A MORAL ALPHABET, Hilaire Belloc. Three complete humor classics in one volume. Be kind to the frog, and do not call him names . . . and 28 other whimsical animals. Familiar favorites and some not so well known. Illustrated by Basil Blackwell.
156pp. (USO) 20749-8 Paperbound $1.50

EAST O' THE SUN AND WEST O' THE MOON, George W. Dasent. Considered the best of all translations of these Norwegian folk tales, this collection has been enjoyed by generations of children (and folklorists too). Includes True and Untrue, Why the Sea is Salt, East O' the Sun and West O' the Moon, Why the Bear is Stumpy-Tailed, Boots and the Troll, The Cock and the Hen, Rich Peter the Pedlar, and 52 more. The only edition with all 59 tales. 77 illustrations by Erik Werenskiold and Theodor Kittelsen. xv + 418pp. 22521-6 Paperbound $3.50

GOOPS AND HOW TO BE THEM, Gelett Burgess. Classic of tongue-in-cheek humor, masquerading as etiquette book. 87 verses, twice as many cartoons, show mischievous Goops as they demonstrate to children virtues of table manners, neatness, courtesy, etc. Favorite for generations. viii + 88pp. $6\frac{1}{2}$ x $9\frac{1}{4}$.
22233-0 Paperbound $1.25

ALICE'S ADVENTURES UNDER GROUND, Lewis Carroll. The first version, quite different from the final *Alice in Wonderland*, printed out by Carroll himself with his own illustrations. Complete facsimile of the "million dollar" manuscript Carroll gave to Alice Liddell in 1864. Introduction by Martin Gardner. viii + 96pp. Title and dedication pages in color. 21482-6 Paperbound $1.25

THE BROWNIES, THEIR BOOK, Palmer Cox. Small as mice, cunning as foxes, exuberant and full of mischief, the Brownies go to the zoo, toy shop, seashore, circus, etc., in 24 verse adventures and 266 illustrations. Long a favorite, since their first appearance in St. Nicholas Magazine. xi + 144pp. $6\frac{5}{8}$ x $9\frac{1}{4}$.
21265-3 Paperbound $1.75

SONGS OF CHILDHOOD, Walter De La Mare. Published (under the pseudonym Walter Ramal) when De La Mare was only 29, this charming collection has long been a favorite children's book. A facsimile of the first edition in paper, the 47 poems capture the simplicity of the nursery rhyme and the ballad, including such lyrics as I Met Eve, Tartary, The Silver Penny. vii + 106pp. (USO) 21972-0 Paperbound
$1.25

THE COMPLETE NONSENSE OF EDWARD LEAR, Edward Lear. The finest 19th-century humorist-cartoonist in full: all nonsense limericks, zany alphabets, Owl and Pussycat, songs, nonsense botany, and more than 500 illustrations by Lear himself. Edited by Holbrook Jackson. xxix + 287pp. (USO) 20167-8 Paperbound $2.00

BILLY WHISKERS: THE AUTOBIOGRAPHY OF A GOAT, Frances Trego Montgomery. A favorite of children since the early 20th century, here are the escapades of that rambunctious, irresistible and mischievous goat—Billy Whiskers. Much in the spirit of *Peck's Bad Boy,* this is a book that children never tire of reading or hearing. All the original familiar illustrations by W. H. Fry are included: 6 color plates, 18 black and white drawings. 159pp. 22345-0 Paperbound $2.00

MOTHER GOOSE MELODIES. Faithful republication of the fabulously rare Munroe and Francis "copyright 1833" Boston edition—the most important Mother Goose collection, usually referred to as the "original." Familiar rhymes plus many rare ones, with wonderful old woodcut illustrations. Edited by E. F. Bleiler. 128pp. $4\frac{1}{2}$ x $6\frac{3}{8}$. 22577-1 Paperbound $1.00

TWO LITTLE SAVAGES; BEING THE ADVENTURES OF TWO BOYS WHO LIVED AS INDIANS AND WHAT THEY LEARNED, Ernest Thompson Seton. Great classic of nature and boyhood provides a vast range of woodlore in most palatable form, a genuinely entertaining story. Two farm boys build a teepee in woods and live in it for a month, working out Indian solutions to living problems, star lore, birds and animals, plants, etc. 293 illustrations. vii + 286pp.

20985-7 Paperbound $2.50

PETER PIPER'S PRACTICAL PRINCIPLES OF PLAIN & PERFECT PRONUNCIATION. Alliterative jingles and tongue-twisters of surprising charm, that made their first appearance in America about 1830. Republished in full with the spirited woodcut illustrations from this earliest American edition. 32pp. 4½ x 6⅜.

22560-7 Paperbound $1.00

SCIENCE EXPERIMENTS AND AMUSEMENTS FOR CHILDREN, Charles Vivian. 73 easy experiments, requiring only materials found at home or easily available, such as candles, coins, steel wool, etc.; illustrate basic phenomena like vacuum, simple chemical reaction, etc. All safe. Modern, well-planned. Formerly *Science Games for Children.* 102 photos, numerous drawings. 96pp. 6⅛ x 9¼.

21856-2 Paperbound $1.25

AN INTRODUCTION TO CHESS MOVES AND TACTICS SIMPLY EXPLAINED, Leonard Barden. Informal intermediate introduction, quite strong in explaining reasons for moves. Covers basic material, tactics, important openings, traps, positional play in middle game, end game. Attempts to isolate patterns and recurrent configurations. Formerly *Chess.* 58 figures. 102pp.   (USO) 21210-6 Paperbound $1.25

LASKER'S MANUAL OF CHESS, Dr. Emanuel Lasker. Lasker was not only one of the five great World Champions, he was also one of the ablest expositors, theorists, and analysts. In many ways, his Manual, permeated with his philosophy of battle, filled with keen insights, is one of the greatest works ever written on chess. Filled with analyzed games by the great players. A single-volume library that will profit almost any chess player, beginner or master. 308 diagrams. xli x 349pp.

20640-8 Paperbound $2.75

THE MASTER BOOK OF MATHEMATICAL RECREATIONS, Fred Schuh. In opinion of many the finest work ever prepared on mathematical puzzles, stunts, recreations; exhaustively thorough explanations of mathematics involved, analysis of effects, citation of puzzles and games. Mathematics involved is elementary. Translated bv F. Göbel. 194 figures. xxiv + 430pp.   22134-2 Paperbound $3.50

MATHEMATICS, MAGIC AND MYSTERY, Martin Gardner. Puzzle editor for Scientific American explains mathematics behind various mystifying tricks: card tricks, stage "mind reading," coin and match tricks, counting out games, geometric dissections, etc. Probability sets, theory of numbers clearly explained. Also provides more than 400 tricks, guaranteed to work, that you can do. 135 illustrations. xii + 176pp.

20335-2 Paperbound $1.75

MATHEMATICAL PUZZLES FOR BEGINNERS AND ENTHUSIASTS, Geoffrey Mott-Smith. 189 puzzles from easy to difficult—involving arithmetic, logic, algebra, properties of digits, probability, etc.—for enjoyment and mental stimulus. Explanation of mathematical principles behind the puzzles. 135 illustrations. viii + 248pp.
20198-8 Paperbound $1.75

PAPER FOLDING FOR BEGINNERS, William D. Murray and Francis J. Rigney. Easiest book on the market, clearest instructions on making interesting, beautiful origami. Sail boats, cups, roosters, frogs that move legs, bonbon boxes, standing birds, etc. 40 projects; more than 275 diagrams and photographs. 94pp.
20713-7 Paperbound $1.00

TRICKS AND GAMES ON THE POOL TABLE, Fred Herrmann. 79 tricks and games— some solitaires, some for two or more players, some competitive games—to entertain you between formal games. Mystifying shots and throws, unusual caroms, tricks involving such props as cork, coins, a hat, etc. Formerly *Fun on the Pool Table*. 77 figures. 95pp.
21814-7 Paperbound $1.25

HAND SHADOWS TO BE THROWN UPON THE WALL: A SERIES OF NOVEL AND AMUSING FIGURES FORMED BY THE HAND, Henry Bursill. Delightful picturebook from great-grandfather's day shows how to make 18 different hand shadows: a bird that flies, duck that quacks, dog that wags his tail, camel, goose, deer, boy, turtle, etc. Only book of its sort. vi + 33pp. 6½ x 9¼.   21779-5 Paperbound $1.00

WHITTLING AND WOODCARVING, E. J. Tangerman. 18th printing of best book on market. "If you can cut a potato you can carve" toys and puzzles, chains, chessmen, caricatures, masks, frames, woodcut blocks, surface patterns, much more. Information on tools, woods, techniques. Also goes into serious wood sculpture from Middle Ages to present, East and West. 464 photos, figures. x + 293pp.
20965-2 Paperbound $2.00

HISTORY OF PHILOSOPHY, Julián Marias. Possibly the clearest, most easily followed, best planned, most useful one-volume history of philosophy on the market; neither skimpy nor overfull. Full details on system of every major philosopher and dozens of less important thinkers from pre-Socratics up to Existentialism and later. Strong on many European figures usually omitted. Has gone through dozens of editions in Europe. 1966 edition, translated by Stanley Appelbaum and Clarence Strowbridge. xviii + 505pp.
21739-6 Paperbound $3.50

YOGA: A SCIENTIFIC EVALUATION, Kovoor T. Behanan. Scientific but non-technical study of physiological results of yoga exercises; done under auspices of Yale U. Relations to Indian thought, to psychoanalysis, etc. 16 photos. xxiii + 270pp.
20505-3 Paperbound $2.50

Prices subject to change without notice.
Available at your book dealer or write for free catalogue to Dept. GI, Dover Publications, Inc., 180 Varick St., N. Y., N. Y. 10014. Dover publishes more than 150 books each year on science, elementary and advanced mathematics, biology, music, art, literary history, social sciences and other areas.